MW00848798

MOSSER/ MUSSER
FAMILY

Anita L. Mott

HERITAGE BOOKS
2008

HERITAGE BOOKS

AN IMPRINT OF HERITAGE BOOKS, INC.

Books, CDs, and more—Worldwide

For our listing of thousands of titles see our website
at
www.HeritageBooks.com

Published 2008 by
HERITAGE BOOKS, INC.
Publishing Division
100 Railroad Ave. #104
Westminster, Maryland 21157

International Standard Book Number: 978-0-7884-1187-8

TABLE OF CONTENTS

(When using the index, please be sure to look up all possible spellings of each name.)

ABBREVIATIONS USED IN THIS WORK

abt. = about
b. = born
bp. = baptized
bur. = buried
chr. = christened
Co. = County
DAR = Daughters of the
    American Revolution

dau. = daughter
div. = divorced
m. = marriage
m. (1) = first marriage
m. (2) = second marriage
m. (3) = third marriage
m. (4) = fourth marriage

(Current legal abbreviations used for states)

iii

1. A Brief History

In order to better understand our confusing **MOSSER/MUSSERS** we must first have some knowledge of the German immigrants, who became known as the Pennsylvania Dutch.

Family surnames were derived from personal names, occupations or the areas where they lived. These names were often Americanized when they reached Philadelphia. A few examples of this are: Huber (small farm owner), Wannemaker (basket maker), Probst (provost), Rau or Rauch (rough), and Pfaff (a priest). Surnames could be changed drastically either by adopting English spelling or using the English translation. An example is the Graff family, who became Graaf, Groff, Groft, Graft and Grove. The most interesting of all were the two brothers who, upon reaching our shores, became known one as Zimmerman and and the other as Carpenter! Our Mossers (the original name being M-O-double S-E-R) became Moser, Muser, Musser, and Messer.

First names were usually Biblical, with families choosing to use the same name for all of their offspring. (In our case, the names were "Hans" or "Johann" for the males and "Maria" or "Anna" for the females). This was possibly done to identify them as "Mosser, son of John", etc. The children became known by their "call" names, which were the middle names. Hence John Paul was listed as simply "Paul" in the records.

While some of our Mossers were highly educated in their native land, most did not speak or write English. We therefore have the added confusion of well-meaning officials trying to write down the names as they heard them. (In the 1850 Trumbull County, Ohio census, for example, we have the elderly Philip Mosser and his wife listed as MASON, living with their son, John, who is listed as Moser!) Another source of confusion is that the double "s" was handwritten *ß* and sometimes translated as a "y" or "fs" by well-meaning researchers hundreds of years later. It is therefore important for the researcher to use some imagination when searching a typed index.

The German exodus to America was influenced both by the Catholic persecution against the Protestants and William Penn, who made three visits to Germany, beginning in 1674. The first colonists were Mennonites from Crefeld on the Rhine who came on 6 October 1683 aboard the *Concord* and established the settlement of Germantown, Pennsylvania, now a section of Philadelphia. Unfortunately, passenger records were seldom kept of these early voyages, and when they were, listed only the adult males. Passengers often had to travel as "steerage", a place usually reserved for the cattle which were butchered to feed the crew during long voyages. Children under sixteen were not counted as passengers, so that a ship designed to carry one hundred adults would often have three times that number of persons aboard.

There were two main currents of Pennsylvania Dutch who came to America in the late 17th and early 18th centuries, settling mostly in what is now Lancaster, Lehigh, Lebanon, York, Northampton and Berks counties. The "plain" or pietist German sectarians who even today shun electricity, cars, and other modern devices are the Brethren, Mennonites, and Dunkers. The "fancy" or "gay" group made up nearly 90 percent of the Pennsylvania Dutch. Most of our Mossers fall into the latter group.

The state of Pennsylvania itself was also changing. It is important to understand that, while our Mossers stayed put, the counties where their records can be found kept changing. For example, Bucks County was formed in 1729; Northampton County was taken from it in 1752; and Lehigh was carved from Northampton in 1812. Centre County was formed in 1800. The town of Coalsdale is located in Schuylkill County today. All of these counties/towns must be searched for the records.

There are many published passengers lists for these early settlers. It is important to look at several of them, as they differ greatly, depending upon the translator. An example is that the Strassburger-Hinke list for the '*Adventure*' which arrived on 23 Sep 1732, has Michael Moser as age 38, while Knittle has him as 40, and poor Evan Barbara ages from 16 to 55! I cannot claim to know the reason for the differences, or even which one is correct. Perhaps what we need is a new translation!

Since it is my personal belief that Hans Martin, Hans Adam (on the '*Goodwill*' in 1728 and the Hans Paul who arrived later on the '*Adventure*' were brothers, I have included information on all of them in this work. However, the main emphasis has been on Hans Martin, who is my direct ancestor. This work is the result of over 40 years of research, which began when the "Bride's Book" that I received as a wedding gift contained a blank family tree.

As our Mosers moved about, some of them, for whatever reason, changed their name to "Musser". To avoid confusion, I have called all the early ones "Mosser" and the ones after 1840 "Moser". Many church records used this spelling, even though the families were using the "Musser" name in public records. To further befuddle the researcher, some of the "Mussers" switched back to "Moser" when they left Pennsylvania and moved westward. Those who kept the Musser spelling are listed in this work by that spelling. A smaller group which went south to North Carolina, Virginia and Tennessee do show up in early census records with very imaginative spellings, including "Mouser", "Mozer", "Mozier", "Mosher", and "Mosier". Some of these branches adopted these spellings, and are known by these names today. However, one must note that there was an entirely separate group of English families which settled in New England one hundred years before the German immigration began. These people are descendants of Hugh Mosier/Mosher, and are no relation to our Mosser/Musser group.

The difficulty in tracing our Mosser/Musser families was made much harder by the amount of false information put out by a coal company in an effort to thwart a law suit. This misinformation has often been copied from generation to generation as gospel truth and can be found in many previously published works.

The purpose of this book is to put as much information into one source as possible, in hopes of helping ease the task of future researchers. To facilitate locating the original sources, I've tried to use the spellings of names as found in those sources.

One last word of caution. Please remember that most of these records were originally written in German and translated by someone else many years later. It is always possible that the translator made mistakes during the translation either in trying to read the German script, in transcribing their own notes, or in the typing itself. Lineages are sometimes guessed at, or even falsified, by those trying to prove membership in a society. Errors can also be made in judgement calls, which are sometimes necessary when absolute proof cannot be found. As with any printed work, this book must be considered as only a "secondary" source. Please check the references for yourself.

Every effort has been made to make this work as accurate and complete as possible. We appologize for any errors of omission, typing, proof-reading, etc. Your comments and/or corrections are invited as we realize that many descendents are still among the missing.

I will be forever grateful to Tricia Dernison for all her help in proof reading this work and for all the fine folks aboard our fictional ship "Samuel" on the Internet for their constant encouragement. Without their efforts, this would never have been completed.

Hans Martin Moser

Hans (Johann, John) **Martin Mosser**, his wife, **Margaretha Kungel**, and a one year old son, (Frederich) arrived in Philadelphia on the ship *James Goodwill*, 11 Sep 1728. The ship, under the command of David Crockett, left from Rotterdam on June 15. Also aboard the ship were **John Adam Mosser** and **Thomas Koppenheffer** (whose son would marry a daughter of John Adam.). While Thomas signed the ship's manifest list with an 'X', Hans Martin and John Adam wrote their whole names. About persons were aboard the ship, but only the men signed the manifest.

morotin suofor

Signature of Hans Martin Mosser

John Martin settled in the Perkiomen Valley at New Goshenhoppen, Philadelphia County, Pennsylvania, near the Berks County border. All three families were members of the New Hanover (Falkner's Swamp) Lutheran Church where the baptism of a son (Michael Moser) took place in 1734. Acting as sponsors at the baptism were John Adam Moser and his wife, Eva. This church is said to be the oldest Lutheran Church in Pennsylvania. Written records at the church did not begin until 1743. (The above baptism was found in Rev. Stoever's private records.)

John Martin died intestate before 1743 when daughter Maria Barbara was confirmed, as her mother was listed as the 'widow Moser'. He was about 44 years old, making his date of birth about 1699. On 8 Apr 1744, John Philip, son of 'widow Moser' was also confirmed. John Michael (age 16) and John Burkhard were confirmed together on 8 Apr 1750. An inventory of the estate was made on 6 Oct 1744, on which Margaretha Mosser, widow of Martin Mosser, placed her mark.

Margaretha ✝ Messer mesek

Signature of Margaretha Mosser

The final accounting of the estate took place on 25 Oct 1749 and named six children as heirs. The six children are as follows:

Johann Frederick Mosser
> b. about 1727 in Europe
> m. **Maria Barbara Loeser**, 22 Apr 1750
> d. 1799, Orange Co., N.C.

Maria Margaretha Mosser
> b. about 1728 in Goshenhoppen, Philadelphia Co., Pa.
> m. **Johann Jacob Steinbruch**

Maria Barbara Mosser
> b. about 1729, Goshenhoppen, Philadelphia Co., Pa.
> confirmed 1743 at New Hanover
> m. _____ **Sittler**

Johann Philip Mosser
> b. 1730, Goshenhoppen, Philadelphia Co.,Pa.
> confirmed 1744 at New Hanover
> m. **Maria Barbara** _____
> d. 26 Jan 1817, Mosserville, Lehigh Co., Pa.

Johann Michael Mosser
> b. 30 May 1734, Goshenhoppen, Philadelphia Co., Pa.
> bp. 6 Jun 1734 at New Hanover
> confirmed (age 16) on 8 Apr 1750 at New Hanover
> m. **Catharina** _____
> d. 1820, Lowhill, Lehigh Co., Pa.

Johann Burkhard Mosser
> b. 1736, Goshenhoppen, Philadelphia Co., Pa.
> confirmed 8 Apr 1750 at New Hanover
> m. **Maria Agatha Lichtenwallner**
> d. 1807, Linn, Northampton Co., Pa.

It is probable that Maria Margaretha was born shortly after her parents arrived in Philadelphia. Her sister, Barbara, should have been about fourteen years old when she was confirmed in 1743, making her date of birth 1729. Since there is no written record of Margaretha having been confirmed, one must conclude that she was the older of the two. With a brother born in 1727 and a sister born in 1729, only 1728 remains for the birth date of Margaretha.

No record has been found of the death of the 'widow Mosser'. It may be that she remarried as pioneer life was very hard for a woman alone. The possibility exists that her mother may have been named 'Burchard', as there were families by that name who also immigrated to Pennsylvania. Johanes Lichtenwallner, who came from Kreuth, Germany aboard the _'Samuel'_ in 1733 was married to Barbara Burchard. One of his daughters would marry Tobias Mosser, who traveled with John Paul Mosser on the _'Adventure'_, while another would marry John Martin's son, Burchard. This would also explain the origin of Burchard's call name.

In 1754 the sons of John Martin went to settle the area of Northampton County which is known as Lynn, Lehigh County today. Lynn (or Linn as it appears in early records) was formed from part of Heidelberg Township.

Hans Adam Mosser

The reader is first cautioned that most of the data concerning Hans Adam Mosser has come to me from other people. I have borrowed heavily from the work of Charles Recker, who made an extensive collection of **Moser** data thru a newsletter called *The People of the Marsh* during the 1970's. The conclusions of this work are available on LDS Microfilm # 1321128, Item # 7. While these conclusions are a valuable tool in the research process, they must not be considered as proof. With appologies to Mr. Recker, many errors have been found in the line of our **Hans Martin Mosser**, due, I am sure, to the limited data available at that time. The magic of photo copiers and computers has opened many doors to the past since the '70's.

It is important to note that while I have spent nearly forty years collecting data concerning Hans Martin, I have not personally conducted much research on the line of Hans Adam. If you are researching this line, please check all references carefully.

According to the <u>Compendium of American Genealogy</u>, the **Hans Adam Mosser** who arrived in Philadelphia on 11 Sep 1728 on the *James Goodwill*, was born in the lower Palatinate area of Germany on 18 Feb 1684. This was his third and final trip to the new world, having been in Lancaster County, Pennsylvania as early as 1717. The Bible he brought with him is located in the Myerstown Library, Lebanon County, Pennsylvania.

Hans Adam and his wife, **Eva** sponsored John Michael , son of **Hans Martin Moser** and **Margaretha Kungel** at Falkner's Swamp in 1734 at New Hanover. Hans Adam signed the Immigration List in 1738/8. In 1745, he purchased 314 acres of land called "Fells Manor" from **Caspar Wistar**, who had purchased it from **William Penn**. The neighboring landowners were: **Thomas Koppenheffer, Tobias Pickle** (who married Adam's daughter, Catharine), **Valentine Hergelrude** (who married an **Elisabeth Moser** of Lebanon in 1747), and **Leonard Rammler**.

Hans Adam made his will on 18 Jan 1770 and died shortly thereafter. He is buried in the old Tulphoecken Cemetery near the Trinity Reformed Church in Millardsville, Lebanon County, Pennsylvania with a **Catherine Ramer**, who may be a second wife. No record has been found of the death of this Eva Mosser.

Several sources claim that Hans Adam married second, **Anna Maria Boehm**, daughter of **Rev. Johann Philip Boehm**, founder of the German Lutheran Reformed Church in America. Rev. Boehm was born in Hochstadt, Germany, in 1683 and died 29 Apr 1749 in Hellertown, Pennsylvania and was a son of **Philip Ludwig Boehm** and **Maria Engelhardt**. He married **Anna Maria Stehler** of Lambsheim, Germany. These same sources claim that this daughter of the Rev. Boehm was married to the Hans Adam, born in 1710, who went to North Carolina and made his will in 1763 in North Carolina. Since the Hans Adam of the *Goodwill* died 1770 in Pennsylvania at the age of 86 and the Hans Adam in North Carolina died there in 1763 at the age of 53, Anna Maria Boehm could not have been the wife of Hans Adam Moser of the *Goodwill*.

The will of our Hans Adam Mosser was probated on 23 Jan 1770 in Lancaster County and mentions ten children and a wife named **Anna Maria** _____. Executors of the will were **Martin Heichold** and **Simon Koppenhefer**.

Children as listed in this will are:
1. **Johann Weyrich (Weirley)**
    b. 16 Mar 1733
    bp. 17 Sep 1733, Evangelish Luttnusche, Cocalico, Lancaster, Pa
    m. **Margaret Epler**
2. **John Adam Musser** (not mentioned in his father's will)
3. **Nicholas Musser**
    b. 1738
    m. (1) **Catherine Ley**
       (2) **Margaret Hahn Ruth**
4. **Henry Musser** m. **Elizabeth** _____
5. **Anna Musser**
    b. 1735, d. 1804
    m. **Michael Ruth**
6. **Catharine Musser**
    m. **Tobias Bickel**
    bur. Row's Cemetery, Penn Twp., Pa.
7. **Peter Musser**
    m. **Catherine Snider**
    d. 1844
8. **Jacob Musser**
    m. **Maria Hostettler**
    d. 1766
9. **Hans Musser**
10. **Elizabeth Musser**
11. **Daniel Musser** m. **Anna Maria** _____

Hans Adam Mosser, Jr. (born about 1736). son of Hans Adam, the immigrant, was shot by indians and died intestate in 1759. He left a wife, **Anna Maria** _____, and a minor son, **John Adam Mosser**. Hans Adam Sr. and Anna Maria Moser guaranteed administration of this estate, along with a **Henry Dups**. It is not known if this Anna Maria was the second wife of Hans Adam, the immigrant, or the young widow who bore the same name. However, Anna Maria, widow of Adam, Moser Jr., married (2) **John Brown** in 1760 in Bethel, Pa.

It has also been claimed that John Adam returned to Germany with the Rev. Boehm and his son, Philip Boehm Jr., returning to Philadelphia on the *Loyal Judith* in 1743. However, a close examination of the signatures by seven experts of early German handwritting has revealed that these were two different men, with the John Adam of the *Loyal Judith* being a much younger man. The two signatures are reproduced here.

Goodwill Signature   *Loyal Judith* Signature

Hans Paulus Mosser

Hans Paulus Mosser is perhaps even more of an enigma than either **Hans Martin Mosser** or **Hans Adam Mosser**, for there appears to have been three immigrants by that name. Many believe that the one who came on the *Adventure*, which sailed from Rotterdam under **Master Robert Carson**, arriving in Philadelphia on 23 Sep 1732 to be the brother of Martin and Adam. For this reason, he is included in this work.

Hans Paul is listed as "under sixteen" in *Pennsylvania Archives, 3rd Series, Vol. 17* passenger lists, but as age twenty-four in the same list as published by a man named **Knittle**. Strassburger-Hinke do not list his age. Since he signed the ship's manifesto, it is would appear that he was at least sixteen. He appears in New Hanover Church records (Montgomery County, Pennsylvania) as having a wife named Elisabeth, who died 8 Apr 1749. She was described at her funeral, conducted by **Rev. Henry Muhlenberg** at the New Hanover Church as being a "young" woman.

Children of Paul and Elisabeth Moser are believed to be as follows:

Michael Mosser
   b. 11 Apr 1739, New Hanover, Pa.
   m. **(1) Elisabeth** _____
       (2) Mary _____
   d. 5 Jun 1814
   They lived in Lancaster Co., Pa. and were known as Musser.

George Mosser, b. 27 Mar 1741, Pa.
   m. **Christina Jung/Young**
   d. 12 Jul 1806, Lancaster Co., Pa.
   They lived in Lancaster County, Pa. and had twelve children. They were also known as Musser.

Eve Mosser
   bp. 18 Dec 1743, New Hanover Church
   m. 19 Dec 1763 **Balthaser Traut**
   They had a son, **George Traut**, b. 8 Sep 1764,
       bp. 4 Nov 1764, New Hanover Church

John Adam Mosser
   b. 31 Oct 1746, Pa.
   bp. 31 Dec. 1746, New Hanover Church
   m. **Christina Prunner**
   d. 26 Jun 1823, Cocalico, Pa.
   They lived in Lancaster County, Pa. They also became known as Musser.

Andrew Mosser
   m. **Maria Magdalena Bign**
   They lived in Easton, Pa. and had nine children.

Jacob Mosser
   m. **Catharine** and/or **Margaret**
   They lived in Plainfield, Pa.

Paul married second, **Eva Beeholt**, on 10 Aug.1749 at New Hanover Church. They were among the first settlers in the Falkner Swamp area, moving there as early as 1752, where his lands joined those of **John Yeager**. By 1767, they were located in Forks Township, Northampton County. His will was probated in 1780 in Northampton County, Pennsylvania. The widow married **John Yeager** in 1785.

Known children of Hans Paul & Eva Mosser:

Magdalena Mosser
> b. abt 1753, Pa.
> confirmed 1767, New Hanover Church
> m. **John Heiter**

Johannes Paulus Mosser
> b. 3 Feb 1756, Pa.
> bp. 7 Mar 1756, New Hanover Church
> m. **Maria (Magdalena or Barbara) Heiter**
> d. 1842, Rye Twp. , Perry Co., Pa.

Tobias Mosser
> b. 26 Feb 1763, Pa.
> bp. 11 Apr 1763, New Hanover Church
> m. **Christina_____**
> They lived in Bethlehem, Pa.

Christina Mosser
> b. 9 Dec 1766, Pa.
> bp. 9 Dec 1767, New Hanover Church
> d. young

John Peter Mosser
> b. 14 Feb 1769, Pa.
> m. **Catharine Miller**, dau. of **Henry Miller**

Catharine Mosser
> m. **Conrad Reiser**
> They lived in Bethel Twp., Pa.

Johannes Mosser
> b. 12 Jul 1771
> m. 14 Jan 1794 **Anna Maria Nickom**
> d. 1839

Johann Philip Mosser + Maria Barbara
(Moserville, Lehigh Co., Pa.)

Philip 1757-1804
Catharine Schunck
to Center Co., Pa.
Musser

Sebastian 1770-1829
Anna Maria Miller
to Center Co., Pa.
Musser

Daniel 1762-1804
Magdalena Oswald
to Center Co., Pa.
Musser

Jacob 1775-1853
Margaretha Hagenbusch
to Center Co., Pa.
Musser

David 1766-1833
Catherine Oswald
stayed in Lehigh Co.

Maria Barbara 1811
1745-
Samuel Everett
to Trumbull Co., Oh.

Catherine 1756-1826
Michael Ohl
to Schuylkill Co., Pa.

Christine 1771
John Matthias Pike
to Center Co., Pa.

Rev. War. Vets
Philip Mosser / Musser
Sebastian Mosser / Musser
Samuel Everett
Michael Ohl

xii

Hans (John) Martin Mosser + Margaretha Kungel

Frederick Mosser 1727-1799
Barbara Loeser/Luser
to Orange Co., N.C.

Margaretha Mosser
Jacob Stanbrook
to Northampton Co., Pa.

Maria Barbara Mosser
Mr. Sittler

Philip Mosser 1730-1817
Maria Barbara
to Northampton Co., Pa.

Michael Mosser 1734-1820

Burkhard Mosser 1736-1807
Maria Agatha Lichtenwallner
to Northampton Co., Pa.

Arrived 1728 on
"James Goodwill"

Rev. War Vets
Philip Mosser
Burkhard Mosser

Jacob   1751-1819
(1) Nellie
(2) Polly Stephens
to Indiana

Abraham   1752
Nellie
to Anderson Co., Tenn.

Michael   1756
Sophie Reinhardt
to Orange Co., N.C.

Philip   1758-1837
(1) Catherine Schneider
(2) Martha
to Floyd, Indiana

Maria Barbara   1760
(1) Samuel Huffman
(2) Mr. Keck

Jurg Frederick 1760-1760

Mary Ann   1761-1838
Conrad Frederick Keck
to Monroe Co., Indiana

Nicholas   1762
Elisabeth Low

Elisabeth 1767-1821
Henry Sharp, Jr.
to Union Co., Tenn

Eve   1768-1822
Peter Sharp
to N.C.

Caty   1769
(1) Barnabus Butcher
(2) Henry Kimbro

John   1771
Margaret Klein

Frederick 1772-1839
Mary Ingold

Johann Frederick Mosser + Maria Barbara Loeser

(1) Henrich Steininger

John Henrich
bp. 1758

Eva Catharina
bp. 1760

Johann Burchard Mosser + Maria Agatha Lichtenwallner   +

Johann Burchard	Johann Philip	Johann Michael	Anna Maria	Jacob	Catherine Barbara
b. 25 Jun 1763	b. Feb. 1765	b. 1767	b. 14 Oct 1769	b. 29 May 1772	b. 1773
m. Catharine Hornberger	m. Elisabeth Oswald	m. Anna Margaretha weber (1)	m. Christian Miller (1)	m. Miss Oswald (1)	m. George Sitler
Catharine Kershner	d. 1849	Elisabeth (2)	John Oswald (2)	Susanna Hunsicker (2)	
d. 1849		d. 1854	d. 18 Apr 1842	d. 18 Apr 1842	
to Centre Co	to Centre Co.	to Centre Co.	to Northampton Co.	to Lehigh Co.	to Lehigh Co.

Hans Adam Mosser + (1) Eva + (2) Anna Maria

Hans Adam
m. Anna Maria
d. 1758

Nicholas
b. 1738
m. (1) Catherine Ley
(2) Margaret Hahn
Ruth

Henry
m. Elizabeth

Anna Mary
b. 1735
m. Michael Ruth

Catharine
m. Tobias Bickel

Jacob
m. Maria Hostettler
d. 1766

Hans

Elizabeth

Daniel
m. Anna Maria

Peter
m. Catherine Snider
d. 1844

Wertley
m. Margaret Foler

Arrived in 1728 on
"James Goodwill"

Hans Paulus Mosser + Elisabeth (1) + Eva Becholt (2)

Arrived in 1732 on "Adventure"

- **Michael** b. 11 Apr 1739, m. (1) Elisabeth, m. (2) Mary, d. 5 Jun 1814, Lancaster, Pa. Musser
- **George** b. 27 Mar 1741, m. Christina Yung, d. 12 Jul 1806, Lancaster, Pa. Musser
- **John Adam** b. 31 Oct 1746, m. Christina Runner, wp 23 Jan 1770, Lancaster, Pa. Musser
- **Andrew** m. Maria Magdalena Bign, Easton, Pa. Musser
- **Jacob** m. Catharine and/or Margaret, Plainfield, Pa.

- Magdalena b. @ 1753, m. John Hiefer
- Johannes Paulus b. 1756, m. Maria Hiefter
- Tobias b. 1763, m. Christina
- John Peter b. 1769, m. Catharine M. ller
- Christina b. 1766, d. young
- Eve m. Balthaser Trout
- Catharine m. Conrad Reiser
- Johannes b. 1771, m. Anna Maria Niekom

Johann Christian Mosser + Anna Maria

Barbara
b.@ 1734 Germany
m. George Neiman

George
b.@ 1740 Germany

Peter
b.@ 1741 Germany
m. Margaret Lamp

Johann Christian Jr.
b. 20 Feb 1758
m. Margaretha

Rev. War Vet
Johann Christian Jr.

Arrived in 1750 on "St. Andrew"

Lorentz Mosser
on "Adventure" 1732
lived Maryland

Kocher

Maria Sarah Binkley

Maria Sara

#1

#2

Anna Margaretha
b. Feb 1745
m.(1) Henry Demuth
(2) Peter Freiser

Leonard
m. Elisabeth
Schenkel

Peter
m.(1) Catherine Folk
(2) Margaret
d. 1 Feb 1831

Jacob
b. @ 1754
m. Elisabeth Orsett
d. 2 Jul 1813

Henry
b. 12 Sep 1769
m. Magdalene
Schenkel
d. 1830

Joseph
b. 21 Jul 1772
d. 17 Apr 1773

John Michael
b. 1 Aug 1759
m. Catherine Koller
d. 11 Jun 1816

Samuel
b. 11 Apr 1761

Francis
b. 15 Mar 1768
m.(1) Elisabeth Miller
(2) Mary Sipes

Christian
b. 5 Jan 1765
m. Elisabeth Fuller

Anna Elisabeth
b. 30 Jan 1767
m. John Jacob Hess

Tobias Mosser + Ursula Margaretha Meyer

Johann Michael
b. 19 Aug 1749
m.(1) Catharina
(2) Eva Burz

John Jacob
b. 25 Jul 1747

Tobias
b. 26 May 1743
m. Christina
Lichtenwallner

Johannes
b. 24 Jun 1741
m. Elisabeth Moyer
d. 11 Oct 1810

Arrived 1732 on
"Adventure"

xiv

Adam Mosser + Maria Strobel

Adam
b. 13 Feb 1675

Anna Maria
b. 30 Apr 1678

Eva
b. 2 Oct 1680

George Philip
b. 24 Apr 1683
m. Eva Ebert
on
Adventure
1732

Maria Barbara
b. 25 Oct 1686

Johann Michael
b. 4 Mar 1690
m. Susanna Barbara
Baumann
on
Adventure
1732

Lived Weissenkiachberg, Germany

Johann Michael Mosser + (?) Anna Barbara Strobel

Ertmann (Adam)
b. 12 Oct 1750
wp 1804

Michael
b. 13 Mar 1752
m. Magdalena
Weimann
d. 1 Jun 1818

Christina Catharina
b. 8 Sep 1754
m. (?) Michael Hochle

Anna Barbara
b. 1756

Johann Frederick Mosser

Johann Frederick Mosser, oldest child of **Hans Martin Mosser** and **Margaretha Kungel**, was born about 1727, in Europe, as the American Compendium states that Hans Martin came to this country with a wife and one child in 1728. Circumstantial evidence (and family tradition) indicates that the family came from Strassburg, Alsace, but that has never been proved. The family settled in New Goshenhoppen, which is located in Upper Hanover Township. They were members of the New Hanover Lutheran Church which is the oldest Lutheran Church in Pennsylvania. Written records were not kept until 1743, but the records of Rev. Stoever have been published. In this work, we find the baptism of Frederick's brother, Michael, and Frederick's marriage on 22 Apr 1750 to **Marie Barbara Loeser (Leeser)**, daughter of **Benedict Loeser** and **Barbara _____**.

Frederick's parentage has long been questioned, but has now been proven by the discovery of the estate papers of Hans Martin, which names all six children. Frederick's name is listed on an old map as once having owned land in Lynn Township, but he does not appear on any of the early tax lists. However, three of his children were christened in Linn (now Lynn, Lehigh County), Northampton County, by Rev. Schumacker. On 4 May 1757 Frederick was among those who signed a petition to Gov. Denny requesting that Fort Franklin (located on the north side of the Blue Mountain) be abandoned.

By 1761 the family was in North Carolina, where daughter Mary Ann was born. Frederick is listed in the 1790 Federal Census for Orange County, North Carolina. Frederick died 21 Feb 1800. His will was probated May, 1800 in Orange County, North Carolina.

Signature of Frederick Moser

Children of Johann Frederick and Marie Barbara Moser:
1. **Jacob Moser**, b. about 1751 in Pa.
   m. **(1) Nellie _____**
   (2) Polly Stephens in Cumberland Co., Tenn.
   d. aft. 1819 in Indiana
2. **Abraham Moser**, b. about 1752 in Pa.
   m. **Nellie _____**
   He served in the North Carolina Militia during the Rev. War. They went to Anderson County, Tenn.
3. **Michael Moser**, b. about 1756 in Northampton Co., Pa.
   m. Aug. 1778 **Sophia Reinhardt**
   d. 1828, Orange County, N. C.
4. **Johann Philip Moser**, b. 26 Nov 1758, Northampton Co., Pa.
   bp. 7 Jan 1759 in the "Organ Church", Linn,
   Northampton Co., Pa. at age six weeks.
   (sponsors were Philip Leideck & Anna Eva Leeser,
   both single)
   m. **(1) Catherine Schneider**
   (2) Martha _____
   d. 1828, Orange Co., N.C.

5. Maria Barbara Moser, bp. 28 Dec 1760, Linn, Northampton, Pa. by Rev.
Schumacher. Sponsors were Barbara Steenbruchen & Jacob Weidmann
    m. (1) 1788, **Samuel Huffman** in N. C.
       (2) _____ **Keck**
6. Jurg Frederick Moser, bp. 7 Feb 1760, Linn, Northampton Co.,
Pa. at age 5 weeks; note says he died. No sponsors
7. Mary Ann Moser, b. about 1761 in Orange Co., N. C. (?)
    m. **Conrad Frederick Keck** in N. C.
    d. 1838, Clear Creek, Monroe Co., In.
8. Nicholas Moser, b. 1 Jul 1762 in Pennsylvania
    bp. 8 Aug 1762, Linn, Northampton Co., Pa.
    (did they really return to Pa for this baptism?)
    m. **Elisabeth Low**
9. Elizabeth "Lizzy" Moser, b. 1767 in Orange Co., N. C.
    m. bef. 1799, **Henry Sharp, Jr.** in Tenn.
    d. Sep 1821, Union Co., Tenn.
    She is buried in Sharp's Chapel, Union Co., Tenn.
10. Eve Moser, b. about 1768, in Orange Co., N. C.
    m. 31 Aug 1795, **Peter Sharp**
    d. Aug 1822 in N. C.
11. Caty Moser, b. abt 1769
    m. 20 Jan 1789 **Henry Kimbro** in Orange Co., N.C.
12. John Moser, b. about 1771 in Orange Co., N. C.
    m. 23 Apr 1805, **Margaret Klein**
    He is not listed in the 1790 N. C. Census.
13. Frederick Moser, b. about 1772 in Orange Co., N. C.
    m. **Mary Ingold**
    d. 15 Aug 1839 in Alamanco, N. C.
    buried in St. Paul Cemetery, Alamanco, N.C.
    He is also not listed in the 1790 N. C. Census.

1. Jacob Moser

Jacob Moser, son of **Johann Frederick Moser** and **Marie Barbara Loeser,** was born about 1751 in Pennsylvania. He went to North Carolina with his parents where he married first, a woman named **Nellie** _____ who was the mother of his children. Nellie and Jacob settled in Cumberland County, Tennessee, where their son, Calvin was born, becoming the first white child born in that territory. Children of Jacob and Nellie:
a. Calvin Moser
    b. 1817, Cumberland Co., Tenn.
    m. 1840 (license # A197) **(1) Margaret Williams**
       (d. 1875)
       (2) Hannah Prosser
    d. Monroe Co., In.
b. Lewis Moser
    m. 1831 (license # A86) **Nancy Hensley** in Monroe Co., In.
    They moved to Brown Co., In. by 1877.
    This couple had no children.
c. Washington Moser
    m. **Deliah Folowell**
    He was killed in the Civil War.
d. John Moser
    b. 1826
    m. 1843 (license # B53) **Eliza Ratliffe** in Monroe Co., In.

e. Patsy "Martha" Moser m. 1846 Rev. John Bridgemann Cox
f. Bertha/Tobetha Moser m. 1825 Jacob Davidson
g. Mary Moser m. 1834 Nathan Hensley
h. Kate Moser m. 1839 Robert Asher
i. Rachel Moser m. Dan McQueen

1a. Calvin Moser

Calvin Moser, the first white child born in Cumberland County, Tennessee, was born in 1817 to Jacob and Nellie Moser. He traveled with his parents to Monroe County, Indiana, where in 1840 he met and married (1) Margaret Williams, who died in 1875. He married (2) Hannah Prosser.   Children of Calvin and Margaret Moser:
1. **Aquilla R. Moser**
    b. 2 Feb1841, Brown Co., In.
    m. 13 Dec1862 **Clarissa Calvin**
2. **Martha A. Moser**, b. 1844
3. **Mary Ann Moser**, b. 1845
4. **James P. Moser, M.D.**
5. **Moses S. Moser**, b. abt. 1847
6. **Isaac B. Moser**, b. 14 Sep 1851, Brown Co., In.
    m. **Jennie C. Stuart** abt. 1875
    known children of Isaac & Jennie Moser:
        John C., b. 1876
        James, b. 1878
7. **Rebecca Moser**
8. **Katherine M. Moser**
9. **N. N. Moser**

1a.1 Aquilla R. Moser

Aquilla R. Moser, son of **Calvin Moser** and **Margaret Williams** was born in Brown (now Monroe) County, Indiana in 1841. He Married **Clarissa** _____ in 1862, and served as the County Commissioner of Monroe County in 1870. Children of Aquilla and Clarissa Moser:
    Alva M. Moser, b. abt 1864
    Haron D. Moser, b. Nov. 1866
    Jennie June Moser, b. June 1869
    Cortez Mexico Moser, b. abt 1871
    Brigham Young Moser , b. 1872
    Tod Moser, b. 1873
    Jack William Moser, b. abt 1878
    Roscoe LeMar Moser

1c. Washington Moser

Washington Moser, son of **Jacob** and **Nellie Moser** was born in Cumberland County, Tennesee. He served in the Civil War and was killed by another member of his own troup, who was court martialed for the deed. Washington married **Deliah Folowell** 24 Mar 1861. Children of Washington and Deliah Moser:
    John Moser
    William Moser
    Polly Ann Moser
    Jane Moser
The widow Deliah Moser had a grandson named **J. E. Moser**.

1d. John Moser

John Moser, son of **Jacob** and **Nellie Moser**, was born in Cumberland County, Tennessee in 1826. He moved to Monroe County, Indiana where he married **Eliza Ratliffe** in 1843 (license # B53). Children of John and Eliza Moser:

> **Calvin Moser**
> **Nancy Jane Moser**
> **John Henry Moser**
> **Mary Elizabeth Moser**
> **Rachel Ellen Moser**
> **Sarah Ann Moser**
> **Martha Moser**
> **Ella Moser**
> **Samuel Moser**
> **George Moser**
> **Sherman Moser**
> **Dora Moser**

1e. Patsy "Martha" Moser

Patsy "Martha" Moser, daughter of **Jacob** and **Nellie Moser** married **Rev. John Bridgeman Cox** in 1846, license #B-104. Children of Rev. John and Patsy Cox:

> **Louisa Cox**
> **Jane Cox**
> **Emily Cox**
> **Milt Cox**
> **Douglas Cox**
> **Clinton Cox**
> **James Cox**
> **Oliver Cox**
> **Thomas Cox**
> **Mack Cox**

1f. Bertha/ Tobetha Moser

Bertha Moser, daughter of **Jacob** and **Nellie Moser** was probably born in Indiana. She married **Jacob Davidson** in 1825, license #A-44. Children of Bertha and Jacob:

> **Sarah Jane "Sally" Davidson**
> **Nancy Davidson**
> **Mary Davidson**
> **Jacob Davidson**

3. Michael Moser

Michael Moser, son of **Johann Frederick** and **Maria Barbara Loeser**, was born about 1756 in Northampton County, Pennsylvania. In 1778 he married **Sophia Reinhardt** in Orange County, North Carolina. In 1779 he served in the North Carolina Militia during the Revolutionary War. The couple settled in Anderson County, Tennessee after the War. Children of Michael and Sophia Moser:

> **a. John Moser**
> > b. 29 Aug 1783, Northampton Co., Pa.
> > m. _____ **Thornburg**
> > They lived in Indiana.
> **b. Rev. Daniel Moser**
> > b. 1790
> > m. **Barbara Moretz**
> > d. 1820

c. **Rev. Jacob Moser** m. **Peggy Counts** of South Carolina
d. **Adam Moser**
    b. 1797
    m. 8 Apr 1816 **Kathrine Deets**
    buried Melanchton Cemetery, near Libety, N.C.
e. **Barbara Moser** m. **Adam Reitzel** in Orange Co., N.C.
f. **Catherine Moser** m. 2 Apr 1799 **Henry Reitzel**
g. **Eve Moser** m. 1808, **Andrew Scherer**
h. **Sara "Saloma" Moser** m. 25 Oct 1810 **John Moretz**
i. **Elizabeth Moser** (1787-1826) m. 15 May 1810 **Rev. Jacob Scherer**
j. **Charity Moser** b. 3 May 1800
    m. **Christian Fox** (1792-1863)
    d. 14 Apr 1864
k. **Clement Burton Moser** m. **Ann Merryweather** of Va.

4. Johann Philip Moser

Johann Philip Moser, son of **Johann Frederick Moser** and **Maria Barbara Loeser** was born in Northampton County, Pennsylvania on 26 Nov. 1758. He was baptized on 7 Jan 1759 at the age of six weeks, in the "Organ Church" of Linn, Northampton Co., Pa. His sponsors were Philip Leideck and Anna Eva Leeser, both single. He married (1) **Catherine Schneider** and (2) **Martha** _____. It is not known at this time which wife was the mother of his children. Johann Philip died in 1828 in Orange County, North Carolina. Children of Johann Philip Moser:

  Mary Moser
  John Moser m. **Polly** _____ in Greenville, Floyd Co., In.
      children: **Sara E. Moser**
            John D. Moser
            Joseph L. Moser
            William Riley Moser
            James P. Moser
            Frederick Moser
            Elizabeth Moser (b. 1785-1793)
                m. **Jacob Yenewin**
            Magdalena Moser
            Eve Moser
            Sally Moser
            Martha C. m. **Dr. G. W. Hartman**
            Nancy D. m. **A.J. Castee**
                (They were murdered on the way to
                Boone Co., Iowa, by **John Thomas**
                who was hung for the crime.)
            Eliza Jane Moser m. **George W. Cory**
Another possible son is **George Moser** (1801-1880) who was listed as a son of a Philip and Martha Moser, and married **Maria** _____. They went to Champaign County, Illinois in 1854 and became the parents of:

        Elijah Moser, d. at age 19
        Elizabeth Moser, m. _____ **Pickett**, d. 1877
        Philip C. Moser b. Harrison Co., In. in 1827
            m. **Dorothea Burton Moser** (b. 1831 Parke Co.,
            In. dau. of **Clement Burton Moser** and **Ann**
            Merryweather of Virginia.
            This couple had no children.

13. Frederick Moser

Frederick Moser, son of **Johann Frederick Moser** and **Marie Barbara Loeser**, was born about 1772 in Orange County, North Carolina. He married (1) **Mary Ingold**, who was the mother of two children and (2) **Barbara Anthony**, mother of eleven. He died in 1839 and is buried in St. Paul's Cemetery in what is now Alamance County, North Carolina. It is not know which wife was the mother of which children. Children of Frederick Moser:

    Barbara Moser m. **Jacob Amick**
    Eli Moser m. 16 Jun 1823, Guilford Co., NC, **Mary Amick**
    Boston Moser m. _____ **Manuel**
    Tobias Moser m. 10 Mar 1829 Lincoln Co., NC, **Catherine Sigmon**
    Nellie Moser m. 29 Oct 1823 Orange Co., NC, **Jacob Fox**
    Nimrod Moser (1809-1897) m. 16 Oct 1840 Guilford Co, NC, **Rachel Ritzel**
    Turleg Moser (1807-1854) m. Orange Co., NC, **William Steele**
    Martin Moser (1812-1875) m. 5 Jun 1848 Orange Co. , NC **Polly Robertson**
    Nancy Moser m. **Martin Fogleman**
    Penena Moser m. **Aquilla Johnson**
    Rebecca Moser m. 3 Jul 1840 Orange Co., NC, **Isaiah Noah**
    Elizabeth Moser m. **Riley Noah**
    Anthony Moser (1823-1906) m. 19 Nov 1845 Randolph Co., NC, **Louisa Brown**

Maria Margaretha Mosser Steinbruch

Maria Margaretha Mosser, daughter of **Hans Martin Mosser** and **Margaretha Kungel**, must have been born shortly after her parents arrival in Philadelphia on 11 Sep 1728 since Hans Martin arrived in Philadelphia with only a wife and a one year old son. Records at the New Hanover Lutheran Church began in 1743, when Margaretha's sister, Maria Barbara was confirmed. Maria Barbara should have been about 14 years old at that time, making her birthdate 1729. Since there is no record of Margaretha's confirmation, she would have to have been older than her sister.

Maria Margaretha married **Johann Jacob Steinbruch** about 1741/2, probably in Goshenhoppen, Philadelphia County, Pennsylvania, but no marriage record has been found. She must have been already married when their son, George Frederick was baptized in 1742 at the St. Paul's Lutheran Church. The next child, Maria Barbara, was baptized at the same church in 1744, but baptism records for the other children have not been found.

Neither the parents of Jacob Steinbruch nor the date of his arrival in America are known at this time. He was granted a land warrent on 9 Dec 1748 in Linn, Northampton County, Pennsylvania. The family probably moved there soon afterwards.

The French and Indian War was in full force by 1756. Jacob had the misfortune of looking out a window during an Indian attack in November, 1756 and was killed. What became of Maria Margaretha after the death of her husband is not known. Her children, Abraham and Anna Barbara, were confirmed at Weisenberg Church, Weisenberg Twp., Northampton County, Pennsylvania. It seems probable that she remarried and moved from Linn to Weisenberg. Children of Johann Jacob Steinbruch and Maria Margaretha Mosser:

    a. **George Frederick Stanbrook**, b. 25 Sep 1742
        bp. 25 Oct 1742, St. Paul's Lutheran Church, Red Hill,
        Philadelphia County, Pa.
        sponsors: Frederich Mosser and Dorothea Freidrich Fug
        m. **Catharina** _____
        d. 12 Feb 1812 in Wayne Twp., Crawford County, Pa.

    b. Maria Barbara Stanbrook, b. 13 Mar 1741
        bp. 1 Feb 1744, St. Paul's Lutheran Church, Red Hill,
        Philadelphia Co., Pa., sponsor: Jacob Drum
        m. **Johann Adam Dietrich**, about 1762
        d. 6 Jun 1821
        buried Zion Moselem Church, Richmond Twp, Berks County, Pa.
    c. Abraham Stanbrook
        confirmed in 1763 at Weisenberg Church, Weisenberg,
        Northampton Co., Pa.
    d. Anna Barbara Stanbrook
        confirmed with her brother in 1763.
There is a possibility that Peter and Christian Stanbrook who appear in Northampton
County records may also be children of Jacob and Maria Margaretha.

a. George Frederich Steinbruch

George Frederich Steinbruch (Stanback) was the oldest child of **Maria Margaretha
Mosser** and **Johann Jacob Steinbruch**. He was born 25 Sep 1742 and baptized
25 Oct 1742 at St. Paul's Lutheran Church. Sponsors at his baptism were Frederich
Mosser (son of Hans Martin) and Dorothea Freidrich Fug. He became fatherless in
1756 when Jacob was killed during an Indian raid on their home. His mother sold off
the land and moved to Weisenburg, Northumberland County, Pennsylvania, where his
younger brother and sister were confirmed in 1763.

Frederich was still single in 1760, but was married to **Catharina** _____ sometime
before 1767 when their son George Friederich was baptized at New Bethel Church in
Greenwich Twp, Berks County. A son John Jacob was baptized on 5 Jul that same year
at Delong's Reformed Church. (Had they become unhappy with New Bethel and joined
the reformed faith?) In 1767 he also appears on the Maxatawny Twp, Berks County,
Pennsylvania tax list, owning one cow, but no land. Frederich served in the
Revolutionary War when he was hired by Nicholas Sawyer to transport military supplies
to Philadelphia. He also was listed as a private 5th class in Col. Daniel Udree's 2nd
Battlion, 4th Company, Maxatawny Militia.

Daughter Elisabetha and son Jacob were baptized at Zion Moselem Church in
Richmond Twp., Pennsylvania in 1781. While there is speculation that they were
twins, it is possible that one or both had been born during the War and that their mother
waited until it was over to have them baptized. The fact that Frederich and Catharina
had two sons baptized in 1767 bears witness that they were not in a hurry to have the
ordinance performed.

At some point the family moved to Crawford County, Pennsylvania, where Frederich
died in Wayne Twp. on 12 Feb 1812. The Orphan's court docket was recorded in
Meedville, Crawford County on 18 Mar 1812, and named the children as Jacob, Henry,
John Adam, Christian, Peter, Catharine, Matty, Elizabeth, Margaret and Susannah. At
the time of this death, he owned 100 acres and was able to leave each of his children
$55.27. Children of George Frederich and Catharina Steinbruch:
    George Friederich Steinbruch
        bp. 1767, New Bethel Church, Greenwich Twp., Berks County, Pa.
        d. 1847
        Moved to Mead Twp., Pennsylvania
    Johann Jacob Steinbruch
        bp. 5 Jul 1767, Delong's Reformed Church, Berks Co., Pa.
        (did he die young, before 1781 when a second Jacob was
        baptized?)

William Henry Steinbruch
    b. 12 Oct 1770, Maxatawny Twp., Berks Co., Pa.
    m. 1808 **Eve Catherine Leffler**
    d. 11 Dec 1853 Brush Creek, Muskinghum Co., Oh.
Johann Adam Steinbruch
    bp. 20 Apr 1777, Delongs' Reformed Church, Berks Co.
    m. Apr 1801 Somersett Co., Pa., **Eizabeth Finley**
    d. 4 Aug 1846, Gallence, Wisconsin Territory
Christian Samuel Steinbruch
    b. 1779
    m. 1 Mar 1800, Crawford Co., Pa. **Esther Trautman**
    d. 1 Nov 1822
    They moved to Mead Twp., Crawford Co., Pa. He was a pvt in Cap.
    James McKnight's Reg. Pennsylvania Militia during the War of 1812.
    After his death, Esther married **George McKnight**
John Steinbruch
    b. about 1780
    d. 1877, Fairfield Twp., Crawford Co., Pa.
    John was a pvt. in Cap. James McKnight's Reg., Pennsylvania Militia
    during the War of 1812. He moved to East Fairfiled, Crawford Co., Pa.
Elisabetha Steinbruch
    bp. 6 Oct 1781, Zion Moselem Church, Richmond Twp.
    m. **Peter Sassman**
Jacob Steinbruch
    bp 6 Oct 1781, Zion Moselem Church, Richmond Twp.
    He was a pvt. in Cap. James McKnight's Reg., Pennsylvania Militia
    during the War of 1812
Susannah Steinbruch
    b. 1785
    m. **Michael Kightlinger**
    d. in childbirth, 1806 had daughter, **Catharine Kightlinger**
Catharine Steinbruch m. _____ **Conrad**
Magdalena "Matty" Steinbruch m. **Peter Conrad**
Margaret Steinbruch m. _____ **Wilhelm**
Peter Steinbruch m. **Mary C. Little**

b. Maria Barbara Steinbruch Dietrich

Maria Barbara Steinbruch was the second born child of **Maria Margaretha Mosser** and **Johann Jacob Steinbruch/Stanbrook.** She was born 13 Mar 1741 in Philadelphia County, Pennsylvania. She married **Johann Adam Dietrich,** son of **Johann Adam Diederich** and **Christina Bieber.** He was born in Wolfskirchen, Germany on 8 Nov. 1740, and came to this country with his parents and seven brothers and sisters aboard the '*Patience*' in 1751. Johann Adam was a weaver and an innkeeper. Barbara and Adam moved to Weisenberg, Northampton County, Pennsylvania where their first three children were baptized. The fourth child was baptized in Heidelberg. Since these two communities are adjacent to each other, there is no indication to believe that they had moved by 1773. Adam Dietrich was naturalized in the fall of 1765. The family later moved to Richmond Twp., Berks County, Pennsylvania and it was here that Maria died on 6 Jun 1821. She is buried in Zion Moselem Cemetery, Richmond Twp., Berks County. Children of Maria Barbara Steinbruch and Johann Adam Dietrich:
    Anna Catharine Dietrich
        bp. 23 May 1763, Weisenberg, Northampton Co., Pa., three days old
        sponsors: Jurg Schneider and Anna Barbara Steinbruch
    Johann Adam Dietrich
        bp. 25 Dec 1764, Weisenberg, Northampton Co., Pa., fourteen days old
        sponsors: Abraham Steinbruch and Barbara Kockin

Johann Simon Dietrich
 bp. 19 May 1766, Weisenberg, Northampton Co., Pa.
 sponsors: Simon and Christina Moser
 died young
Johann Georg Deitrich
 bp. 24 May 1767, Heidelberg, Northampton, Co., Pa.
 sponsors: Simon and Christina Moser
Anna Christina Dietrich
 bp. 5 May 1771, Weisenberg, Northampton Co., Pa.
Johann Jacob Dietrich
 bp. 13 Aug 1773, Heidelberg, Horthampton Co., Pa. three weeks old
 sponsors: Sebastian and Maria Margaretha Werner

Johann Philip Mosser

Johann Philip Mosser, the third child of **Hans Martin Mosser** and **Margaretha Kungel**, was born in Goshenhoppen, Philadelphia County, Pennsylvania in 1730. He was confirmed on 8 April 1844 at New Hanover Church. He is named among the heirs of Hans Martin in the settlement of the estate on 25 Oct 1749.

Soon after the settlement of the estate, Philip and his brothers, Frederich, Burchard and Michael purchased land in Northampton County, Pennsylvania in the area that is Lynn, Lehigh County today. He married **Maria Barbara*** before 1751 when daughter, Christina was born.

During the Revolutionary War, a Loyalist named William Thomas tried to unite the German Colonists of Lynn Twp. into a league to oppose both the draft and a new law requiring them to turn in their firearms. On 15 Dec 1776 he brought Jacob Oswald to the home of Philip Mosser where they drafted a document, which was signed the next day at the home of Burchard Mosser. The group was then arrested by the "Council of Safety" and held prisoner at Reading Goal. They were later paroled after giving money as security for the promise of good behavior. Philip later served as a pvt. in Captain Adam Stahler's Company, Sixth Batallion, Northampton Militia.

Philip built a log cabin on the Ontelaunee Creek, which was used as a mill. An adjoining saw mill was added later, which was operated by the family until at least 1893. The log cabin was still standing in 1991. This mill has earned Philip the nickname "Millowner" by Moser researchers today.

In 1794 two companies of New Jersey soldiers, on their return from western Pennsylvania where they were putting down the Whiskey Insurrection, encamped on the farms of Philip Mosser, Jacob Oswald and Peter Hunsicker. As they were very tired and hungry, Maria Barbara was kept busy baking for the soldiers, who stood outside the door waiting for the bread to come out of the oven.

Maria Barbara Moser died about 1816, as her will was probated in Mosserville on 16 Nov 1816. Philip died 26 Jan 1817 in Mosserville, Lehigh County, Pennsylvania. Children of Johann Philip and Maria Barbara Moser:

---

* An article published by Charles Recker has given evidence that <u>Krangelich,</u> long thought to be the maiden name of Maria Barbara, was merely a misreading of the word "Evangelish" which was often used by the German people to mean "Lutheran".

1. **Christina Moser**
   b. Oct. 1751, Pa.
   m. **John Matthais Pike**
   d. 11 Mar 1833
2. **Maria Barbara Moser**
   b. 27 Dec 1753, Linn, Northampton Co., Pa.
   bp. 7 Jan 1754, New Hanover Church
   m. **Samuel Everett**
   d. 1 Sep 1811, Liberty, Mahoning Co., Ohio
   buried Girard Cemetery, Girard, Mahoning Co., Ohio
3. **Catharina Moser**
   b. 1756, Linn, Northampton Co., Pa.
   m. **Michael Ohl**
   d. 1826, Lehigh Co., Pa.
   buried Heidelberg Cemetery, Heidelberg, Lehigh Co., Pa.
4. **Johann Philip Moser**
   b. Jul 1757, Linn, Northampton Co., Pa.
   m. **Catharina Margaret Schuck**
   d. 19 Jul 1804, Gregg Twp., Centre Co., Pa.
   buried Heckman Cemetery, Penn Valley, Centre Co., Pa.
5. **Johann Sebastian Moser**
   b. 3 Jan. 1760, Linn, Northampton Co., Pa.
   bp. 25 Jan 1761, age 3 weeks
   sponsors: Sebastian & Maria Margaretha Werner
   m. **Anna Maria Miller**
   d. 29 Nov 1829
   buried Heckman's Cemetery, Penn Valley, Centre Co., Pa.
6. **John Daniel Moser**
   b. 1762, Linn, Northampton Co., Pa.
   bp. 19 Sep 1762, age 4 weeks
   m. 18 Dec 1784 **Magdalena Oswald**
   d. 16 Jul 1804 in Haines Twp., Centre Co., Pa.
   buried Wolf's Chapel Cemetery, Penn Valley, Centre Co.
7. **David Moser**
   b. 30 Dec 1766, Linn, Northampton Co., Pa.
   m. Jan 1775, **Catharine Oswald**
   d. 18 Oct 1832, Lynn, Lehigh Co., Pa.
8. **Jacob Moser**
   b. 30 Aug 1775, Linn, Northampton Co., Pa.
   m. **Mary Krause** (or **Margaretha Hagenbach**)
   d. 28 Aug 1833 Mosserville, Lehigh Co., Pa.
   buried Ebeneezer Cemetery, Lynn, Lehigh Co., Pa.

2. Marie Barbara Mosser Everett

Marie Barbara Mosser, the oldest child of **Johann Philip Mosser** and **Maria Barbara**, was born 27 Dec 1753 in Lynn (when it was still called Linn), Northampton County, Pennsylvania and baptized on 7 Jan 1754 at New Hanover Lutheran Church. (The reader is cautioned that her head stone in Ohio claims she was born in 1760.) She married about 1772 in Linn, **Samuel Everett**, son of **Thomas Everett** and **Catherine Albrecht** born 1745 in Linn. She had three children, one of them only a tiny baby, when Samuel went to fight in the Revolutionary War. After the War, she had eight more children born in Lynn before the family decided to head for Ohio around 1797. They later settled in Liberty Township, Trumbull County, Ohio. Maria Barbara died 1 Sep 1811 and is buried in the Girard Cemetery, Mahoning County, Ohio. Children of Maria Barbara Mosser and Samuel Everett:

a. Samuel Everett
    b. about 1773, Linn, Northampton Co., Pa.
    m. **Sarah Pheil** in 1818
    d. 1858
    Children of Samuel & Sarah Everett:
    Azariah Everett (became an occulist, married and
        had a son, **Henry B.**)
    Samuel Everett (of Cleveland)
    Henry Everett (of Cleveland)
    Mary Everett (m. **D. Marshall** of Cleveland)
    Sarah Everett, b. abt. 1831 in Ohio
        m. _____ **Delenbaugh** of Cleveland
    Peter Root Everett, MD, b. abt. 1834 in Ohio
        (m. **Lucy Hewett**, lived in Cleveland, Ohio)
    Charles David Everett, b. abt. 1836 in Ohio
        (a Cleveland lawyer)
    Sylvester Everett, b. abt. 1838 in Ohio
        (m. **(1) Mary Everett**, daughter of his
            of his uncle, Charles
        (2) a daughter of **Jephthah D. Wade**
        (They lived in Cleveland)
    Franklyn Everett, b. abt. 1842 in Ohio
        (He also lived in Cleveland)
        Living with Samuel and Sarah in Liberty, Trumbull County,
        Ohio in 1850 was **Mary Arts**, age ten, from New York.
b. Michael Everett
    b. about 1775, Linn, Northampton Co., Pa.
    m. (1) **Margaretha Kieffer** 12 Apr 1803
        (2) **Rebecca** _____
    He became a merchant in Philadelphia, Philadelphia Co., Pa.
    Children of Michael Everett (mother unknown):
    Samuel Everett, disappeared before 1850, when his
        wife, **Matilda** _____ (b. abt. 1810 in
        Suitland Co., Vt.) was living in the
        Trumbull County Poor House
        with her children **Jeptha** (10), **John** (8) and
        Mary Jane (6).
    Rebecca Everett
    Elizabeth Everett, m. **John Drake**
    Sarah Everett, married _____ **Rubicum**
c. Charles Everett
    b. about 1777, Linn, Northampton Co., Pa.
    m. **Elizabeth** _____
    Children of Charles & Elisabeth Everett:
    Joseph Everett
    Charles Everett
    Margaret Everett
    Mary Everett m. **Sylvester Everett**
    Catharine Everett
d. Catherine Everett
    b. about 1783, Linn, Northampton Co., Pa.
    m. **Jacob Kistler**
    d. in Lehigh Co., Pa.

e. **Sarah "Sally" Everett**
    b. Apr 1785, Linn, Northampton Co., Pa.
    m. (1) **John Hake** 18 Mar 1810 in Trumbull Co., Ohio
        (2) **George Hake** 10 Aug 1843
    d. 12 Sep 1845, Howland, Trumbull Co., Ohio
    Children of Sarah & John Hake:
    John Hake
    Samuel Hake m. **Margaret Patterson**
    Daniel Hake m. 30 Jul 1848 **Lemira Atwood**
    David M. Hake m. 4 Oct 1860 **Malinda Hayden**
    Mary B. Hake
    Rebecca Hake m. 8 Jul 1852 **Milo M. Combs**
    Phoebe Hake m. 9 Apr 1845 **James W. Wilson**
    Nancy Hake
    Sarah Hake m 7 May 1840 **Sylvester Brewster**
f. **Mary Elisabeth "Betsy" Everett**
    b. 16 Jun 1783, Linn, Northampton Co., Pa.
    m. **Jacob Oswald** 22 Feb 1802 in Lehigh Co., Pa
        (she is listed as EBRIT on the marriage record)
    d. 11 Mar 1844, Girard, Mahoning Co., Ohio
    buried in Girard Cemetery, Mahoning, Co., Ohio
    Known children of Elisabeth & Jacob Oswald:
    Charles Oswald, b. 1804
    Catharine Oswald b. 1806
    Leodia Oswald b. 1808
    David Oswald b. 1811
    Jonathan Oswald b. 1815
    Eliza Oswald, b. 1819 m. **James Sechler**
    Mary Oswald, b.1824 m. **Solomon Everett**
    Jacob Oswald, b. 19 Jun 1827
g. **Daniel Everett**
    b. Nov.1790, Linn, Northampton Co., Pa.
    m. (1) **Sarah Cline** 5 Jul 1814, Trumbull Co., Ohio
        (2) **Mrs. Jane Stephens White**, 16 Jul 1857
    d. 7 Apr 1855, Hubbard, Trumbull Co., Ohio
    Children of Daniel and Sarah Everett:
    Mary Everett b. 1817, m. **Frederick Christian Becker**
    Samuel Everett b. 1819, m. **Catherine Fenstamaker**
    Peter Everett
    Caroline Everett
    Emanuel Everett b. abt. 1824, Ohio
    Solomon Everett b. abt 1824, Ohio, **Susan Fenstamaker**
    Known children of Solomon and Susan Everett:
        Daniel Everett b. abt. 1853. Ohio
        Charles Everett b. abt. 1855, Ohio
        Mary A. Everett b. abt. 1863, Ohio
        Irene Everett b. abt. 1865. Ohio 19
        Daniel Everett b. abt 1829
        Rebecca Everett b. abt. 1830, m. **Mr. Geist**
        Michael Everett b. abt. 1832, m. **Matilda Hood**
        Charles Everett b. abt. 1836, m. **Susannah Crum**
    Known children of Jane White:
    John White, b. abt. 1842
    Rebecca White, b. abt. 1846
    James M. White, b. abt. 1852

h. Magdaline "Mattie" Everett
    b. 1791, Linn, Northampton Co., Pa.
    m. (1) **Philip Wannamaker** 30 Nov 1813, Trumbull Co, Ohio
      (2) **John Bates/Betz**
    d. 1853 Mahoning Co., Ohio
    Children of Mattie & Philip Wannamaker:
        Julia Wannamaker b. 1814
        Maria Wannamaker b. 1816
    Children of Mattie & John Bates:
        Sophia Bates m. 1830 **John Myers**
        William Bates m. 24 Nov 1831 **Rachel Winter**
        Lucy Bates m. 24 Sep 1849 **Ervin Black**
        Judith Bates

i. Maria Everett
    b. 1795, Linn, Northampton Co., Pa.
    m. **Jonathan Oswald**
    d. 22 Feb 1859 in Girard, Mahoning Co., Ohio

j. Maria Barbara Everett/Ebrit
    b. 1790, Linn, Northampton Co., Pa.
    m. **Christian Wannamaker** 22 Feb 1803, Trumbull Co.
    (Her name is spelled Ebrit in the marriage record).
    d. 4 Jul 1842 Lordstown, Trumbull Co., Ohio
    buried in Girard Cemetery, Girard, Mahoning Co., Ohio
    Known children of Maria Barbara & Christian Wannamaker:
        John Wannamaker m. 1 Dec 1842 **Delly Fusselman**
        Daniel Wannamaker (twin) m. **Persona Lutz**
        Rebecca Wannamaker (twin)

k. Rebecca "Peggy" Everett
    b. abt. 1795 in Linn, Northampton Co., Pa.
    m. **John Moser** 20 Jun 1819, Trumbull Co., Ohio
    d. 1864, Weathersfield, Trumbull Co., Ohio
    Children of Rebecca & John Moser:
        Timothy Moser
        Samuel Moser
        Cornelius Moser, b. 18 Jul 1820
        Philip Moser
        John Moser
        Michael Moser
        Charles Moser
        Mary Moser
        Elizabeth Moser
        Lucy Moser

l. Susanna Everett
    b. 1798, Weathersfield, Trumbull Co., Ohio
    m. **Daniel Moser** 20 Jun 1819, Trumbull Co., Ohio
    d. 9 Jun 1857, Trumbull Co., Ohio
    buried in Girard Cemetery, Girard, Mahoning Co., Ohio
    Children of Susanna & Daniel Moser:
        Phoebe Moser, b. abt 1821
        Solomon Moser, b. abt. 1824
        (He is called 'Lemuel' in the 1850 census)
        Mary Barbara Moser, b. abt.1826
        Charles E. Moser, b. abt 1828
        Sarah Moser, b. abt 1829
        Henrietta Moser, b. 4 Dec 1832
        Angelinus Moser, b. abt 1833

Sarah Moser, b. abt. 1836
Sylvanius S. Moser, b. 1837
Samuel E. Moser, b. abt 1838 *
Horace Moser, b. abt 1840
(Is he the one called Harrison in later records?)
P.N. Moser (male), b. abt. 1841 *
(Note: P. N. Moser, while listed in the Everett Genealogy, is not listed on the 1850 census when he should have been about 9 years old. Another problem is that Samuel was listed as only 12 in the 1850 census, yet the Everett work has him born in 1818.)

m. Lydia Everett (twin)
b. 16 Oct 1799, Weathersfield, Trumbull Co., Ohio
m. Horatio Nelson Pringle/Prindle 18 Aug 1822 in Trumbull Co., Ohio
d. 1837
Children of Lydia & Horatio Pringle:
Samuel Pringle b. 1826 (married a Boston lady
and moved to California)
Charles Pringle b. 1828 m. 31 Aug 1852 Martha Ann
Stoddard (remained in Girard, Ohio)

n. Esther Everett (twin)
b. 16 Oct 1799, Weathersfield, Trumbull Co., Ohio
m. 2 Sep 1820 Jonas Wannamaker (her first cousin)
d. 31 Jan 1875 in Boscobeh, Grant Co., Wisc.
bur. Steele Cemetery, Boscobeh, Wisc.
Children of Esther and Jonas Wannamaker:
Charles E Wannamaker, b. Dec. 1820 m. Mary Bacon
Susan Elizabeth Wannamaker, b. 23 Mar 1821
m. Dr. William Fry
Samuel W. Wannamaker, b. 23 Feb 1822 m. Maria J. Hill
Sarah A. Wannamaker, b. 1 Nov 1824 m. Ethan Bowen
Mary Barbara Wannamaker, b. 1825 m. Eli Emmons
Jonas Everett Wannamaker, 30 Apr 1827
m. Elizabeth Angeline Hill
Lydia Wannamaker, b. 1829 m. Isaac Clark Jones
Rebecca Elizabeth Wannamaker, b. 23 Mar 1833
m. Chauncey Harrison Steele
Clarice Magdalene Wannamaker, b. 8 Jul 1835
m. Leonard Fry
Catherine Esther Wannamaker, b. 18 Jan 1838
m. James Bradford Newcomb
Nelson Daniel Wannamaker, b. 12 Feb 1840
m. Mary Magdaline Mounts
Emma Gertrude Wannamaker, b. 12 Oct 1844
m. Robert Wyley Dennis

3. Catherine Moser Ohl

Catherine Moser, the second child of Johann Philip Moser and Maria Barbara, as born in 1756, in Linn, Northampton County, Pennsylvania. Shortly after the Revolutionary War, she married Michael Ohl (b. 1750, d. 1825), son of Michael Ohl (b. 26 Jun 1729, d. 4 Jul 1804 at age 74) and Elisabeth Barbara _____ (d. age 37). Catherine died in 1826 and they are buried in Heidelberg Cemetery, Heidelberg, Lehigh (now Schulykill) County, Pennsylvania near his parents and stepmother, Maria _____ (b. 23 Dec 1751, d. 27 Apr 1829). Supposed children of Catherine Moser and Michael:

George Ohl, Jun 1792, d. 11 Mar 1862
Elisabeth Ohl m. **John Dietrich** (1779-1830)
Eve Ohl
Christine Ohl
Catherine Ohl, b. 28 Jan 1790
  m. 1802 **John Strausburger**
  d. 25 Mar 1848 Pickaway County, Ohio
Samuel Ohl, b. 1833

(Note: both Catherine and Michael were deceased before the birth of Samuel in 1833!)

A **Michael Ohl**, age 66, b. Pa., a miller by trade, shows up in the Trumbull Co., Ohio 1850 census, wife Elisabeth (65) and Julia (19). Nearby is **Michael Ohl, Jr.**, age 31, a farmer, with wife **Eliza**, age 30 and a son, Edward, who was born in September of that year. (Michael Jr. m. **Eliza Jane Campbell** 8 Mar 1849 in Trumbull County, Ohio.)

There is a **Henry Ohl** (b. 1762, d. 21 Oct 1857, age 87-5-16) who may be the brother of Michael. He is buried in Weiland Private Cemetery, near Lima, Mahoning County, Ohio, and is the father of the Michael above (b. 1784) from whom the DAR members have based their membership.

A **Michael & Elisabeth Barbara Ohl** had a daughter, **Eva Catharina** (b. 9 Jan 1753) bp. at the Egypt Reformed Church. Sponsors were **Andreas Ohl** (son of **Henrich Ohl**), **Henrich Roeder** son of the late **Henrich Roeder** & **Eva Elisabeth Gucker** (daughter of **Bardell Gucker** & **Anna Catharina Ohl**, daughter of **Henrich Ohl**.)

4. Johann Philip Moser

Philip Moser, oldest son of **Johann Philip Moser** and **Maria Barbara**, was born Jul 1757 in Linn, Northampton County, Pennsylvania. After the Revolutionary War (in which he served as a private in the 3rd Bat., Northampton Militia) he married **Catharina Margaret Schuck** and they moved to Centre County. Catharina had a brother named **Johannes Schuck** (b. 15 Sep 1761, d. 11 Feb 1799) who also went to Centre County. Soon after their arrival, they began to call themselves by the name of **MUSSER**. The reason for the change is unknown, but lies buried with them. Perhaps a quarrel erupted over who would inherit their father's mill. Perhaps they wanted to leave the "plain" Lutheran religion of their father to join the less rigid terms of the "fancy" or Reformed Lutherans. Or perhaps they just wanted the opportunities in the less settled Centre County. Whatever the reason, the fact remains that three sons of Philip, the millowner, left their homes in Linn and became the Mussers of Centre County.

Philip and Catharina were married about 1784. Their first three children may have been born before the move, as baptism records were not found for them in Centre County. Philip does not appear in the 1790 Census for Northampton County. Although two Philips lived in Linn, the number and ages of the children do not match this Philip. In 1790, our Philip had a wife, a son age 7 and a daughter age 5.

Philip died 19 Jul 1804; Catharina, born in Jul 1759 died 14 Apr 1839 (cemetery stone reads 13 Apr 1839). They are buried together in the Heckman Church cemetery, Penn Valley, Centre County, Pennsylvania. Children of Philip and Catharina:
  a. John Philip Moser
    b. 1783, probably Linn, Northampton Co., Pa.
    m. **Elisabeth Kraemer** @ 1810
    d. 21 Jun 1835, Centre Co., Pa.
    buried Heckman Cemetery

b. **Catharina Moser**
    b. 2 Feb. 1785, probably Linn, Northampton Co., Pa
    m. **Michael Moser**
    d. 1822, Centre Co., Pa.
    buried Heckman Cemetery
c. **David Moser**
    b. 29 Jan 1791, in Penn Valley, Centre Co., Pa.
    m. **Magdalena Seiss**
    d. 5 Nov 1862 Centre Co., Pa.
    buried Heckman Cemetery
d. **Johannes Moser**
    bp. 8 Jan 1793, Haines Twp., Northumberland Co., Pa.
    m. **Susanna Fielder** 15 May 1822
    d. 1880, Bellefonte, Pa.
e. **Elisabeth Moser**
    b. abt. 1799, Pa.
    m. **John Housman**
    d. 1861 in Trumbull Co., Ohio
f. **Barbara Moser**
    b. 16 May 1795, Northumberland Co., Pa.
    m. **Johannes Harter**
g. **Sarah Moser**
    b. 16 Feb1797, Northumberland Co., Pa.
    m. **George Schwartz**
h. **Maria Eva "Polly" Moser**
    b. 11 Aug 1789, Northumberland Co., Pa.
    m. **George Ilgen** They went to Stephenson Co., Illinois
i. **Mary Magdalena Moser**
    b. 29 Jan 1802, Centre Co., Pa. She never married

4a. John Philip Moser, Jr.

John Philip Moser, Jr., born 1783, is the first known child of **Johann Philip Moser** and **Catharina Margaret Schuck**. Although Charles Recker, in the *"People of the Marsh"* newsletters, stated that he was their third son. no older children have been found. Philip married **Elisabeth Kraemer** about 1810, by whom he had five children. Children of John Philip Moser and Elisabeth Kraemer:

a. 1 **Samuel Moser**
a. 2 **Johann Philip Moser**
    b. 4 Sep 1813
    bp. Penn Creek Church, Gregg Twp., Centre Co., Pa. (No date given)
        sponsors: Johannes & Anna Maria Miller
a. 3 **Johannes Moser**
    b. 26 Oct 1825, Centre Co., Pa.
    bp. 20 Nov. 1825, Penn Creek Church, Gregg Twp.
a. 4 **George Moser**
    b. 6 Mar 1827, Centre Co., Pa.
    bp. 11 Mar 1827, Penn Creek Church, Gregg Twp.
a. 5 **David Moser**
    b. 19 Mar 1829, Centre Co., Pa.
    bp. 30 Mar 1829, Penn Creek Church, Gregg Twp.
    m. **Catharine** _____, b. abt. 1828, Pa.
    Had daughter **Alice Moser**, b. 1850.
Philip died in 1835 and Elisabeth died 1843. They are buried together in Heckmans Cemetery, Penn Valley, Centre Co., Pennsylvania.

NOTE: Some sources claim that John Philip married (2) **Catherina Reichard** and had children: **Philip Timotheus Moser, Md.** b. 10 Nov 1828, Centre Co., Pa. and **Rachel Moser**, b. 23 Jun 1830, Centre Co., Pa., m. **John Lord.** Other sources claim that Philip Timotheus was two separate people. However, Dr. Philip Timotheus Moser lived in Haines Township, Centre County, Pennsylvania in 1850. He was not married. Unless Philip had practiced polygamy, he could not have been the Philip married to Catherina Reichard, as her two children were born before the death of Philip's first wife, Elisabeth. Catherina was therefore married to an unidentified Philip Moser.

4c. David Moser

David Moser, son of **John Philip Moser** and **Catharina Margaret Schuck**, was born 29 Jan 1791 in Penn Valley, Centre County, Pennsylvania. He married about 1818 **Magdalena Seiss** (b. 19 Dec 1786, d. 29 Mar. 1856). They had two children baptized in Heidelberg, Lehigh County, Pennsylvania. No other records have been found for this family. David died on 5 Nov 1862 and is buried in Heckman's Cemetery with his wife, where there is a War of 1812 marker on his grave. Known children of David and Magdalena Moser:

Matilda Moser
b. 22 Jun 1819, Lehigh Co., Pa.
bp. 29 Jul 1819, Heidelberg Reformed Church,
Heidelberg, Lehigh Co., Pa.
sponsor: Philip Moser
Fianna Moser
b. 9 Aug 1821, Lehigh Co., Pa.
bp. 2 Sep 1821, Heidelberg Lutheran Church,
Heidelberg, Lehigh Co., Pa.
sponsors: Michael Frey and Elisabeth Moser

4d. Johannes Moser

Johannes Moser, son of **John Philip Moser** and **Catharina Margaret Schuck**, was baptized 8 Jan 1793 in Haines Township, Northumberland County, Pennsylvania. On 15 May 1822 he married **Susanna Fielder**, daughter of **Johann Jacob Fielder**. They moved to Spring Township, Centre County, Pennsylvania by 1850. The surname in the census is written with the old-style double S. Johannes died in 1880 in Bellefonte, Pa. Children of Johannes and Susanna Moser:

d.1 Philip Moser
b. 19 Jan 1823 in Centre Co., Pa.
m. **Sara Hanebike**
d. 1909 in Illinois
He was a carpenter, and went to Stephenson Co., Illinois.
d.2 Catharine Moser
b. 6 May 1824, Centre Co., Pa.
bp. 6 Jun 1824, Penn Creek Church, Gregg Twp., Centre Co.
m. **Joseph Keller**
d. 1887 in Rudd, Stephenson Co., Illinois.
d.3 Magdalena "Molly" Moser
b. 6 Nov 1825, Centre Co., Pa.
bp. 27 Dec 1825, Penn Creek Church, Gregg Twp.
sponsors: Michael and Catharina Moser
m. **John George Breon**
They went to Lena, Illinois

d.4 Rebecca Moser
>b. 12 Aug 1827, Centre Co., Pa.
>bp. 25 Sep 1827, Penn Creek Church, Gregg Twp.
>sponsors: Johannes & Barbara Harter
>m. **William Kaslin (or Kerlin)**
>d. 1893
>They went to Rudd, Iowa.

d.5 John J. Moser
>b. 10 Mar 1829 in Brush Valley, Centre Co., Pa.
>(bap. record not found.)
>m. 1857 (1) **Nancy J. Baird** (1836-1879)
>   (2) **Sarah J. Miller** (1857-1938)
>d. 1901

d.6 Susanna Moser
>b. 26 Jan 1831, Centre Co., Pa.
>bp. 3 Apr 1831, Penn Creek Church, Gregg Twp.
>sponsor: her maiden aunt, Magdalena Moser
>m. **Johannes Wentzel**
>d. 1911 in Spring Twp., Centre Co., Pa.
>She is listed as only 17 in the 1850 census record.28

d.7 Samuel D. Moser
>b. 7 Oct 1832, Haines Twp., Centre Co., Pa.
>m. 1870 **Sarah J. Cantner**
>He is listed as only 15 in the 1850 census record.
>d. 1915, buried in Milheim Cemetery in Scranton.
>Samuel served in the Civil War. They went to Scranton, Luzerne Co., Pa.

d.8 Michael M. Moser
>b. 11 Oct 1834, Miles Twp., Centre Co., Pa.
>m. Sep 1863 **Catherina Fisher**
>He is listed as only 13 in the 1850 census record.
>He served as a Lieutenant during the Civil War.

d.9 Israel Moser
>b. 30 Jan 1838, Centre Co., Pa.
>bp. 27 Feb 1838, Penn Creek Church, Gregg Twp.
>sponsor: his maiden aunt, Magdalena Moser
>He is listed as 11 in the 1850 census record.
>He was killed in 1863 while serving as a Lieutenant during
>the Civil War. He never married.

d.10 Maria J. Moser
>b. 1 Jul 1842, Centre Co., Pa.
>bp. 30 Oct 1842, Penn Creek Church, Gregg Twp.
>m. **Rev. William Schoch** (Lutheran)
>d. 1921
>She is listed as 8 in the 1850 census record.
>They lived in New Berlin, Snyder Co., Pa. and in Ogle Co., Ill.

4d.3 Magdalena "Molly" Moser Breon

Magdalena "Molly" Moser, daughter of **Johannes Moser** and **Susanna Fielder**, was born in Centre County, Pennsylvania on 6 Nov 1825. She was baptized 27 Dec 1825 at Penn Creek Church, Gregg Township, Centre County, Pennsylvania. She married **John George Breon**, son of **Jacob** and **Maria Breon**. He was born 6 Dec 1818 in Centre County Pennsylvania and baptized 14 Feb 1819 at Penn Creek Church. They moved to Illinois. It is possible that Magdalena was his second wife. There was a **George Breon** with a wife named **Catharine** who had the following three children baptized at Penn Creek Church:

Jonathan Breon
    b. 23 Sep 1832
    bp. 22 Nov 1832
    sponsors: Anna Maria and George Confer
Wilhelm Breon
    b. 28 Aug 1835
    bp 11 Oct 1835
    sponsors: Maria and Wilhelm Graff
Susanna Breon
    b. 10 Feb 1838
    bp. 16 Oct 1838
    sponsors: Daniel and Maria Breon
George and Catharine are listed in the 1850 census records with a family of 10 children. It is not known when the family left for Lena, Stephenson County, Illinois. Did this George Breon marry the much younger Magdalena before they headed west?

4d.5 John J. Moser

John J. Moser, son of **Johannes Moser** and **Susanna Fielder** was born in 1829 in Brush Valley, Centre County, Pennsylvania. No baptism records were found for him. He was married in 1857 to **Nancy J. Baird**. Childr of John and Nancy Moser:
    Frank W. Moser
After Nancy's death, John married **Sarah J. Miller** and had two more children:
    Eva Moser m. **Dr. _____ Kirk**
    Children of Dr. and Eva Kirk:
        Harold Kirk
        Norman Kirk
        Lois Kirk
    Katie (or Carie) S. Moser m. **Daniel Rhinesmith**
    Children of Katie and Daniel Rhinesmith:
        Mary Rhinesmith
        Nannie (Nancy?) Rhinesmith

4d.6 Susanna Moser Wentzel

Susanna Moser, daughter of **Johannes Moser** and **Susanna Fielder** was born 26 Jan 1831 in Centre County, Pennsylvania. She was baptized at Penn Creek Church, Gregg Township on 3 Apr 1831. Her sponsor was Magdalena Moser, the unmarried sister of her father. She married **Johannes Wentzel**, son of **Johannes** and **Christina Wentzel**. He was born 5 Aug 1829 in Centre County and baptized at Penn Creek Church on 7 May 1830. His sponsor was Johannes Schmidt, a single man.

4d.7 Samuel D. Moser

Samuel D. Moser, son of **Johannes Moser** and **Susanna Fielder** was born 7 Oct 1832 in Haines Township, Centre County, Pennsylvania. No baptism record has been found. He married **Sarah J. Cantner**, daughter of **John Cantner** and **Mary Ellen Briggs**. Children of Samuel and Sarah Moser:
    Mabel Moser married **Walter Price**
    Walter Moser married **Mary Hoover**
    Marian Moser married **Paul Sheffer**
    Marion Herbert M. Moser

4d.8 Michael M. Moser

Michael M. Moser, son of **Johannes Moser** and **Susanna Fielder**, was born 11 Oct 1834 in Miles Township, Centre County, Pennsylvania. No baptism record has been found. He married Sep 1865 **Catherina Fisher**, daughter of **Adam Fisher** and **Mary Brussman**. Children of Michael M. Moser and Catherina Fisher:

William S. Moser, 20 Jul 1866, Gregg Township, Centre Co., Pa.

Irene C. Moser (twin), b. 8 Oct 1867, Haines Township, Centre Co., Pa.

Charles H. Moser (twin), 8 Oct 1867, Haines Township, Centre Co., Pa.

Mary S. Moser

        b. 17 Apr 1870, Centre Co., Pa.

        m. _____ **Mertis**

Edward Moser

4f. Barbara Moser Harter

Barbara Moser, daughter of **John Philip Moser** and **Catharina Margaret Schuck** was born in Centre County, Pennsylvania 16 May 1795. She married **Johannes Harter**, son of **Andrew** and **Salome Harter**. A daughter, **Maria Catharina Harter**, was born on 16 Aug 1820 and baptized 10 Sep 1820 at Penn Creek Church, Gregg Township, Centre County, Pennsylvania. The sponsor was Barbara's mother, Catharina Moser, now a widow. Johannes and Barbara sponsored a child of her sister, Sarah Schwartz in January 1823. Since there is no further mention of this couple in Gregg Township, they probably left the area. A John Harter (b. 15 Dec 1792, d. 11 Feb 1884) is buried in Aaronsburg, Centre County, Pennsylvania.

4g. Sarah Moser Schwartz

Sarah Moser, daughter of **John Philip Moser** and **Catharina Margaret Schuck** was born 16 Feb 1797 in Northumberland (now Centre) County, Pensylvannia. She married **George Schwartz** (b. about 1797) about 1821. They were farming in Haines Township, Centre County, Pennsylvania in 1850. Sarah died 5 Sep 1873 in Centre County, while George died 10 Dec 1979. Children of Sarah and George Schwartz:

Johannes Schwartz

        b. 20 Dec 1822, Gregg Twp., Centre Co., Pa.

        bp. 26 Dec 1822, Penn Creek Church, Gregg Twp.

        Sponsors: John and Barbara Harter (his mother's sister)

Philip Schwartz

        b. 13 Apr 1824, Gregg Twp., Centre Co., Pa.

        bp. 9 May 1824, Penn Creek Church

        Sponsors: Henrich and Elisabeth Hausman (his mother's sister).

Catharina Schwartz

        b. 8 Oct 1825, Gregg Twp., Centre Co., Pa.

        bp 8 Nov 1824, Penn Creek Church

        Sponsor: Widow Catharina Musser, grandmother

George Schwartz

        b. about 1828

Daniel Schwartz

        b. about 1832

Sarah Rose Schwartz

        b. about 1837

4h. Maria Eva "Polly" Moser Ilgin

Maria Eva "Polly" Moser, born 11 Aug 1789 in Northumberland (now Centre) County, Pennsylvania, was a daughter of **John Philip Moser** and **Catharina Margaret Schuck** married **George Ilgen (Elgin)** who was probably a son of **Rev. Ludwig Albert Wilhelm Ilgen**. They had six children born in Centre County, Pennsylvania before moving to Illinois. Children of Maria and George Ilgen:

Wilhelm Emanuel Ilgen
> b. 27 Aug 1822, Centre Co., Pa.
> bp. 29 Aug 1822, Penn Creek Church, Gregg Twp.
> sponsors: Rev. L. A. W. & Anna Barbara Ilgin

Johan Joseph Emanuel Ilgen
> b. 11 Mar 1824, Centre Co., Pa.
> bp. 11 Apr 1824, Penn Creek Church, Gregg Twp.
> Sponsors: Philip Ludwig and Elisabeth Moser

Henrietta Ilgen
> b. 7 Sep 1827, Centre Co., Pa.
> bp. 7 Oct 1827, Penn Creek Church, Gregg Twp.
> Sponsors: Michael and Catharina Moser

Ludwig Thomas Ilgen
> b. 6 Sep 1829, Centre Co., Pa.
> bp. 18 Oct 1829, Penn Creek Church, Gregg Twp.
> Sponsors: Thomas and Anna Foster

Sarah Johanna Ilgen
> b. 16 Dec 1831, Centre Co., Pa.
> bp. 4 Mar 1831, Penn Creek Church, Gregg Twp.
> Sponsor: Magdalena Moser, her mother's sister

David Ilgen
> b. 5 Jul 1839, Centre Co., Pa.
> bp. 23 Feb 1839, Penn Creek Chruch, Gregg Twp.
> Sponsors: David and Magdalena Moser (His mother's brother)

5. Johann Sebastian Mosser

Johann Sebastian Moser, son of **Johann Philip Mosser** and **Maria Barbara**, was born on 3 Jan 1760 in Linn, Northampton County, Pennsylvania. He was baptized on 26 Jan 1761. Sebastian served in the Revolutionary War as did his brothers. He married 12 May 1783 **Anna Maria Miller** who was born 15 Jul 1762, also in Linn. They moved to Centre County shortly after the War, where they became known as **'Musser'**. They were a highly respected couple, and were often called upon to act as sponsor at baptisms . Sebastian died 29 Nov 1829. His wife survived him for several years to enjoy her many grandchildren. She died in 1842. They are buried together in Heckmans Cemetery, Penn Valley, Centre County, Pennsylvania. Only child of Sebastian and Anna Maria:

Philip B. Moser
> b. 27 Aug 1795 in Northampton Co., Pa.
> m. Elisabeth Ilgin, 4 Nov 1806 in Centre Co., Pa.
> d. 1873 in Milheim, Centre Co., Pa.

5a. Philip B. Moser

Philip B. Moser, only child of **Rev. Johann Sebastian Moser** and **Anna Maria Miller**, was born 27 Aug 1795 in Northampton County, Pennsylvania. Philip was an avid hunter and was said to have got six hundred deer and forty bear in his lifetime. By occupation, he was a miller. He moved to Centre County, Pennsylvania with his family. On 4 Nov 1806 he married **Elisabeth Ilgen**, daughter of **Rev. Ludwig Albert Wilhelm Ilgen** and **Anna Barbara _____**. According to the 1850 census, Anna Barbara was born in New Jersey in 1790.

Philip and Elisabeth made their home in Gregg township, Centre County until after 1839 when they moved to Aaronsburg, Centre County, Pennsylvania. After Elisabeth's death on 15 Jul 1854, Philip moved to Milheim, still in Centre County, where he died in 1873. Children of Philip and Elisabeth Moser:

1. **Johan Sebastian Moser**
   b. 29 Mar 1808, Gregg Twp., Centre Co., Pa.
   bp. 24 Apr 1808, Penn Creek Church, Gregg Twp.
   Sponsors: Sebastian and Anna Maria Moser
   m. **Maria Neese (or Meese)**
   d. 9 Jan 1887, Penn Twp., Centre Co., Pa.
   He became a Lutheran minister

2. **Ludwig Albright Wilhelm Moser**
   b. 10 Apr 1810, Gregg Twp., Centre Co., Pa.
   bp. 20 May 1810, Penn Creek Church, Gregg Twp.
   Sponsors: Rev. L.A.W. and Anna Barbara Ilgen
   m. (1) 1835, **Elisabeth Hubler**
      (2) 1846, **Elisabeth Yeager**
      (3) 1850, **Rebecca Stine**
   d. 4 Oct 1889, Milheim, Snyder Co., Pa.

3. **Marie Elisabeth Moser**
   b. 10 Oct 1811, Centre Co., Pa.
   bp. record not found
   m. **George Moser** (1804-1846) son of **Michael Moser** and **Anna Margaretha Weber**
   d. 7 Jan 1846, Gregg Twp., Centre Co., Pa.

4. **John Philip Moser**
   b. 4 Sep 1813, Gregg Twp., Centre Co., Pa.
   bp. 4 Nov 1813, Penn Creek Church, Gregg Twp.
   Sponsors: Johannes and Anna Maria Miller
   d. 1814

5. **Philip Andrew Moser**
   bp. 9 Dec 1815, Penn Creek Church, Gregg Twp.
   no sponsors listed
   d. 11 Oct 1894, Penn Twp., Centre Co., Pa.
   He was a farmer.

6. **Anna Barbara Moser**
   b. 3 Jul 1818, Gregg Twp., Centre Co., Pa.
   bp. 2 Aug 1818, Penn Creek Church, Gregg Twp.
   m. **John Huber**
   buried in Brush Valley, Pa.

7. **John G. Moser**
   b. 12 Dec 1820, Centre Co., Pa.
   baptism record not found
   m. **Julia Huber**
   They are buried in Milheim, Pa.

8. **Daniel Emanuel Moser**
   b. 28 Jun 1822, Gregg Twp., Centre Co., Pa.
   bp. 24 Jul 1822, Penn Creek Church, Gregg Twp.
   sponsors: Daniel and Susanna Oswald
   m. 29 Jun 1851 **Lydia Sheffler**
   d. 30 Jun 1888, Mifflinburg, Snyder Co., Pa.
9. **Maria Catharina Moser**
   b. 16 Feb 1827, Gregg Twp, Centre Co., Pa.
   bp. (date not given), Penn Creek Church, Gregg Twp.
   Sponsor: Lidia Ilgen, single
   m. **Thomas Frank** (1821-1886)
10. **Lydia Eva Moser**
   b. 16 Mar 1828, Gregg Twp., Centre Co., Pa.
   bp. 9 Apr 1828, Penn Creek Church, Gregg Twp.
   Sponsors: Jacob and Eva Hering
11. **John Friedrich Ilgen Moser**
   b. 23 Jan 1830, Gregg Twp., Centre Co., Pa.
   bp. 28 Jan 1830, Penn Creek Church, Gregg Twp.
   Sponsors: Friedrich and Catharine Abele
12. **James Jacobi Moser**
   b. 19 Nov 1834, Union County, Pa.
   bp. 26 Dec 1834, Penn Creek Church, Gregg Twp.
   Sponsors: his parents (Name in baptism record is "Noa Jacobi")
   m.(1) **Catharine Albert** (1836-1885)
       (2) **Mary A. Musser**
   They went to Hartletown, Union Co., Pa.
13. **Samuel Moser**
   b. abt 1835 (age 13 in 1850 census)
   baptism record not found
14. **Sarah C. Moser**
   b. 20 Feb 1839, Pa.
   baptism record not found
   m. **Fredrick Catherman** (1823-1912)
   She is listed as 14 in the 1850 census

5a1 Rev. Johann Sebastian Moser

Johann Sebastian Moser, son of **Philip B. Moser** and **Elisabeth Ilgen**, was born in Gregg Township, Centre County, Pennsylvania on 29 Mar 1808. He was baptized at the Penn Creek Church on 29 Mar 1808, with his grandprents, **Johann Sebastian Moser** and **Anna Maria Miller** acting as sponsors. He followed in the footsteps of his maternal grandfather, the **Rev. Ludwig Albert Wilhelm Ilgen** and became a Lutheran minister. He married about 1829 **Maria Neese (or Meese)**. They had one child born in Greeg Township. It is believed he went to service a church in Union County, Pennsylvania, so the other children may have been born there. However, he was living in Harter Township, Centre county during the 1850 Federal Census, where his occupation was listed as "farmer". He died in Penn Township on 9 Jan 1887. Known children of Johann Sebastian and Anna Maria:

Sarah Moser
   b. 13 Sep 1830
   bp. Penn Creek Chutch, Gregg Twp., Centre Co., Pa.
John Moser b. abt 1831, Pa.
Rebecca Moser b. abt. 1836, Pa.
Samuel Moser b. abt 1838, Pa.
William Moser b. abt 1840, Pa.

5a2. Ludwig Albright Wilhelm Moser

Ludwig Albright Wilhelm Moser, son of **Philip B. Moser** and **Elisabeth Ilgen**, was born on 10 Apr 1810 in Gregg Township, Centre County, Pennsylvania and baptized on 20 May 1810 at the Penn Creek Church, with his maternal grandparents, **Rev. Ludwig Albright Wilhelm** and **Anna Barbara Ilgen** acting as his sponsors. He married (1) **Elisabeth Huber** about 1836 and they moved to Milheim, Union County, Pennsylvania. Children of Ludwig and Elisabeth Moser:

Maggie Moser
        b. 1837, Union Co., Pa.
        d. 1854, Union Co., Pa.
Elisabeth Moser
        b. 1840, Union Co., Pa.
        m. **Elias Condo**
Sarah J. Moser
        b. 1843, Union Co., Pa.
        m. **Samuel Resman**
        They went to Nebraska

Elisabeth died about 1845, and Ludwig married **Elisabeth Yeager** as his second wife. She died in 1848, giving birth to twin daughters, **Clara** and **Emma Moser**. Ludwig then married **Rebecca Stine** who became the mother of his daughters. Of the twins, Clara died young, but Emma grew to maturity and married **Captain Heimbach**. There are not any known children born to Ludwig and Rebecca. Ludwig died in Milheim, Union (now Snyder) County, Pennsylvania on 4 Oct 1889.

5a7 John G. Moser

John G. Moser, son of **Philip B.** and **Elisabeth Ilgen**, was born in Centre County, Pennsylvania on 12 Dec 1820, probably in Gregg Township, but his baptism record has not been found. John married **Julia Huber** (born about 1817). They lived in Milheim, Union (now Snyder) County, Pennsylvania, where John was a farmer. John died in Milheim. Children of John G. and Julia Moser:

Ralph M. Moser (b. 1843)
Clarence Moser (d. 1846)
Emma C. Moser (b. 1846) m. **J.H. Swartz/Schwartz**
Andrew Clark Moser (b. 1848) m. **Margaret Kistler** (dau of **Jeremiah Kistler**
        and **Elizabeth Miller**, born 15 Mar 1841)
        Children of Andrew and Margaret Moser:
                Bertha E. Moser
                Norman Lester Moser
                Thomas B. Moser
                Frederick W. Moser
                John F. Moser
                Grover G. Moser
                Lizzie Moser
                Orvis Moser
                Paul Moser
                Mary Moser
                Claude E. Moser
Charles Moser (b. 1850)
James B. Moser (went to California to look for gold, but returned to Pennsylvania.
        Source didn't say if he found any, though!)
Anna Moser

5a8 Daniel Emanuel Moser

Daniel Emanuel Moser, son of **Philip B. Moser** and **Elisabeth Ilgen**, was born 28 Jan 1822 in Gregg Township, Centre County, Pennsylvania and baptized at the Penn Creek Church on 24 Jul 1822, with Daniel and Susanna Oswald acting as sponsors. On 29 Jun 1851, Daniel married **Lydia Sheffler**, daughter of **Daniel Sheffler** and **Rachel Moyer** in Mifflinberg, Union County, Pennsylvania. She was born 2 Mar 1826 in Milheim, Union County, Pennsylvania. Daniel died 30 Jun 1888. Children of Daniel Emanuel and Lydia Moser:

Pierce Moser
> b. 31 Oct 1852, Pa.
> d. 1915
> He had a daughter, **Maude Moser** m. _____ **Breneman**

Janie A. Moser
> b. 5 Aug 1855, Pa.
> m. **A. Walter** of Milheim

Elizabeth A. Moser
> b. 16 Sep 1857, Pa.
> died young

Jane Mary Belle Moser
> b. 4 Apr 1860, Pa.
> m. **C.A. Sturgis**
> They went to West Union Co., Iowa

Rose E. Moser
> b. 4 Aug 1863, Pa.
> m. **T.R. Stamm**
> They went to West Union Co., Iowa

Clymer Moser
> b. 6 Sep 1866, Pa.
> He also went to Iowa.

Milton O. Moser
> b. 2 Feb 1870, Pa.

Went to Union Co., Iowa

6. Daniel Moser

Daniel Moser, son of **Johann Philip Moser** and **Maria Barbara**, was born on 14 Aug 1762 in Mosserville, Northampton County, Pennsylvania. He was baptized on 19 Sep 1762 at age four weeks by Rev. Schumacher. Like his brothers, he served in the Revolutionary War. He married 17 Oct 1787 **Magdalena Oswald**, born 15 Dec 1767, daughter of **Daniel Oswald** and **Catharine Everett**. They went to Haines Township, Center County where they became known as **"Musser"**.

Daniel died 16 Jul 1804 and is buried in Wolf's Chapel, Penn Valley, Centre County, Pennsylvania. His will was probated in 1807. Magdalena, b. 15 Dec 1767, survived him for nearly forty years, leaving this earth on 16 Nov 1842. She is buried with her husband. Children of Daniel and Magdalena Moser (Musser):

a. Philip Jacob Moser
> b. 17 Oct 1787, Pa.
> m. (1) **Kathryn Lutz**
>   (2) **Elizabeth Weber**
> d. 1865 Center Co., Pa.

b. Daniel Moser
>> b. 6 Nov1790, Northampton County, Pa.
>> bp. 26 Dec 1790, Heidelberg Church, Heidelberg
>>> Northampton Co., Pa.
>>> Sponsors: **Bastian & Anna Maria Moser**
>> m. **Rebecca or Margaret** _____
>> d. 1868, Pine Grove Mills, Centre Co., Pa.

c. David Moser
>> b. 1791, Pa.
>> m. **Mary Magdalena Homan**
>> d. 1852, Centre Co., Pa.
>> buried Heckman's Cemetery, Centre Co., Pa.

d. Maria Magdalena "Polly" Moser
>> b. 16 May 1794, Pa.
>> m. (1) **Daniel Condo**
>>> They had 13 children before he died
>>> (2) **Philip Moser**, son of **Philip** (1763) and **Elisabeth Oswald**
>> d. 1850, Pa.

e. Sara Moser
>> b. 4 Dec 1795, Pa.
>> m. **Nicholas Condo**

f. John Moser
>> b. 4 Dec 1797, Pa.
>> m. **"Polly"** _____
>> d. 1871, Pa.

g. Rosine Moser
>> (There is a Rosine Moser who was confirmed at age 15 in 1810 in
>> the Lutheran Reformed Church in Reading, Pa.)

h. William Moser
>> b. 7 Jan1802, Musser's Valley, Centre Co., Pa.
>> m. 12 Apr 1829 **Kathryn Hess** in Haines Twp.
>> d. 14 Mar 1870 Pine Grove Mills, Centre Co. Pa.

6b. Daniel Moser

Daniel Moser, son of **Daniel Moser** and **Magdalena Oswald**, was born
6 Nov 1790 in Northampton County, Pennsylvania. He was baptized at the Heidelberg
Church on 26 Dec 1790, with his Uncle Johann Sebastian and Aunt Anna Maria Moser
acting as his sponsors. He married about 1816 **Rebecca** _____ by whom he had
two known children. Daniel died in 1868 in Pine Grove Mills, Centre Co.,
Pennsylvania. No further data is available on this couple at this time. Known children
of Daniel and Rebecca Moser:

Johannes Moser
>> b. 11 Mar 1817, Pa.
>> bp. 8 Jun 1817, Penn Creek Church, Gregg Twp., Pa.
>> Sponsors were Philip Jr. & Hanna Moser

Daniel Moser
>> b. 18 Dec. 1820, Pa.
>> bp. 28 Jan 1821, Penn Creek Church, Gregg Twp., Pa.
>> Sponsors were Jacob & Catharina Moser

6d. Maria "Polly" Magdalena Moser Condo

Maria "Polly" Magdalena Moser, daughter of **Daniel Moser** and **Magdalena Oswald**, was born in 1794, probably in Centre County, Pennsylvania. She married (1) **Daniel Condo**, by whom she had at least thirteen children. Daniel was born in 1794 and died in 1844. Known children of Daniel and Magdalena Condo:

1. **Rebekka Condo**
   b. 27 Apr 1836, Centre Co., Pa.
   bp. 17 Jul 1836, Penn Creek Church, Gregg Twp.
   Lived with Philip and Mary Moser in Haines Twp. in 1850.
2. **Elias Condo**
   b. 25 Mar 1838, Centre Co., Pa.
   bp. 15 Apr 1838, Penn Creek Church, Gregg Twp.
   m. **Elisabeth Moser** (b. 1840)
3. **Susan Condo** m. **Philip Moser**
4. **Lydia Condo**
   m. **George Moser** (son of **Jonas**)
5. **Sarah Condo**
   m. **Christian Moser**
   Moved to Ohio

Magdalena married about 1845 **Philip Moser**, son of **Philip Moser** and **Elisabeth Oswald**, her second cousin, as his third wife. There were no children. Magdalena died in 1850. Living with Philip in Gregg Township at the time of the 1850 census, were his wife, **Mary** (54), **Hannah Moser** (18), **Rebecca Condo** (15) and **Elias Condo** (13).

6f John Moser

John Moser, son of **Daniel Moser** and **Magdalena Oswald**, was born in 1791 in Pennsylvania. It is not known if he was born in Linn, Northumberland County before his parents settled in Haines Township, Centre County or not. (His wife's name was **Mary** in the 1850 Centre County, Pennsylvania census). He died in 1871. Children of John and Mary "Polly" Moser:

Elisabeth Moser
   b. abt. 1821, Pa.
   m. **Jacob Stover** of Haines Township, Centre Co., Pa.
Margaret Moser
   b. abt. 1823, Pa.
   m. **Jonathan Kreamer** before 1850
   They went to Effingham, Effingham Co., Illinois
Jonathan Moser . 1826, Pa.
John David Moser
   (A possibility exists that John David and Jonathan (above) only one person, that he married a **Catharine**, age 22, and had a daughter, **Alice**, age 6 mos. in 1860.)
Mary Moser b. 1831, Pa. m. _____ **Shirk**
Rachel Moser b. 1833, Pa.
Susan Moser
   b. 1839, Pa.
   m. **Adam F. Hosterman**
Christina Moser b.1843, Pa.
Diana Moser
   b. 1845, Pa.
   m. **William Cook Huber**
   (She was not found in the 1850 census)
Magdalena Moser b. 1845, Pa.

6h William Moser

William Moser, son of **Daniel Moser** and **Magdalena Oswald** was born on 7 Jan1802, in Musser's Valley, Centre County, Pennsylvania. He married 12 Apr 1829 in Haines Township, **Katherine Hess**, daughter of **John Michael Hess** and **Maria Catherine Kreider**. She was born in 20 Jan1805 near Pine Grove Mill, Centre County, Pennsylvania. William died 14 Mar.1870 in Pine Grove Mills, Centre County, Pa. and Katherine died 24 May1882 in Pleasant Gap, Centre County, Pa. Children of William and Katherine Moser:

1. **Samuel Moser**
   b. 13 Feb1830, Pine Grove, Centre Co., Pa.
   m. 10 Dec 1854 **Nancy Rider**
   d. 12 Aug 1902, Tyronne, Blair Co., Pa.

2. **John Moser**
   b. 15 Dec 1831, Haines Twp., Centre Co., Pa.
   m. **Katharine Dale**
   d. 1904

3. **Rebecca Moser**
   b. 9 Oct 1833, Ferguson Twp., Centre Co., Pa.
   m. **William J. Dale**

4. **Anna Moser**
   b. 26 Apr 1835, Ferguson Twp., Centre Co., Pa.
   m. **John F. Drebs**

5. **Catherine Moser**
   b. 7 Aug 1837, Ferguson Twp., Centre Co., Pa.
   m. **Christian Dale**

6. **Mary Magdalena Moser**
   b. 31 May 1839, Ferguson Twp., Centre Co., Pa.
   m. **Frank B. Stover**

7. **William Henry Moser**
   b. 20 Aug 1841, Ferguson Twp., Centre Co., Pa.
   m. **Sarah Elizabeth Shiffer**
   d. 9 Jan 1916, Bellefonte, Pa.

8. **George Daniel Moser**
   b. 18 Aug 1843, Ferguson Twp., Centre Co., Pa.
   He was killed in the Civil War

9. **Nathan C. Moser**
   b. 24 May 1848, Ferguson Twp., Centre Co., Pa.
   d. 1853

6h.1 Samuel Musser

Samuel Musser, son of **William Musser** and **Katherine Hess**, was born 13 Feb 1830 in Pine Grove Mills, Centre County, Pennsylvania. He married 10 Dec 1854 in Rider Farm, Gatesburg Township, Centre County, Pennsylvania, **Nancy Rider**, daughter of **Michael G. Rider** and **Barbara Kreider**. Nancy was born 13 Aug 1830 in Rider Farm and died 10 Dec 1914 at the Houser Residence in Baileyville, Pennsylvania. Samuel preceded her in death on 12 Aug 1902 in Tyrone, Blair County, Pennsylvania.
Children of Samuel and Nancy Musser:

1. **Ellen Martha Musser**
    b. 11 Sep 1855, The Branch, Centre Co., Pa.
    m. 12 Oct 1882 **John Timothy Reamy**
    d. 4 Apr 1916
2. **Anna Catharine Musser**
    b. 6 Jan 1857, Marengo, Centre Co., Pa.
    m. 4 Jun 1889 **Luther Murry Houser**
    d. 6 Mar 1937, Baileyville, Pa.
3. **Edward Rider Musser**
    b. 9 Jan 1859, Marengo, Centre Co., Pa.
    m. 22 Sep 1886 **Harriet Elizabeth Gardner**
    d. 18 Oct 1916, Tyrone, Blair Co., Pa.
4. **William Franklin Musser**
    b. 27 Oct 1860, Marengo, Centre Co., Pa.
    m. **Edith E. Moore**
    d. 30 Nov 1894
5. **Mary Ida Musser**
    b. 1863, Marengo, Centre Co., Pa.
    m. 8 Dec 1891, Musser Farm, Fairbrook Co., Pa.
    William Neff Van Tries
    d. 25 Jan 1912, Tyrone, Blair Co., Pa.
6. **Irvin Michael Musser**
    b. 26 Dec 1864, Marengo, Centre Co., Pa.
    m. 27 Sep 1893, Pennsylvania Furnace, Huntington, Pa.
    Myra Almeda Geist
    d. 15 Nov 1934, State College, Centre Co., Pa.
    Children of Irvin and Myra Musser:
    a. **Robert Stewart Musser**
        b. 9 May 1895, Pa.
        m. (1) 19 Nov 1917, Williamsport, Pa.
        Olga Elizabeth Richter
        (2) **Kathryn G. First**
        d. 4 Sep 1966, Harrisburg, Pa.
    b. **Curry Marshall Musser**
        b. 11 Oct 1905, Barnsboro, Pa.
        m. 8 Nov 1933, Brooklyn, New York City, NY
        Nellie Georgia Tuttle Jul 1907, New York City
        d. 15 May 1977, Orange, Orange, Tx, dau. of **Henry Frank Tuttle** and **Sarah Janice Jacob**
        Child of Curry and Nellie Musser:
        Michael Tuttle Musser
            b. 31 Jan 1942, Williamsport, Lycoming, Pa.
            m. 26 Mar 1966, Lafayette, Tippecanoe, Ind.
            Shirley Ann Stahlhut
            Child of Michael and Shirley:
            Kathleen Musser

7. Walter Scott Musser
  b. 3 Sep 1867, Marengo, Centre Co., Pa.
  m. Tyrone, Pa. **Anna Smith**
  d. 26 Dec 1944, Tyrone, Blair Co., Pa.
8. Emma Francis Musser
  b. 10 Sep 1869, Mareng, Centre Co., Pa.
  m. 19 Jul 1893 Camden, NJ **Emory Ellsworth McClintock**
  d. 26 Aug 1944
9. John Howard Musser
  b. 14 Jan 1872, Furguson Twp., Centre Co., Pa.
  m. 22 Dec 1898, Campbell Farm, Fairbrook Co., Pa.
    Mary Ann Pennington Campbell
  d. 31 Oct 1953, State College, Centre Co., Pa.
10. Barbara Bella Musser
  b. 24 Sep 1873, Marengo, Centre Co., Pa.
  m. 26 Sep 1901, Baileyville, Pa. **Curry H. Love**
  d. 15 Dec 1920, Pennsylvania Furnace, Huntington Co., Pa.
11. Marshall Clemson Musser
  b. 6 Nov 1876, Marengo, Centre Co., Pa.
  m. (1) Jan 1906, Clearfield,, Pa. **Enid Bilger**
    (2) **Annella Bilger**
  d. 2 May 1946, State College, Centre Co., Pa.

7. Jacob Moser

Jacob Moser, son of **Johann Philip Moser** and **Maria Barbara**, was born in 1775 in Northampton County, Pennsylvania. Like his brothers, he moved to Centre County and became known as **'Musser'**. He married about 1804 **Margaretha Hagenbach** who was born in 1779. His will mentions nine children, but only five are known at this time. Jacob died in 1853. Margaretha died in 1851 and is buried in Wolf's Cemetery in Centre County, Pennsylvania. Jacob and Margaretha were found in the 1850 census, living in Haines Township, Centre County, Pennsylvania. A **Lydia Musser**, age 20 was living with them. Known children of Jacob and Margaretha Moser (Musser):

a Mary Magdalena Moser
  b. 1805, Pa.
  m. (1) **Michael Hess**
    (2) **Samuel Hess**, his brother
  d. 1855
b Andrew Moser
  b. 1807, Pa.
  m. **Rachel Huber**
  d. 1865
c Philip Moser
  b. 1812, Pa.
  m. abt. 1836 **Mary Huber**
  d. 1895, Pa.
  (He was listed as age 32 in the1850 census)
d John Moser
  b. 1821, Pa.
  m. **Susan Dale** about 1845
  d. 1895, Pa.
  buried in Wolf's Cemetery, Buffalo Run, Pa.
e Michael Moser
  b. 1824, Pa.
  m. (1) **Elizabeth Homan**
    (2) **Mary Homan** (1824-1865)
  d. 1898 5

7b. Andrew Moser

Andrew Moser, son of **Jacob Moser** and **Margaretha Hagenbach**, was born in 1807 in Pennsylvania, probably Centre County. He married **Rachel Huber**, daughter of **John Huber** and **Christine Johnsonburg**, about 1826. Andrew died in 1865 and Rachel died in 1873. Children of Andrew and Rachel Moser:

Noah Moser
    b. 1828, Pa.
    m. (1) **Louisa Roush**
       (2) **Addie Foltz**
    d. 1890, Pa.
    buried Myers Cemetery, Buffalo Run, Centre Co., Pa.

Michael Moser
    died young

Samuel Moser
    b. 1834, Pa.
    Went to Kansas City, Clay Co., Mo.

John H. Moser
    b. 1839, Pa.
    d. 1908, Centre Co., Pa.
    He was the sheriff of Centre County, known as 'Devil John'

Anna Maria Moser
    b. 1842, Pa.
    m. **John Reeser**, b. 1842 (her second cousin)
       (son of **Henry** and **Rebecca Reeser**)

Phoebe Moser
    m. **Landis Gerbrich** of Lebanon, Lebanon Co., Pa.

Sara Ellen Moser
    b. 1845, Pa.
    m. **Silas Mansheiger** of Saxton, Bedford Co., Pa.

Mary Moser
    b. 1849, Pa.

James G. Moser
    b. 1850, Pa.
    d. 1939
    He was called 'James of Fillmore'. He never married.

7c. Philip Moser

Philip Moser, son of **Jacob Moser** and **Margaretha Hagenbach**, was born about 1812 in Pennsylvania. He married **Mary Huber** (b. about 1815) about 1836. Philip was a farmer in Centre County, Pennsylvania. Mary died in 1846 and is buried in Wolfs Cemetery, Buffalo Run, Centre County, Pennsylvania. Philip died in 1895 and is buried with his wife. Philip is listed as age 32 in the 1850 Centre Co. census, when there is a **Susannah Huber**, age 20, living with them. Children of Philip and Mary Moser:

Julia Moser
    b. abt. 1837, Pa. m. **Charles Bower**

Emanuel Henry Moser
    b. abt. 1839, Pa.
    m. **Elisabeth Shirk**
    d. 1912, South Dakota
    They had eight children. A daughter, **Ida Moser** married **William Homan**. (A **David Moser** was born in Muskingham County, Ohio in 1827 claimed he was a son of Elisabeth Shirk. Since his father died in 1864 in Muskingham County, Ohio at the age of 66, his father was born about 1798. David cannot be a son of this Elisabeth Shirk!)

Phoebe C. Moser
>   b. abt. 1843, Pa.
>   m. **George Mahlon Stover** (1838-1920)
>   d. 1902, Pa.
>   Both are buried in Aaronsburg Cemetery, Aaronsburg, Centre Co.

Rebecca Moser
>   b. abt. 1845, Pa.
>   d. 1863
>   Not listed in 1850 census with parents

Diane E. Moser
>   b. 1847, Pa.
>   (She is called 'Hannah' in the 1850 census)
>   m. **Charles Bower**, widower of her sister, Julia.
>   d. 1876

Susan Louisa Moser
>   b. 1850, Pa.
>   m. **John Jacob Fielder**
>   They had five children. One was **Henry Oliver Fielder**
>   who married **Daisy Moser**, a granddaughter of
>   **Rev. Johan Sebastian Moser** and **Anna Neese**

7d. John Moser

John Moser, son of **Jacob Moser** and **Margaretha Hagenbach**, was born in 1821 in Pennsylvania. He married about 1845 **Susan Dale**, daughter of **Christian Dale** and **Hannah Sheenberger**. The family lived in Grove Mills, Centre County, Pennsylvania. Children of John and Susan Moser:

Hannah Moser
>   b. 1846, Pa.
>   She never married.

George Washington Moser
>   b. 1848, Pa.
>   m. **Mary Emma Sellers** (1846-1917)
>   d. 1924
>   They had four children.

Mary Catherine Moser
>   b. 1851, Pa.
>   m. **Caleb Sellers**

Elizabeth Moser
>   b. 1852, Pa.
>   m. **James Waddle**
>   d. 1933

William John Moser
>   b. 1854, Pa.
>   m. **Agnes Zettle**
>   d. 1929
>   They had six children.

Charles R. Moser
>   b. 1856, Pa.
>   m. **Elizabeth M. Farher** (1858-1913)
>   They had three children.

Aggie Priscilla Moser
>   b. 1856, Pa.
>   m. **John Rupp**
>   d. 1935
>   They had one daughter

Henry Lincoln Moser
  b. 1861 Pa.
  m. **Gertrude Salt (or Saltz)**, dau. of **David** and **Fannie Salt**
  d. 1940
Christian Moser
  b. 1864 Pa.
  m. **Mary Swartz**
  d. 1940
Francis M. Moser
  b. 1867 Pa.
  m. **Mary Ellen Meek**
  d. 1935

8. David Moser

David Moser, son of **Johann Philip Moser** and **Maria Barbara**, was born in Mosserville, Northampton County, Pennsylvania on 30 Dec 1766. He was not baptized until shortly before his marriage in 1795. He married **Catharine Oswald**, daughter of **Daniel Oswald** and **Catherine Everett**, born 7 April 1775 -- did she influence him to become a member of her church? David went to work in his father's mills. Unlike his brothers, David stayed in Mosserville and would later inherit his father's sawmill. He operated the mill very successfully for forty years. In addition, David owned 180 acres of farm land. In 1798, he purchased his father's farmland and rebuilt the grist mill, which he passed on to his son, Joseph. He divided his land between his sons, John and Joseph. This family adopted the surname **"Moser"**, dropping the double "S" of their ancestors.

David died on 18 Oct 1832 in Mosserville, (now Lehigh County), Pennsylvania and is buried in the Ebeneezer Cemetery, located in New Tripoli, Lynn Twp., Lehigh County. Catharine died on 14 May 1857 and is buried with her husband. Children of David and Catharine Moser:

a. Magda Moser
  b. 1797, Mosserville, Northampton Co., Pa.
  Is she the Magda who married **Jacob Kistler**
  (16 Sep 1780 - 2 Apr 1855)? They are buried
  in the old Ebeneezer Cemetery.

b. John Moser
  b. 17 Jan 1796, Mosserville, Northampton Co., Pa.
  m. 9 Jul 1820 **Sophia Ebert (Everett)** (1798-1883)
  d. 29 Oct 1852, Mosserville, Lehigh Co., Pa.

c. Jacob Moser
  b. 29 Jan 1798, Mosserville, Northampton Co., Pa.
  m. 1 Jun 1821 **Salome Kistler** (1801-1874)
  d. 10 Feb 1877, Allentown, Lehigh Co., Pa.

d. Elisabeth Moser
  b. 9 Apr 1800, Mosserville, Northampton Co., Pa.
  m. (1) **Christian Kistler**
    (2) **Henry Guin (Grim)**
  d. 15 Apr 1852, New Tripoli, Pa.

e. Lydia Moser
  b. 21 Mar 1807, Mosserville, Northampton Co., Pa.
  m. **William Kaul**

f. William Moser
  b. 18 May 1802, Mosserville, Northampton Co., Pa.
  m. 8 May 1825 **Susanna Kuhns**
  d. 5 Feb 1879, Steinsville, Berks Co., Pa.

g. Magdaline Moser
>b. 1807, Mosserville, Northampton Co., Pa.
>m. 17 Nov 1822 **Daniel Kistler**
>d. 27 May 1789 (bur. Zion Cemetery)

h. Joseph Moser
>b. 29 May 1810, Mosserville, Northampton Co., Pa.
>m. 30 Mar 1833 **Mary Krause** (1813-1911)
>d. 23 Apr 1893, Mosserville, Lehigh Co., Pa.

i. Catherine Moser
>b. 9 May 1813, Mosserville, Northampton Co., Pa.
>m. **Joseph Seiberling**, son of **John** and **Catharine Seiberling**
>d. 13 Sep 1883, Seiberlingsville, Pa.
>(A Catherine is also listed as wife of **Joshua Seiberling**,
>son of **Christian** and **Magdalena Seiberling**.)

j. Esther Moser
>b. 24 May 1816, Mosserville, Northampton Co., Pa.
>m. 6 Jun 1837 **Stephanus Kistler** (1815-1880)

k. Sara "Sally" Moser
>b. 6 Mar 1819, Mosserville, Northampton Co., Pa.
>m. **James Seiberling**, son of **Christian** and **Magdalena**

l. David O. Moser
>b. 4 Apr 1822, Mosserville, Northampton Co., Pa.
>m. 4 Apr 1845 **Susan Breinig**
>d. 23 Feb 1861, Breinigsville, Lehigh Co., Pa.

7b. John Moser

John Moser, son of **David Moser** and **Catharine Oswald**, was born 12 Jan 1796 in Mosserville, Northampton County, Pennsylvania. He married **Sophie Ebert (Everett)** who was born 19 Sep 1798, also in Mosserville.

John was the leading tanner in the entire country, having inherited the tanning mill from his father in 1832. He was able to offer employment to many of his neighbors at the mill, which was powered by a horse walking around the outside. John retired from the tanning business and moved to Lynn where he died on 29 Oct 1852, with Sophie outliving him by thirty years. She died on 18 Sep 1883. They are buried in Ebenezer Cemetery, Lehigh County, Pennsylvania. Children of John and Sophie Moser:

b1 Catharine Moser
b2 Polly Moser m. **Nathan Wetherold**
b3 Mary Moser b. 1824
b4 David Moser *
>b. 30 Dec 1825
>m. **Mary A _____** (b. 1823, d. 1907)
>d. 3 Apr 1892
>He became a tanner

---

* Other researchers have claimed that this David married **Eliza Houseman**, daughter of Jacob, on 25 Dec 1849. However, David, the son of John Philip and Sophie Everett was a single man, age 25, living with his parents at the time of the 1850 census. David and Eliza (Houseman) Moser are buried in Lock Haven, Huntington Co., Pa.

b5 John J. Moser
> b. 6 May1828
> m. aft. 1850, **Rebecca Rauch**
> (dau of **Reuben Rauch** and **Lucy Anne Weber**)
> d. 2 Jul 1904
> He was a farmer

b6 Aaron E. Moser
> b. 1 Jun 1845, Mosserville, Lehigh Co., Pa.
> m. aft. 1850, **Jane A Breinig**
> 17 Jun 1876, Allentown, Lehigh Co., Pa.

7b6 Aaron E. Moser

Aaron E. Moser, son of **John Moser** and **Sophie Ebert (Ebrit, Everett)**, was born on 1 Jun 1834 in Mosserville, Lehigh County, Pennsylvania. John clerked in a general store in Breinigsville, Pennsylvania where he met and married **Jane A. Breinig**, daughter of **Jacob Breinig** and **Catharine Trexler**. They established a general store in Mosserville which they operated for six years. They then moved to Allentown, where Aaron joined with **Frank Hersh** to found the firm of Hersh & Moser Hardware.

Aaron died on 17 Jun 1876 in Allentown, Lehigh County, Pennsylvania. Jane died 30 Sep 1913. They are buried in Union Cemetery, Allentown. Children of Aaron and Jane Moser:

> **Mary A. Moser**
>> b. 16 Oct 1858
>> d. 26 Nov 1939
>> She never married
> **John J. Moser**
>> b. 21 Nov 1861
>> d. 13 Mar 1883
> **George E. Moser**
>> b. 1864 in Mosserville, Lehigh Co., Pa.
>> m. 1890 **Elisabeth A. Rau** (daughter of
>> **Charles Rau** and **Mary Newhard**)
>> Children of George and Elisabeth Moser:
>>> **Margaret M. Moser** (d. at age 5)
>>> **Aaron R. Moser** m. **Mary Margaret Jacobi**
>>> **George W. Moser**
> **Annie Moser**
>> b. 26 Jan 1867
>> d. 29 Jan 1922
>> m. **Oscar Trexler**
> **Jennie Moser**
>> m. **James Gladhill**
> **Harry Moser**
>> b. 28 Apr 1873
>> d. 17 Apr 1911
>> m. **Nellie** _____
> **May Moser**
>> b. 12 Dec 1870
>> d. 2 Oct 1873

7d Elisabeth Moser Kistler

Elisabeth Moser, daughter of **David Moser** and **Catharine Oswald**, was born 9 Apr 1800 in Mosserville, Northampton County, Pennsylvania. She married first **Christian Kistler** (b. 1794) about 1819. They moved to Albany Township, Berks County, Pennsylvania and then to Lynn, Lehigh County by 1850. Children of Elisabeth and Christian Kistler:

David M. Kistler
> b. 20 Apr 1820, Albany Township, Berks Co., Pa.
> bp. 25 Jun 1820, Jordan Lutheran Church
> m. abt. 1826 **Lovina** _____
> Known children of David & Lovina Kistler:
>> **Sylvesta Kistler**, b. abt. 1847
>> **Masena Kistler**, b. abt. 1849
> Also living with them in 1850 were:
>> **Magdalena Kistler**, age 69
>> **Carolina Kistler**, age 14
>> **Lewis Kistler**, age 8

Sara Ann Kistler bp. 23 Nov 1823, Jordan Lutheran Church
Catharine Kistler b. 1830
Mary Ann Kistler b. 1833
Thomas Kistler b. 1836

After Christian's death, Elisabeth married **Henry Grim** and moved to Allentown, Lehigh County, Pennsylvania.

7f. William Moser

William Moser, son of **David Moser** and **Catharine Oswald**, was born 8 May 1802 in Mosserville, Northampton County, Pennsylvania. He married **Susanna Kuhns**, daughter of **Daniel Kuhns**, and settled near the Berks/Lehigh County line. He operated a mill on the Onetelajnee river. Their fourteen children were born there; three of the children died young and their names are unknown at this time. Surviving children of William and Susanna Moser:

> f1. **Thomas Moser**, moved to Sayersville, Pa
> f2. **Lucy Moser** m. **Joseph Clauss** of Allentown, Pa
> f3. **Catharine Moser** m. **Wilson Peter** of Slatington, Pa
> f4. **James K. Moser** m. **Cordelia Wannamaker**
>> b. 21 Dec 1834, Moser's Mill, Lehigh Co., Pa
>> m. 1859 **Cordelia Wannamaker** dau of **Daniel Wannamaker**
>>   and **Persena Lutz**
>> d. 1912, Allentown, Lehigh Co., Pa
>> Then had no children
> f5. **William K. Moser** m. **Sara Lutz**
> f6. **Amanda Moser** m. **Owen Hoffman** of Allentown, Pa
> f7. **Ellen Moser** m. **Abraham Kistler** of Allentown, Pa
> f8. **Albert Moser**, lived in Allentown, Pa
> f9. **Charles Moser**, went to Missouri
> f10. **Sarah Moser** m. **Dr. Aaron Miller** of Saegersvile, Lehigh Co., Pa
> f11. **Mary Moser** m. **Owen Miller** of Philadelphia, Pa

8c. Jacob Moser

Jacob Moser, son of **David Moser** and **Catharine Oswald**, was born
29 Jan 1798 in Mosserville, Northampton County, Pennsylvania. He married **Salome Kistler** (b. abt. 1801) and moved to Trexlerville, Lehigh County by 1829. By 1849 the family was living in Allentown, where he died in 1877. Jacob was a tanner like his brother. Children of Jacob and Salome Moser:

1. **Catherine Moser**
   b. 9 Mar 1823, Pa.
   bp. Upper Milford Church, Zionsville, Lehigh Co., Pa.
   m. **Samuel Albright**
2. **William Kistler Moser**
   b. 4 Apr 1822, Allentown, Lehigh, Pa
   m. 12 May 1845 **Lusiana "Lucy" Fisher**
   Children of William and Lucy:
   > 2a. **Mary Moser**
   > b. 9 Jul 1852, Allentown, Pa
   > m. 22 Jan 1885 **Harry Clay Trexler**
   > 2b. **Jacob Fisher Moser**, b. 6 Nov 1855, Allentown
   > 2c. **William F. Moser**, b. 12 Jun 1860, Allentown
3. **Charles Kistler Moser**
   m. bef. 1850 **Annie E. Mink**
   They had eight children.
4. **Elizabeth Moser**
   b. 1827, Lehigh Co., Pa.
   m. aft. 1850 **Peter Knaff Grim**
   d. 1899
   They had six children
5. **James Kistler Moser**
   b. 1830, Mosser's Mill, Lehigh Co., Pa.
   m. aft. 1850 **Marie E. Keck**
   d. 1904

In 1850, living with Jacob and Salome in Allentown, Pa. was **Eliza Jane Mertz**.

8c3. Charles Kistler Moser

Charles K. Moser, son of **Jacob Moser** and **Salome Kistler**, was born in Lehigh County, Pennsylvania, and was married prior to the 1850 census to **Anna E. Mink**. The couple had eight children, but only three are known at this time:

Emma C. Moser
   b. 20 Dec 1850, Trexlertown, Lehigh, Pa.
   m. 3 Jun 1876 **Henry M. Schell** (b. 11 Jun 1848,
            Old Zionsville, Pa., d. 26 Jan 1934, Macungie,
            Lehigh, Pa., son of **George & Lydia Schell**)
   d. 3 Jan 1928, Trexlertown, Lehigh, Pa.
   bur. St. Paul's Union Cemetery in Trexlertown, Pa.

Frank H. Moser
   b. 1 Oct 1857, Trexlertown, Lehigh, Pa.
   m. 7 Jun 1879, _____ **Weaver** (b. 14 Apr 1860,
            Lowhill, Lehigh, Pa., d. 2 Mar 1897,
            Trexlertown, Pa., dau of **Edwin Weaver & Sarah Peters**)
   d. 24 Mar 1912, Allentown, Lehigh, Pa.
   bur. St. Paul's Union Cemetery, Trexlertown, Pa.

Children of Frank Moser:
>> (female) **Moser** (died young)
>> **William A. Moser**
>> **Jacob H. Moser**
>> **Charles P. Moser**
>> **Edward J. Moser**
>> **Sadie E. Moser** (b. 1885, c. 1953) m. **Fred J. Romig**

Alice Ida Moser
> b. 2 May 1862, Trexleertown, Lehigh, Pa
> m. 12 Dec 1895 **Irwin W. Schmoyer** (b. 8 Aug 1860
>> (d. 16 May 1939, son of **Willouby Schmoyer**
>> and **Henrietta Smith**)
> Children of Alice and Irwin Schmoyer:
>> **Lloyd M. Schmoyer**
>> **Charles W. Schmoyer**

8c5. James Kistler Moser

James Kistler Moser, son of **Jacob Moser** and **Salome Kistler**, was born 6 Feb 1830 in Trexlertown, Lehigh County, Pennsylvania. He was married in Allentown, Lehigh County, Pennsylvania on 24 Nov 1856 by Rev. B. M. Schmucker to **Marie E. Keck**, daughter of **Solomon Keck** and **Anna Saeger**. Marie was born 12 Oct 1830 in Allentown and died 25 Sep 1915. James worked as a tanner in Allentown. He died 6 Feb 1905. They are buried in the Fairview Cemetery in Allentown. Children of James and Marie:

Henry Solomon Moser
> b. 15 Sep 1857, Allentown, Pa.
> m. 9 Oct 1879 **Mary Grim**
> Children of Henry and Mary Moser:
>> **Helen Moser**
>> **James Moser**
>> **Henry Moser**
>> **Miriam Moser**

Jacob S. Moser
> b. 4 Dec 1859, Allentown, Pa.
> m. **Sallie Seiberling**
> Children of Jacob and Sallie Moser:
>> **Anna Seiberling Moser**
>> **Paul Moser**
>> **Karl Edward Moser**
>> **Harris Moser**
>> **John Moser**
>> **Catharine Moser**
>> **Philip Moser**
>> **Charles Moser**

George Keck Moser
> b. 7 Dec 1862, Allentown, Pa.
> m. 14 Jun 1884 **Ida Hausman**
> d. 22 Nov 1953, Allentown, Pa.
> Children of George and Ida Moser:
>> **Fred Moser**
>> **Robert Moser**
>> **Mary Moser**
>> **Frederick Moser**

Lucy Elizabeth Moser
>   b. 6 Jun 1866, Allentown, Pa.
>   m. 12 Oct 1897 **Victor I. Huebner**
>   d. 9 Sep 1953, Allentown, Pa.
>   Children of Victor and Lucy Huebner:
>   **James K. Huebner**
>   **Richard Huebner**
Joseph Andrew Moser b. 1 Sep 1885, Allentown, Pa.

8f1 Thomas K. Moser

Thomas K. Moser, son of **William K Moser** and **Susanna Kuhns**, was born 10 Apr 1826 in Jacksonville, Lehigh County, Pennsylvania. He married (1) **Caroline German** on 13 Jun 1852. He married (2) in Saegersville, Lehigh County, Pennsylvania, 5 Jun 1860 **Maria Peter**, daughter of **Godfrey Peter**. She was born in Saegersville on 24 Oct 1821 and died in Heidelberg, Lehigh County, Pennsylvania on 26 Feb 1898. Thomas died 2 Jan 1884 in Saegersville. They are buried in Heidelberg. Child of Thomas and Maria Moser:

Oliver G. Moser
>   b. 14 Jun 1861, Saegersville, Lehigh, Pa.
>   m. 9 Sep 1885, **Alice E. Kern**
>   d. 23 Sep 1926, Heidelberg, Lehigh, Pa.

8f7. William K. Moser

William K. Moser, son of **William Moser** and **Susanna Kuhns**, was born 24 Jul 1838 in Lehigh County, Pennsylvania. He inherited the homestead of his father, Moser's Mill and farm, along with another 102 acre farm. He was a very successful potato farmer. He and **Dr. James Graber** erected the Jacksonville Creamery. With **Wilson P. Krum**, he operated the slate quarries in Slatesville, Williamstown and Jacksonville, Pennsylvania. He married 11 May 1862 **Sara Lutz**, daughter of **Joseph Lutz** and **Maria Wannamaker**. She was born in New Tripoli, Lehigh County, Pennsylvania and died 10 Jan 1912 in Reading, Lehigh County, Pennsylvania. They were members of the Lutheran Church in Jacksonville, Lehigh County, Pennsylvania. William died 15 Dec. 1905. They are buried in the Jacksonville cemetery. Children of William K. and Sara Moser:

a. **Lena Moser**, b. 4 Dec 1863, Pa., m. **Francis S. Keller**
b. **Adda Moser**, b. 12 Jan 1865, Pa.
c. **Charles L. Moser**, b. 12 May 1866, d. 22 Jan 1890
d. **William J. Moser**, b. 5 Jan 1869
>   m. **Caroline A. Straub**
e. **Sallie Moser**, b. 24 Dec 1871, drowned 28 Mar 1873
f. **Clara Moser**, b. 30 Mar 1874, m. **Louis Lenhart**
g. **Albert Moser**, b. 12 May 1875, m. **Millie G. Oswald**
h. **Edward Moser**, b. 7 Feb 1876
i. **Nellie Ann Moser**, b. 22 Oct 1878
j. **Robert L. Moser**, b. 18 Oct 1879
k. **Daisy E. Moser**, b. 16 Jul 1884
l. **Esther Moser**

8f7d. William J. Moser

William J. Moser, son of William K. Moser and Sara Lutz, was born
5 Jan 1869 in Jacksonville, Lehigh County, Pennsylvania. He inherited his father's
homestead and continued with the farming and milling businesses. He married
Caroline A. Straub, daughter of Moses Straub and Caroline Long. Children of
William J. and Caroline Moser:

> Warren Lee Moser, b. 11 Nov 1888, m. Verna Loy
> Milo William Moser, b. 2 Apr 1890
> Harry Straub Moser, b. 30 Jul 1892
> Esther Caroline Moser, b. 26 Sep 1893, d. 21 Apr 1894
> Robert Moser
> Marguerite Moser
> George Moser
> Florence Moser
> Frederick Thomas Moser, b. 6 May 1906
> Frank S. Moser, b. 18 Aug 1909

8g. Magdaline Moser Kistler

Magdaline Moser, daughter of David Moser and Catharine Oswald, was born
12 Jun 1804 in Mosserville, Northampton County, Pennsylvania. She married
17 Nov 1822 Daniel Kistler, son of Samuel Kistler and Catherine Brobst. Daniel
was born 27 May 1789 in Lehigh County, Pennsylvania and died 28 Jun 1866.
Magdaline died 1 Apr 1861. They are buried in Zion Cemetery, West Penn, Schuylkill
Co., Pennsylvania. Children of Daniel and Magdaline Kistler:

> Jacob Kistler
> > b. 6 Oct 1827, Albany Twp., Berks Co., Pa.
> > bp. Jordan Lutheran Church, Berks Co., Pa.
> Charles Kistler m. Elizabeth Peters
> John M. Kistler m. Mary Moser
> Daniel Kistler m. Catherine Whetstone
> David Kistler m. Mary Mantz
> Noah Kistler m. Sarah Moser
> Hettie Kistler m. David Zehner
> Fianna Kistler m. Daniel Yingst
> Kate Kistler m. Benjamin Bohner

8h. Joseph Moser

Joseph Moser, son of David Moser and Catharine Oswald, was born on
28 May 1810 in Mosserville, Northampton County, Pennsylvania. Joseph inherited the
grist mill and saw mill from his father in 1823, which he operated successfully for
nearly forty years, making two frame additions to the grist mill. In 1862 he erected a
two-story brick home near the mill. It was said that the ceiling and the walls in the
parlor had been decorated with handpainted butterflies, no two of which were alike.

He married Mary Krause, daughter of Philip Krause and Salome Peter,
30 Mar 1833 in Lehigh County, Pennsylvania. She was born 1 Nov 1813. They were
members of the Ebeneezer Lutheran Church. Joseph died 23 Apr 1893 while Mary died
6 Feb 1911.

Children of Joseph and Mary Moser:
1. **William Franklin Mosser**
    b. 26 Dec 1833, Mosserville, Lehigh Co., Pa.
    m. **Louisa Seiberling**, dau. of
        Peter Seiberling of Schuylkill Co., Pa.
    d. 6 Jan 1908, Allentown, Lehigh Co., Pa.
    Children of William and Louisa Moser:
    a. **Alvena L. Mosser**
        b. 6 Jun 1857, Mosserville, Lehigh Co., Pa.
        m. 10 May 1881 **George W. Eckert**
        d. 18 Nov 1947, Hollywood, Ca.
        Children of George and Alvena Eckert:
            Charles Mosser Eckert b. 2 Feb 1882
            Robert W. Eckert, b. 14 Apr 1884
            Kathryn Eckert, b. 16 Feb 1890 m. **Ward Drake**
    b. **Amanda L. Mosser**
        b. 7 Jan 1859, Mosserville, Lehigh Co., Pa.
        m. 1 Jun 1881 **Thomas E. Bechtel**
        d. 3 Oct 1938, Allentown, Lehigh Co., Pa.
        They had no children.
    c. **Emma L. Mosser**
        b. 10 Oct 1860, Mosserville, Lehigh Co., Pa.
        m. 18 Sep 1899 **William G. Keck**
        d. 19 Jan 1944, Allentown, Lehigh Co., Pa.
        Children of William and Emma Keck:
            Elizabeth Keck
                b. 22 Jun 1900
                m. **G. Edward Leh**
            Andrew Sager Keck
                b. 15 Feb 1902
            Paul G. Keck
                b. 20 Jul 1904
    d. **Rosa L. Mosser**
        b. 7 Jun 1862, Mosserville, Lehigh Co., Pa.
        m. 7 Oct 1896 **George T. Roth**
        d. 21 Jan 1941, Elkin, Surry Co., NC
    e. **Joseph D. Mosser**
        b. 12 Dec 1863, Mosserville, Lehigh Co., Pa.
        d. 13 Jun 1865, Mosserville, Lehigh Co., Pa.
    f. **Charles Franklin Mosser**
        b. 14 Nov 1867, Allentown, Lehigh Co., Pa.
        m. 16 Apr 1890 **Flora Bohlen**
        d. 5 Feb 1934, Allentown, Lehigh Co., Pa.
        Children of Charles and Flora Mosser:
            Hannah Mosser
            Joseph Mosser
            Ruth Mosser
            William Mosser
    g. **Joseph Peter Mosser**
        b. 17 Mar 1865, Allentown, Lehigh Co., Pa.
        d. 27 Dec 1866, Allentown, Lehigh Co., Pa.
2. **Rosa Anna Moser**
    b. 12 Dec 1836, Mosserville, Lehigh Co., Pa.
    m. 31 Mar 1857 **Edwin Camp**
    d. 22 May 1913, Mosserville, Lehigh Co., Pa

3. Lewis F. Moser
>> b. 6 Nov 1840, Mosserville, Lehigh Co., Pa.
>> m. 20 Apr 1860 **Sarah A. Bachman**
>> d. 9 Apr 1923, Mosserville, Lehigh Co., Pa.
>> Children of Lewis and Sarah Moser:
>>> **Alice Moser** m. **Alvin J. Ziegler**
>>> **Mary Moser** m. **Rev. George Richards**
>>> **Ellen Sarah Moser** (unmarried)
>>> **Annie Moser**
>>>> b. 14 Apr 1870
>>>> m. **Granville Snyder**
>>> **Ida Victoria Moser**, b. 11 Jul 1872 (unmarried)

8i. Sara "Sally" Moser Seiberling

Sara "Sally" Moser, daughter of **David Moser** and **Catharine Oswald**, was born in Mosserville, Northampton County, Pennsylvania on 6 Mar 1819. She married **James Seiberling** (b. 1819), son of **Christian Seiberling** (b. 1785) and **Magdalena** ———— (b. 1792). In 1850, they were farming in Lynn, Lehigh County, Pennsylvania and had the following children:

Ritzen (male) Seiberling
>> b. abt. 1841 in Pa.

David Seiberling
>> b. abt. 1842 in Pa.

Owen Seiberling
>> b. abt. 1845 in Pa.

Peter Seiberling
>> b. abt. 1847 in Pa.

James Seiberling
>> b. abt. 1849 in Pa.

Also living with them was **Jonas Seiberling**, age 15, either a younger brother or a cousin of James.

8j. David O. Moser

David O. Moser, son of **David Moser** and **Catharine Oswald**, was born 4 Apr 1822 in Mosserville, Lehigh County, Pennsylvania. David was a doctor in Breinigsville, Lehigh County, Pennsylvania. He married **Susan Breinig**, daughter of **Jesse Breinig**, who was born 4 Jul 1828. Susan died 16 Aug 1871.

In 1850, the family was living in Upper Maccungi, Lehigh County, Pennsylvania. Their name is listed as **MAFSER** in the 1850 Federal Index. Living in their household at that time were: **Permellia Marston** (age 8) and **William Trexler** (age 14). Children of Dr. David and Susan Moser:

Oliver Moser
>> b. 1848, Upper Maccungi, Lehigh Co., Pa.

Hannah Moser
>> b. 1849, Upper Maccungi, Lehigh Co., Pa.
>> m. 5 May 1874 **Dr. Beldon** of Akron, Ohio

Ida V. Moser
>> b. 17 Dec 1854
>> d. 12 Apr 1872 in Savannah, Georgia
>> bur. Alburtus, Pa.

Johann Michael Mosser

Johann Michel Mosser, third son of **Hans Martin Mosser** and **Margaretha Kungel** was born 30 May 1734 in Goshenhoppen, Philadelphia County, Pennsylvania. He was baptized at the New Hanover Lutheran Church on 6 Jun 1734 with John Adam Mosser and his wife, Eva, acting as sponsors. When he was only nine or ten years old, his father died unexpectedly. Life must have been very hard for Margaretha and her five children during the five years it took to settle the estate. The following spring, she took her two youngest sons to be confirmed on 8 Apr 1750 at the New Hanover Church. The oldest son, Frederick, was married there on 22 April 1750 and the family left Goshenhoppen for the unsettled territory which is now Lynn, Lehigh County, Pennsylvania. On 8 Jun 1754, Michael, now a young man of twenty years, became the owner of fifty-four acres of land. If he is the Michael (surname spelled "Mooser" in the record) who had children baptized in Zion Moselem Church in Richmond Township, Berks County, Pennsylvania, then he is the father of the following:

1. **Adam (Ertmann) Mooser**
   b, 12 Oct 1750
2. **Michael Mosser**
   b. 13 Mar 1752 (his father is called "Michael of Atolhoe")
   m. **Catharina Weiman**
3. **Christina Catharina Mooser**
   b. 2 Sep 1754
   m. **Michael Hochnle**
   (She is called Catharina Looser in the record)
4. **Anna Barbara Mooser**
   b. 27 May 1756

Did our young Michael become a father at sixteen? No record of his marriage has been found. However, a child with no name was born 2 Jan 1757 and baptized 20 Mar 1757 at the New Hanover Church, whose parents were Michael Mosser and **Anna Barbara Strobel**. The sponsors were **Johann Ludwig Strobel** and **Johannes Luppold**. If this child was also a child of "Michael of Atolhoe", than our Michael is married to Anna Barbara Strobel. Since he is believed to have had a daughter named **Eva Moser**, she could be the child born and baptized in 1757.

Michael of Atolhoe served in the Revolutionary War as a lieutenant in Capt. Jacob Weston's Company, 4th Pa. Battalion. Two Michael Mosers received Bounty Land Warrants for Reveolutionary War service. Record #R7450 is Michael and his wife, Catherine, of Maryland, while record #R7451 is Michael of Pennsylvania. Our Michael is believed to be the one who owned a one hundred acre farm on the boundary between Bern and Tulpehocken Townships in Lancaster (now Schuylkill) County, Pennsylvania.

By 1768 Michael owned another sixty acres and a still. He also had acquired other acreage which he called "White Oake Thicket". Although his land was located next to that of an Amishman, **Jacob Hochstetler**, it would appear from the above baptisms that Michael was of Lutheran persuasion.

In 1790 Michael's household consisted of himself and one female over sixteen. When he sold off his last in 1809, he was listed as "Michael of Bern, widower" on the deeds. It would appear from this that his wife died between 1790 and 1809.

This Michael is believed to be the ancestor of the Mosers who went to Crawford County, Pennsylvania and founded the town of Mosiertown.

1. Michael Moser

Michael Moser, son of **Johann Michael Moser** and (?) **Anna Barbara Strobel**, was born 13 Mar 1752 in Goshenhoppen, Philadelphia County, Pennsylvania and died 1 Jun 1818. His father was called "Michael of Atolhoe" in the church records. He married **Catharine Weihmann** and is buried with his wife in the cemetery of the Old Red Church in W. Brunswick Township, Schuylkill County, Pennsylvania. During his lifetime, Michael operated a tavern, where he sold some of the "spirits" from his father's still. In 1780, he was taxed on 260 acres of land and a grist mill in Schulykill County. The following year, he was identified as an innkeeper. By 1813, Michael and Catharine had sold the land in Lancaster County which he received from his father.

This Michael is thought to be the one who served as a 2nd lt. in Whetstone's Company, Berks County Militia.

According to the 1790 Federal Census, Michael's household consisted of three males over sixteen, one male under sixteen and five females. A Michael and Catharine Moser had a son, **John Moser**, born 3 Jul 1763 and baptized 14 Jul 1763 in the Jordan Church with Mrs. Michael (Maria Barbara) Leubert as sponsor. This John is **believed** to have been the John who went to Crawford County in 1830. **Daniel Moser** and **Abraham Moser** took their families there at about that same time. They may be the other two males from the 1790 census. There is no knowledge of the four daughters of Michael Moser at this time. The following pages are of the Mosers found in early Crawford County records. Crawford County was still Indian Territory as late as 1788, when it became part of the new Allegheny County. It did not become a county until 1810. Records prior to 1810 should be sought in Allegheny County.

Possible children of Michael and Catharine Moser:
    a. Margaretha Magdalena Moser
        b. 21 Jul 1779, Pa.
        bp. 29 Aug 1779
        sponsor: **Margaretha Magdalena Weiman**
        m. **Jacob Miller**
        d. 1817
        Children of Margaretha and Jacob Miller:
            Samuel Miller
                b. 6 May 1800
            William Miller
                b. 10 Mar 1804
    b. Michael Moser
        b. 13 Feb 1782, Pa.
        m. **Catharina** _____
        d. 2 Jun 1818
        Children of Michael and Catharina Moser:
            1. Manuel Moser
                b. abt. 1812, Pa.
            2. Rebecca Moser
                m. **John McClure**
            3. Christina Moser
            4. Catharina Moser
                m. **Samuel Kepner**
            5. Martin Moser
                b. 5 Jun 1815 Pa.
                d. Aug 1822

The following are thought by many to be children of this Michael and Catharina Moser. They are more likely to have been cousins, as Michael was only nine years old when Fhae was born. They are included here for your consideration.

    *6. Fhae Moser
        b. 6 Sep 1791, d. young
    *7. Isaac Moser
        b. abt. 1793 Pa.
        m. **Kate Kepner**
        Known children of Isaac and Kate:
            Priscilla Moser m. _____ **Lebo**
            Missouri Moser m. **Joseph Edwards**
            Rebecca Moser m. **Hugh Koch**
            Matilda Moser m. **Mr. Koch**
                (had a son, **Thomas Koch**)
            Erastus Moser
    *8. George Moser, b. 9 May 1794, Pa.
        confirmed 12 Apr 1811
        m. **Hannah Davis** (b. 18 Aug 1793/5)
        They had three children by 1820
    *9. Daniel Moser
        b. 16 Sep 1796, Pa.
        confirmed 1813
        m. **Rachel** _____ d. 21 Apr 1834
        d. 22 Aug 1840 of consumption
        Children of Daniel and Rachel:
            1. Elisabeth Moser
                b. 11 Mar 1823
            2. Catharina Moser
                b. 19 Jul 1825
            3. Margareth Moser
                b. 14 Aug 1827
            4. Elias Moser
                b. 11 Mar 1830
                m. **Maria Kramer**
                  (b. 15 Aug 1828)
                They went to North Dakota
                Children of Elias and Maria:
                Elisabeth Moser, b. 16 Sep 1851
                Daniel Moser b. 18 May 1853
                Susanna Moser b. 28 Nov 1854
                George Washington Moser
                  b. 15 Jul 1856
                Catharine Moser b. 2 Nov 1857
                John Moser b. 18 Apr 1860
                Thomas Moser b. 5 Jun 1863
                Henry Francis Moser
                b. Sep 1865
                Mary D. Moser b. 26 Jan 1870
                Charles Moser b. 4 Oct 1872

Abraham Moser

In the 1850 Crawford County, Pennsylvania census, **Abraham Moser**, age 52, was living in Beaver Township with his wife **Sarona**, age 43. He is listed as a farmer with two children, **Abram Moser**, age 4, and **Daniel**, age 10. If these ages are correct, Abraham was born in Pennsylvania in 1798, and would not have been listed in the 1790 census as a son of our Michael.

An **Abraham Moser** m. **Catharine Miller** on 25 Jun 1804, and had a son, (b. 6 May 1807) christened on 20 Oct 1807 at the Lutheran Reformed Church in Reading, Pennsylvania.

On 18 Nov 1810, an **Abraham** and **Catharine Moser** were the sponsors of **Jacob Moser**, son of **Michael** and **Elisabeth Moser** who was born on 12 Sep. 1810. This couple had a younger son, **John Moser**, b. 1806, christened on 28 Sep 1806 with **John** and **Anna Maria Semmel** acting as the sponsors. (An **Elisabeth Moser** married **Thomas Semel** in 1784 at Whitehall Twp., Pa.)

Living on the neighboring farm appears a **Nathaniel Moser**, b. abt. 1818, who has a wife, **Eliza** (b. abt. 1830) and a son, **Archibald Moser** who is six months old. Nearby is another Moser family, who list their birth place as New York. They are **Franklin** (b. about 1816), **Caroline** (age 33) and **Nancy** (age 4).

Daniel Moser

Daniel Moser, a farmer, is also found in the 1850 Beaver Township Crawford County, Pennsylvania Census. He was born in Pa. and is listed as 53 years of age, making him born about 1797. He also would not have been listed in the 1790 census as a son of our Michael. He is shown with a wife, **Susanna**, age 49, and children, **Aaron** (18), **Lydia** (16), **Rueben** (14), **Rebecca** (12) and **Sarona** (9).

It is also important to note that there was a **Daniel Moser**, b. 11 Nov. 1796 and bp. 16 Dec 1796 at Schlosser's Church in Whitehall Twp., (now Lehigh County), Pa. His parents were **John** and **Barbara Moser**, with **Daniel** and **Catharine Imbody** acting as the sponsors. The Beaver Township Daniel is the right age to belong to John and Barbara.

John Moser

John Moser, an innkeeper, is found in the 1850 Beaver Township, Crawford County, Pennsylvania Census. John is 63 years of age, (b. abt.1787), making him only 3 in 1790. He could be the "under sixteen" son of Michael. This John has a wife named **Catharine** (age 61) and children as follows:

William Moser, a clerk, age 23
Mary Moser, age 21
David Moser, also a clerk, age 19
Thomas Moser, age 16
Louisa Moser, age 13
John Moser, age 12

The next listing is for **Amos Moser** (age 24) a farmer with a wife, **Catharine** (age 20) and no children. He is possibly another son of John and Catharine.

In Woodcock Township, Crawford County, Pennsylvania, we also find a **John Mozer**, a farmer, age 41, with a wife named **Catharine** (age 40). His children are **George** (age 17), **Barbara** (age 15), **Leah** (age 12), **William** (age 7) and **Augustus** (age 1). This John is the right age to have also been a son of the John and Catharine.

Also in Woodcock Township we find **Sarah Moser** (age 17) living with the **Jonathan Yeager** family, a **Mary Mosier** (age 22) living next door to them with the **Abraham Duchman** (a 37 year old physician) family, and a **Joel Mosier** (age 24) who has a wife named **Elizabeth** (age 22).

The presence in Woodcock County of a **John** and **Catharine Moyer** should also be mentioned as there is a possibility that the extractor might have misread a double "s" as a "y", making them really Mosers.

A **John Moser** married **Catharine Yost** at the Lutheran Reformed Church in Reading, Pennsylvania on 17 Sep 1809. A **John** and **Catharine** (surname spelled **Mouner)** had a son, **Henrich** (b. 13 Aug 1803) christened on 21 Nov. 1803. Sponsors were **Frederick** and **Maria Magdalene Maurer**.

The *American Compendium of Genealogy, vol. 5, p. 154* claims that **John Moser**, the inkeeper above, was born in 1788 in Whitehall, Pennsylvania and is the son of **Michael Moser**. It also mentions two additonal sons, (1) **Eli Moser** and (2) **Gideon Moser**, born in 1819, who married **Adelia Rice**. John is credited with the founding of Mosiertown, Pennsylvania.

Johann Burchard Mosser

Johann Burchard Mosser was the youngest child of **Hans Martin Mosser** and **Margaretha Kungel**. He was born in 1736 at Goshenhoppen, Philadelphia County, Pennsylvania and confirmed along with his brother Michael at the age of fourteen on 8 Apr 1750 in the Faulkner Swamp Lutheran Church. By this time, his mother had been a widow for nearly six years. After his oldest brother's marriage later that month, the family went to the area that is known as Lynn, Lehigh County, Pennsylvania today.

Burchard married about 1760 **Maria Agatha Lichtenwallner**, daughter of **Johannes Lichtenwallner** and **Barbara Burchard** who came to Philadelphia aboard the *"Samuel"* in 1733. Maria was born 3 Feb 1734 in Pennsylvania and baptized 6 Feb 1734. Sponsors at her baptism were Tobias and Margaretha Moser. She was the widow of **George Henrich Steininger**, whom she married 5 Feb 1754 at the Jordan Reformed Church. Her father and her first husband's father were among the first trustees at the church. Children of Maria Agatha and Heinrich Steininger:

> **John Heinrich Steininger**
> > bp. 1758, New Hanover Church, Northampton Co., Pa.
> **Eva Catharina Steininger**, b. 1760
> > bp. Jordan Reformed Church, Northampton Co., Pa.

On 15 Dec 1776 the Tory sympathizer, William Thomas held a meeting at the home of Philip Mosser, Burchard's brother. A document was protesting a requirement of turning in of all firearms was drawn up and signed the next day at Burchard's home. As a result of this, Burchard and his brother were arrested by the Council of Safety and sent to jail in Reading, Pennsylvania. They were released after paying a heavy fine. Burchard later served as a private in the 1st Company, 6th Battalion, Northampton County Militia.

In 1771, Burchard and Agatha purchased a lot in the town of Sunbury, Pennsylvania from the family of William Penn, which they sold in 1798. Burchard is found on the County Commisioner's tax list, 27 Dec 1781 in Linn Township. An early map of the area shows that he owned land in the southern part of Linn, bordering on the land of his brother-in-law, Abraham Steinbrook on the north and Jacob Leaser (Jacob is the one who hid the Liberty Bell from the British during the Revolutionary War) on the west. He also had acreage in the northern part of the township. Much of this area is Leaser Lake today. One of these was a 112 acre track which he called "Richmond". He also owned a 220 acre tract in Rush Township called "Amsterdam".

Maria Agatha was living in Lynn at the time of the 1800 census. Burchard died in 1807. A deed dated 8 Jan 1807 identified six children of Maria and Burchard, as follows:

1. **Johann Burchard Mosser**
   b. 25 Jun 1763 Lynn, Northampton Co., Pa.
   bp. 10 Jul 1763 by Daniel Schumacher
   m. **(1) Catharine Hornberger** abt 1789
   (2) Catharine Kershner
   d. 1849, West Penn Twp., Centre Co., Pa.
2. **Johann Philip Mosser**
   b. Feb 1765 Lynn, Northampton Co., Pa.
   bp. 3 Mar 1765 at 5 weeks of age
   sponsors: Johann Philip and Barbara Moser
   m. 11 Nov 1785 **Elisabeth Oswald**
   d. 1849, Gregg Twp., Centre Co. Pa.
   buried Heckman's Cemetery, Haines Twp.
3. **Johann Michael Mosser**
   b. 18 Jun 1767, Lynn, Northampton Co., Pa.
   bp. 30 Jun 1767
   m. **(1) Anna Margaretha Weber** 14 Jan 1801
   (2) Elisabeth _____
   d. 1854, Centre Co., Pa.
   lived in Haines Township by 1807
4. **Anna Maria Mosser**
   b. 14 Oct 1769, Lynn, Northampton Co., Pa.
   m. **(1) Christian Miller**
   (2) John Oswald 29 Jan 1799, Milford
   Twp,Northampton Co.
   d. 18 Apr 1842
5. **Jacob Mosser**
   b. 29 May 1772, Lynn, Northampton Co., Pa.
   m. **(1) _____ Oswald**
   (2) 6 Apr 1800 **Susanna Hunsicker**
   d. 30 May 1855, New Tripoli, Lehigh Co., Pa.
6. **Catherine Barbara Mosser**
   b. 1773, Lynn, Northampton Co., Pa.
   m. **George Sittler**
   lived in Lehigh County in 1807

1. Johann Burchard Moser

Johann Burchard Moser, oldest son of **Johann Burchard Moser** and **Maria Agatha Lichtcnwallner**, was born 25 Jun 1763 in Lynn, Northampton County, Pennsylvania and baptized 10 Jul 1763 in Lynn, by Rev. Schumacher. Sponsors at his baptism were Johannes Moser and Christina Lichtenwallner. He acquired the land known as "Amsterdam" in Rush Township from his father, and built a log cabin in 1801 which was still standing in 1990. He also patented land which he called "Northfarm" in Penn Township. Both of these properties were in Northampton County, Pennsylvania, but are now in Schuykill County. "Amsterdam" is now Tamaqua and "Northfarm" is Coaldale.

Burchard is believed to have had two wives, both named Catharine. The first is thought to be **Catherine Magdelena Hornberger** (daughter of **Carl** and **Barbara Hornberger** of West Brunswick, b. 1752) . Did he really marry a twenty-seven year old woman when he was but a boy of sixteen? Children of Burchard and Catherine Moser:
  a. **Mary Magdalena Moser**
         b. 21 Jul 1779, probably in Lynn
         bp. Old Red Church
         m. **Nicholas Boyer**
  b. **Maria Barbara Moser**
         (a son's bp. rececord calls her Maria Agatha)
         b. 7 Jan 1780, Whitehall Twp., Northumberland Co.
         bp. 4 Feb 1780, Scholssers Church
         Sponsors: Burkhard and Maria Agatha Moser
         m. **John Kershner**
         d. 1840

If there were two wives, the second one is believed to be **Catharine Kershner**. Because of the eight year gap in the birth of the children, The first wife must have died before 1788 when the second Catharine began having children. No burial has been found for the first Catharine Moser. The second Catharine died in 1822. The question now arises: Were there really two Catharines? Perhaps our lady is Catharine Hornerberger, widow of _____ Kershner and mother of two children. Perhaps Burchard did not marry at sixteen, but married her at twenty-five and adopted her two Kershner children. That could also explain the existance of two daughters named 'Barbara' and two named 'Magdalena'. It is an interesting thought to ponder!

Burchard was a wheelwright, a farmer, a lumberman, a coal miner, and in the 1790's served as a captain of the 1st Co., 1st Battilion and then as 1st Lieutenent of the light horse in the Northampton Militia. In 1799 he built a saw mill at the junction of the Tamaqua River and Panther Creek.

In 1817 Burchard and his son, Jacob, discovered coal on their Rush Township property. They began to mine it and started selling it locally to blacksmiths. Therein lies the beginning of all our problems with our Moser research! The Lehigh Coal & Navigation Company somehow managed to run them off their land and then forged many public documents to "prove" that Burchard had never married. The property was still in litigation as late as 12 Jun 1929, but was dropped during the Depression.

The fake Burchard was supposed to have been a son of **Hans Michael Moser** who arrived 16 Oct 1752 aboard the *"Duke of Wurtemberg"* with four children, Peter, Barbara, Burkhard and Christian. (Straussberg-Hinke gives his surname as **Mauer**). However, the will of Hans Michael does not mention a son named Burkhard. The story goes on that this Burkhard was an eccentric old hermit, that he served in the Revolutionary War and sent his money to his younger brother, Peter (born in this country), that he went away into the mountains in 1800 and died there in 1828. The coal company paid the taxes for two years, then built the log cabin and claimed it on a squatter's claim.

Our real Burchard is said to have had at least thirteen children. Other known children are:

    c. Marie Magdalena Moser
        b. 4 Jan 1788, Lynn, Northampton Co., Pa.
        m. **Abraham Miller**
        d. 20 Mar 1859
        buried Ebeneezer Church Cemetery
    d. Marie Elisabeth Moser
        b. 14 Oct1789, Lynn, Northampton Co., Pa.
        m. **Philip Brobst**
        d. 18 Apr 1842, Schoenersville, Lehigh Co., Pa.
    e. Jacob Moser
        b. 24 Aug 1790, Lynn, Northampton, Co., Pa.
        m. (1) **Margaret Schwepp**
            (2) **Sarah** _____
        d. 17 Mar 1883, Tamaque, Schulykill Co., Pa.
        buried Dutch Hill Cemetery, Tamaque, Schuylkill Co., Pa.
    f. Philip Moser
        b. 20 Dec 1793
        d. 12 Jan 1840
        buried Ebenezer Church Cemetery
    g. Michael Moser
        b. 1794, Lynn, Northampton Co., Pa.
    h. Barbara Moser
        b. 22 Jul 1796, Lynn, Northampton Co., Pa.
        (mother's name given as **Catherine Hornberger**)
        m. 25 Dec 1820 **John Whetstone**
        d. 12 Jan 1879, Schuylkill Co., Pa.
        buried Dutch Hill Cemetery, Tamaque, Schuylkill Co.
    i. Burchard Moser
        b. 3 Feb1800, Lynn, Northampton Co., Pa.
        m. **Rebecca Wartman**
        d. 22 Jun 1863
        buried Dutch Hill Cemetery, Tamaque, Schuylkill Co.
    j. John Moser
        b. 24 May 1805, Lynn, Northampton Co., Pa.
        m. (1) **Catharine Wartman**
            (2) **Polly** _____
            (3) aft. 1850 **Elisabeth Acker**
               (widow of **John Kershner, Jr.**
        d. 27 Dec 1893, West Penn Twp., Schuylkill Co., Pa.
        Buried Dutch Hill Cemetery, Tamaque, Schuylkill Co., Pa.
    k. Rebecca Moser
        b. 1 Dec 1798
        m. **Abner Robinold**
        d. 11 Apr 1848
    l. Polly M. Moser m. **George Longenberger**
    m. Catherine Moser m. **Henry Frey** 24 Jun 1838

In 1840, Burchard was living in West Penn Township (now Coaldale), Schuylkill Co., Pennsylvania with his son, John. He attended church at St. John's Lutheran Church in Tamaqua. In the 1820 census, Burchard no longer owned land, but had to pay taxes on it anyway. Catharine is believed to have died after she signed a deed in 1811, as she did not sign one in 1814. However, it is also believed that these two deeds are forged, since they are typed and the typewriter was not invented until 1868. Burchard died before the 1850 Federal Census was taken.

b. Maria Barbara Moser Kershner

Maria Barbara Moser, daughter of **Johann Burchard Moser** and **Catherine Hornberger**, was born 7 Jan 1780 and baptized on 4 Feb 1780 at Schlosser's Reformed Lutheran Church in Whitehall Township, Northampton County, Pennsylvania. (Her name is listed as 'Maria Agatha' by some researchers, but the record named her as 'Maria Barbara'). She married about 1804 **John Kershner.** As there were four John Kershners living in Tamaqua at that time, it is unclear which one was the father of the John who married Mary Barbara. The family lived in Tamaqua, where their child was born. She died in 1840. Only one child is known of Mary Barbara and John:

1. **John Kershner**
   b. 1805, Tamaqua, Pa.
John worked as a teamster and lived in Tamaqua, Pennsylvania. In 1850, he was living with **Elisabeth (Acker?) Kershner**, a widow, and her children, Julia E (15), John (14), Thomas (12), Jacob (9), William(6), Hannah (4) and Samuel (1). Also living with with Elisabeth were **Richard Shiner** (26) and **Christina Sharp** (57).

This Elisabeth would later become the third wife of **John Moser** .

e. Jacob Moser

Jacob Moser, oldest son of **Johann Burchard Moser** and **Catherine Hornberger**, was born 1790 in Lynn, Northampton County, Pennsylvania. He married first about 1823 **Margaretta Schwepp**, who was born in 1795. They lived in Tamaqua, Schuylkill County, Pennsylvania where their six children were born. Jacob was with his father when coal was discovered on their land. He inherited the land, but was put off it by the coal company. After Margaretha's death in 1848, he married a woman named **Sarah**, born about 1793 in Pennsylvania. Jacob died 17 Mar 1883 in Tamaqua and is buried in the Dutch Hill Cemetery there in row #139. Margaret is buried in row #138.
Children of Jacob and Margaretta Moser:

1. **Ephraim Moser**
   b. abt 1824, Tamaqua, Schuylkill Co., Pa.
   m. **Catherine** _____
   lived Mauch Chunk Twp., Carbon Co., Pa.
   Had at least five children
2. **Lauretta "Redde" Moser**
   b. 7 Jul 1827, Tamaqua, Schuylkill Co., Pa.
   bp. St. John's Lutheran Church, Tamaqua, Pa.
   m. **David Landback** abt 1850
   Children of Redde & David Landback:
   > **Ellen Landback** (b. abt 1851)
   > **Mary Landback** (b. abt 1854)
   > > m. **Charles Koch** (b. abt 1843)
   > > children: **Rettia Koch** (b. abt 1875)
   > > > **Lizzie Koch** (b. abt 1878)
   > > Lived Tamaqua, Schuylkill Co., Pa.
   > **Alice Landback** (b. abt 1858)
   > **Clara Landback** (b. abt 1862) m. **Louis Heisler**
   > > Lived Tamaqua, Schuylkill Co., Pa.
3. **David Moser**
   b. abt 1828, Tamaqua, Schuylkill Co., Pa.
   Lived Coaldale, Schuylkill Co., Pa. in 1850
   with brother, John and sister Margaret
4. **John Burkhard Moser**
   b. 28 Aug 1830, Tamaqua, Schuylkill Co., Pa.
   Lived Coaldale with brother and sister in 1850

5. **Margaret Moser**
    b. abt 1831, Tamaqua, Schuylkill Co., Pa.
    m. aft. 1850 **Simon Lutz** of Rush Twp.
    Known children of Margaret & Simon Lutz:
        Mary Lutz (b. 1856)
        William Lutz (b. 1858)
        Josephine Lutz (b. 1860)
6. **Leah Moser**
    b. 16 May 1834, Tamaqua, Schuylkill Co., Pa.
    m. aft. 1850 **James Moyer**
    Lived Rush and Walker Twps., Schuylkill Co., Pa.
    In 1850, Leah lived with Mary Kersner, a widow and her
    children in Tamaqua, Schuylkill Co., Pa.
    Known children of Leah and James Moyer:
        Mary Moyer (b. abt 1853)
        William Moyer (b. abt 1854)
        Daniel Moyer (b. abt 1856)
        Margaret Moyer (b. abt 1858)
        Elizabeth Moyer (b. abt Jul 1860)
        Henry A. Moyer (b. abt 1863)
        Anna A. Moyer (b. abt 1867)
        Mabel A. Moyer (b. abt 1873)
        Clayton H. Moyer b. abt 1876)

During the 1850 Federal Census, Jacob and his wife, Sarah were living in the South Ward of Tamaqua. Living with them was a **Samuel Moser**, age three.

h. Barbara Moser Whetstone

Barbara Moser, daughter of **Johann Burkhard Moser** and **Catherine Hornberger**, was born 22 Jul 1796 in Lynn, Northampton Co., Pennsylvania and baptized 25 Jul 1796 by Rev. Miller. Sponsors at her baptism were George and Catherine Barbara Sittler. Her mother's name is given as Catherine Hornberger, and the baptismal certificate is displayed at the Schuylkill County Historical Society. Barbara married in Tamaqua 25 Dec 1820/1 **John Whetstone**, son of **Isaac Whetstone**. Barbara died 12 Jan 1879 and John died 1 Nov 1898. They are buried in Dutch Hill Cemetery. Children of John and Barbara Whetstone:

1. **Gideon Whetstone**
    b. 1823 Pa.
    m. **Catherine Bougher** (b. abt. 1822)
    d. 1907
2. **John Whetstone**
    b. abt 1825, West Penn Twp., Centre Co., Pa.
    m. **Esther** _____
3. **Susan Whetstone**
    b. abt 1826 Pa.
    m. _____ **Britsman** (b. abt 1826)
    One known child: **William Britsman**, b. abt 1848
4. **Elijah Whetstone**
    b. 1827
    bp. St. John's Lutheran Church, Tamaqua, Pa.
    m. **Hannah** _____

g.4 Absalom Whetstone
   b. 1833, Tamaqua, Pa.
   m. **Rebecca** _____

g.5 Amos Whetstone
   b. abt 1835
   Still single in 1850

g.6 Emanuel Whetstone
   b. 1839, Tamaqua, Pa.
   m. abt. 1862 **Elmira Moyer**
   lived in Tamaqua, Pa.

h.1 Gideon Whetstone

Gideon Whetstone, son of **John Whetstone** and **Barbara Moser**, was born in 1823 and died in 1907. He worked as a hotel-keeper, a farmer, a coal operator, a lumberman, a merchant, a Justice of the Peace, a constable, a postmaster and a census-taker. Gideon married about 1845 **Catherine Bougher**. The family lived in Schuylkill Township, Walker Township, West Penn Township and Tamaqua (all in Centre County), Pennsylvania. Children of Catherine and Gideon Whetstone:

    Anna C. Whetstone, b. about 1846
    Mary E. Whetstone, b. about 1853
    Louisa Whetstone, b. about 1855
    Cladius Whetstone, b. about 1858
    Martha Whetstone, b. about 1861
    Jennie Elmira Whetstone, b. 1865,Tamaqua
        m. **William H. Snyder**, moved to Hagerstown, Maryland

h.2 John Whetstone

John Whetstone, son of **John Whetstone** and **Barbara Moser** was born about 1825 in West Penn Township, Centre County, Penssylvania. He was a farmer in West Penn. His wife was named **Esther** (b. about 1829). Children of John and Esther Whetstone:

    John W. Whetstone, b. about 1848, farmer
    Thomas W. Whetstone, b. about 1851
    Mary Jane Whetstone, b. about 1853
    James F. Whetstone, b. about 1855
    Amos Whetstone, b. about 1856
    Catharine Whetstone, b. about 1859
    Emanuel Whetstone, b. about 1861
    Gideon Whetstone, b. about 1863
    Elisabeth Whetstone, b. about 1866
    Pierce Whetstone, b. about 1868

h.4 Elijah Whetstone

Elijah Whetstone, son of **John Whetstone** and **Barbara Moser**, was born in 1827 and baptized in St. John's Lutheran Church in Tamaqua, Pennsylvania. By profession he was a hotel keeper and a farmer. His wife was named **Hannah** (b. abt 1826). They lived in West Penn Township, Centre County, Pennsylvania in 1850 and had moved to Schuylkill Township, Centre County, Pennsylvania by 1860.

Known children of Elijah and Hannah Whetstone:
> **Emalina Whetstone**, b. about 1850
> **John Whetstone**, b. about 1853
> **James Whetstone**, b. about 1855
> **Hannah Whetstone**, b. about 1857
> **Amanda Whetstone**, b. about 1858

h. 5 Absalom Whetstone

Absalom Whetstone, son of **John Whetstone** and **Barbara Moser**, was born 1833 in Tamaqua, Pennsylvania and died in Schuylkill Township, Centre County, Pennsylvania in 1916. He was a school teacher and a farmer. His wife was named **Rebecca** (b. 1843, d. 1902). Known children of Absalom and Rebecca Whetstone:
> **Alice Whetstone**, b. about 1867
> **Louella Whetstone**, b. about 1870
> **Milton Whetstone**, b. about 1872
> **Darwin Whetstone**, b. about 1878

h.7 Emanuel Whetstone

Emanuel Whetstone, son of **John Whetstone** and **Barbara Moser**, was born in 1838 in Tamaqua, Pennsylvania. He married **Elmira Moyer** (b. about 1842), daughter of **Susan Moyer** in 1862. They lived in Tamaqua, Schuylkill County, Pennsylvania. Known children of Emanuel and Elmira Whetstone:
> **Emma Whetstone**, b. about 1863
> **George L. Whetstone**, b. about 1865
> **Laura Whetstone**, b. about 1867
> **Katie Whetstone**, b. about 1874

i. Burkhard Moser

Burkhard Moser Jr., son of **Johann Burkard Moser** and **Catharine Hornberger**, was born 3 Feb 1800 in Lynn, Northampton County, Pennsylvania and died 22 Jun 1863. He married about 1825 **Rebecca Wartman**. She was born in Pennsylvania in 1806 and died in 1888. They lived in Lynn Township, Lehigh County, Pennsylvania until after 1840. They were in Summit Hill, Carbon County, Pennsylvania by 1850, but left there and moved to Coaldale, Schuylkill County, Pennsylvania where they died and are buried in the Dutch Hill Cemetery. They were the parents of twelve children, but only eleven are known. Known children of Burchard and Rebecca Moser:

1. **Daniel Moser**
   b. 1827, Lehigh Co., Pa.
   bp. 1 Jul 1827 Upper Milford Lutheran Church, Zionsville
   m. (1) **Caroline Hoering**
   (2) **Maria Hollerbach**
2. **William Moser**
   b. about 1828, Lehigh Co., Pa.
   moved to Scranton, Pa.
3. **Joseph Moser**
   b. about 1830, Lehigh Co., Pa.
   m. about 1870 **Lydia** _____
   served in the Civil War, in the 11th Infantry, Co. H.
4. **Abraham Moser**
   b. about 1832, Lehigh Co., Pa.
   m. **Sarah MacIntosh**

5. **David W. Moser**
    b. about 1834, Lehigh Co., Pa.
    m. 21 Apr 1859 **Sarah Rickert** of Mount Oakes, Luzern Co., Pa.
6. **Elias Moser**
    b. 1837, Lehigh Co., Pa.
    d. 9 Oct 1868, age (31y 11m 10d)
    buried Dutch Hill Cemetery, Tamaqua, #269
    He may have been the father of **Ely Moser** (b. 1868) and
             Mary Moser (b. 1866).
7. **Gideon Moser**
    b. about 1838, Lehigh Co., Pa.
    m. about 1870 **Clara Tiffany**
    They lived in Summit Hill, Coaldale and Scranton, Pa.
    Gideon also served in the Civil War as a Corporal in the 28th
    Pennsylvania Reg. They had three known children:
        Burchard Moser
        Wallace Moser
        Carrie Moser
8. **Aaron Moser**
    b. about 1840, Pa.
    d. 1864 in Georgia during the Civil War after
        the battle of Mill Springs Gap, during which he served
        as a Sgt. in the 28th Regt., with his brother Gideon.
9. **Lewis Moser**
    b. about 1847, Pa.
    m. **Bridget Barrett**
    He served in the 11th Infantry, Co. H., during the Civil War and moved
    to Scranton, Pa.
10. **Catherine "Kate" Moser**
    b. about 1845, Pa.
    m. about 1870 **(Thomas?) Whetstone**
11. **Mary "Polly" Moser**
    b. 1849, Summit Hill, Pa.
    m. **Rossiter Raymond Chase** about 1875
    d. 1912, probably in Scranton, Pa.

i.1 Daniel Moser

Daniel Moser, son of **Burkhard Moser** and **Rebecca Wartman**, was born in 1827 and baptized at Upper Milford Reformed Lutheran Church, Zionsville, Lehigh County, Pennsylvania on 1 Jul 1827. His occupation is listed as "ostler" in the 1850 Coaldale census. He married (1) **Caroline Hoering**, (born 1828, died 4 Jan 1859) and (2) **Maria Hollerbach** on 16 Feb 1859. By 1870, he had become a slate boss and was living in Rahn Towhship, Coaldale, Schuylkill County, Pennsylvania. Only son of Daniel and Caroline Moser:
    A. J. Moser
        b. 1849, Coaldale, Pa. (Not found in other census records)
Known children of Daniel and Maria Moser:
    Emma Moser b. about 1852
    William Moser b. about 1854
    Elias Moser b. about 1857
    John Moser b. about 1860
    Gideon Moser b. about 1863
    Daniel Moser b. about 1865
    Elizabeth Moser b. about 1871
    Mary Moser b. about 1875
    Ida Moser b. about 1877

i.3 Joseph Moser

Joseph Moser, son of **Burkhard Moser** and **Rebecca Wartman**, was born in 1830 in Pennsylvania, probably in Lynn, Lehigh County. He served in the Civil War in the 11th Pennsylvania Infantry, Co. H., with his brother, Lewis. He married late in life to a woman named **Lydia**. She may have been the widow of a Moser cousin with a daughter, **Mary Moser**, born in 1864. A Mary Moser, age 16 was living in their household in the Coaldale, Schulykill County, Pennsylvania Census. Joseph worked as a carpenter. Only known child of Joseph and Lydia Moser:

> **Aaron Moser**
>> b. about 1872, probably Coaldale, Schulykill Co.
>> He Lived in Lansford, Pennsylvania and had a
>> daughter, **Isabel Moser**.

i.4 Abraham Moser

Abraham Moser, son of **Burkhard Moser** and **Rebecca Wartman**, was born about 1832, probably in Lynn, Lehigh County, Pennsylvania. He married about 1862 **Sarah MacIntosh**. He was a carpenter and lived in Summit Hill, Pennsylvania. Children of Abraham and Sarah Moser:

> **Aaron Moser**, b. 1863, died young
> **Minnie Moser**, b. 1866
> **Nathan Moser**, b. 1868, died young
> **Mabel Moser**, b. 1871, m. **Chalmer Longstreet**
> **Ada Moser**, b. 1873, m. **John McCready**

i.5 David W. Moser

David W. Moser, son of **Burkhard Moser** and **Rebecca Wartman**, was born about 1834, probably in Lynn, Lehigh County, Pennsylvania. On 21 Apr 1859 he married **Sarah Rickert** of Mount Oakes, Luzern County, Pennsylvania. They lived in Scranton, Pennsylvania, where he was a mining boss. Known children of David and Sarah Moser:

> **Clara Moser**, b. 1861
> **W. T. Moser**, b. 1862
> **Clinton Moser**, b. 1872
> **John W. Moser**, b. 1875
> **Rutherford Moser**, b. 1877

Did they really have a ten year break between children? While such a thing is entirely possible, perhaps we should search for others.

i.9 Catharine Moser Whetstone

Catharine Moser, daughter of **Burkhard Moser** and **Rebecca Wartman**, was born about 1845, probably in Lynn, Lehigh County, Pennsylvania. When she was fifteen, she was living with the Whetstone family in Coaldale, and married about 1880 **(Thomas?) Whetstone** , a teamster, born in 1836. They were living in Coaldale in 1880, but moved to Scranton. Known children of Catharine and (Thomas?) Whetstone:

Mary A. Whetstone, b. 1871
William Whetstone, b. 1870
Emma Whetstone, b. 1875
George Whetstone, b. 1877
Elias Whetstone, b. 1880

i.10 Lewis Moser

Lewis Moser, son of **Burkhard Moser** and **Rebecca Wartman**, was born about 1847. He married **Bridget Barrett**, daughter of **Thomas Barrett** and **Mary Moser** (daughter of **John Moser** and **Catherine Wartman**), his double second cousin. They lived next door to his brother, David, in Scranton, Pennsylvania where Lewis was a coal miner. Children of Lewis and Bridget (sometimes called Elisabeth) Moser:

Dora Moser, b. 1870, Pa.
Ella Moser, b. 1872, Pa.
Thomas Moser, b. 1878, Pa.
Guy Louis Moser
      b. 23 Jan, 1886, Pa.
      d. 9 May 1961, Amityville, Berks Co., Pa.
      buried Amityville Cemetery
      Served in the 75th, 76th and 77th Congress
      He was a Democrat.
Burkhard Moser
Maude Moser

i.11 Mary "Polly" Moser Chase

Mary "Polly" Moser, daughter of **Burkhard Moser** and **Rebecca Wartman**, was born 21 Apr 1849, Summit Hill, Pennsylvania. She married **Rossiter Raymond Chase** in May 1874 and moved to Scranton, Pennsylvania. Rossiter was the fifth child, but only son, of **Beverly Chase** and **Mary Ann Green**, born at Syracuse, New York on 18 Aug 1852. He was a traveling sales man for his Nettleton brother-in-law, selling Nettleton shoes and miners' boots. Mary died in Scranton, Pennsyvania on 7 Oct 1898. Rossiter died at Bryn Mawr Hospital (near Philadelphia) on 28 Dec 1912. Children of Mary and Rossiter Chase:

Beverly Moser Chase
      b. 18 Aug 1876, Scranton, Pa.
      m. **Mertie May Frommfelter**
      They had a daughter, **Mary Beverly Chase** m. **Derwood Newhart**
Alton Irving Chase
      b. 11 Jul 1878, Scranton, Pa.
      m. **Florence Mary Sayer**
      Children: **Harold Alton Chase**
               Arthur Leroy Chase
               Harry (died, age 2)
               Beverly Chase
               Dorothy Florence Chase m. **Loren Davis**
               Marion Ethel Chase m. **Clayton Castles**
               Mable Louise Chase m. **Hal Sicling**

William Moser Chase
      b. 25 Mar 1880, Scranton, Pa.
      d. 8 May 1881, Scranton, Pa.
Kate Nettleton Chase
      b. 1 May 1882
      m. **Walter Carl Benedict**
      Children: **Walter Carl Benedict, Jr.**
                Jannette May Benedict m. **Olof Lundberg**
                George Beverly Benedict
Mable Chase
      b. 29 Jul 1884, Scranton, Pa.
      d. 15 Jul 1885, Scranton, Pa.
Clyde Naylor Chase
      b. 10 May 1886, Scranton
      m. **Nettie Wirth**
      Children: **Clyde Naylor Chase, Jr.**
                Charles Chase
                Dorothy Chase
                William Chase
                Catherine Chase m. **Ferdinand Chamoni**
                Warren Chase

j. John Moser

John Moser, son of **Burchard Moser** and **Catharine Hornberger**, was born 24 May 1805, probably in Lynn Township, Northampton County, Pennsylvania. He married first **Catharine Wartman**, younger sister of his brother, John Moser's first wife, Rebecca. Catharine was born 17 Aug 1811 and died 30 May 1859. They lived in Penn Township, Schuylkill County, Pennsylvania (from which Rahn Township was formed later) and had moved to Coaldale (which is now part of Tamaqua) by 1907. Children of Catharine and John Moser:

Elizabeth Moser
      b. about 1834
      m. _____ **Houser**
      She had the following grandchildren:
                Edna Stevens
                Edith Houser
                Helen Houser
                Gretchen Houser
                Lida Houser
                Christine Houser
Esther Moser
      b. about 1836
      m. _____ **Brobst**
Catherine Moser
      m. _____ **Kuntz**
Mary Moser
      b. about 1839
      m. 1850, **Thomas Barrett**
      Their daughter, **Bridget Barrett**, m. **Lewis Moser**, (son of John's brother Burkhard) her double second cousin.

2 Philip Moser

Philip Moser, son of **Johann Burchard Moser** and **Maria Agatha Lichtenwallner**, was born 26 Jan 1765 in Lynn, Northampton County, Pennsylvania and baptized 3 Mar 1765 at five weeks of age by Rev. Daniel Shoemaker. Sponsors at his baptism were Johann Philip and Barbara Moser. He married 11 Nov 1785 **Elisabeth Oswald** who was born in 1771. She was probably the daughter of **Jacob Oswald** who had the neighboring farm. They moved to Haines Township, Centre County, Pennsylvania. Philip is referred to as "Philip of Haines" in his father's will. They were in Gregg Township by 3 Apr 1803. Elisabeth died in 26 Feb 1843 and Philip died in 1835. They are buried in Heckmans Cemetery, Haines Township, Centre Co., Pennsylvania. Children of Philip and Elisabeth Moser:

- a. **John Moser**
  - b. 24 Jul 1788, Lynn, Northampton Co., Pa.
  - m. **Rebecca "Peggy" Everett** 20 Jun 1819
  - d. 6 Nov 1876, Southington, Trumbull Co., Ohio
  - Buried Oakwood Cemetery, Warren, Trumbull Co., Ohio
- b. **Philip Moser**
  - b. Sep 1790, Lynn, Northampton Co., Pa.
  - m. (1) **Hannah "Catharine" Wallborn**
    - (2) **Susan Rush** (widow of _____ **Peters**)
    - (3) **Maria Magdalena "Polly" Moser**,
      - widow of **Daniel Condo**
    - (4) **Susan Miller** (widow of **David Oswald**)
- c. **Daniel Moser**
  - b. 1 Oct 1792, Lynn, Northampton Co., Pa.
  - m. 20 Jun 1819, **Susanna Everett**
  - d. 10 Dec 1872, Liberty, Trumbull Co., Ohio
  - Buried Girard Cemetery, Girard, Mahoning Co., Ohio
- d. **Elisabeth Moser** m. **John Durst**
- e. **Hannah Moser** m. **Adam Shaffer**
- f. **Lydia Moser**
  - b. 8 Nov 1807, Centre Co., Pa.
  - bp. 5 Dec 1807, Penn Creek Church
    - Sponsors: Philip and Elisabeth Moser
  - m. **Michael Rheim (Ream)**
- g. **Catherine Moser**
  - m. **Elias Wasser** (b. 15 Apr 1822)
  - They went to Kansas.

a. John Moser

John Moser, son of **Philip Moser** and **Elisabeth Oswald**, was born 1788 in Lynn, Northampton County, Pennsylvania. It is unclear when he left Pennsylvania, but he and his brother **Daniel** were married in a double ceremony on 28 Jun 1819 to their second cousins, daughters of **Samuel Everett** and **Maria Barbara Moser**. John was married in Trumbll County, Ohio to **Rebecca "Peggy" Everett** (born 1795 in Lynn). They settled in Southington, which is still a small farming community north of Warren, the county seat. Rebecca died in Weathersfield, Trumbull County, Ohio in 1864 and John died 6 Nov 1867 on his farm in Southington. They are buried in a lovely moseleum in Oakwood Cemetery, Warren, Trumbull County, Ohio.

Children of John and Rebecca Moser:
1. **Timothy Moser**, b. abt. 1820
2. **Lucy Moser**
   b. 1823, Trumbull Co., Ohio
   m. 22 Oct 1850 **William Rayen, Jr.** at the
      Presbyterian Church, Liberty Twp, Mahoning Co., Oh.
3. **Philip Moser**
   b. 1824
   m. 24 Apr 1860 **Emma Drift**
   In 1880, Philip & Emma and their children Elizabeth E . (17), Frank J.
   (14), William R., (9) and Lucy Grace (5) were living in Girard, Trumbull
   County, Ohio.
4. **John Moser**
   b. 1829
   m. 22 May 1856 **Catharine Hezlep/Hezlys**
   d. 27 Oct 1906
   buried Oakwood Cemetery, Warren, Trumbull, Oh.
5. **Elizabeth Moser**
6. **Cornelius Moser**
   b. 18 Jul 1830
   m. 24 Jun 1847 **Elizabeth McKee**
   d. 16 May 1861
   buried Oakwood Cemetery, Warren, Trumbull, Oh.
7. **Michael Moser**, b. abt. 1835
8. **Charles Moser**, b. abt. 1837
9. **Mary Moser**, b. abt. 1839

2b. Philip Moser

Philip Moser, second son of **Philip Moser** and **Elisabeth Oswald**, ws born Sep. 1790
in Centre County, Pennsylvania. He married about 1813 (1) **Hannah Wallborn**, who
may be the **Hannah Moser** (1793-1819) that is buried in Heckmans Cemetery, Penn
Valley, Centre County, Pennsylvania. Philip married (2) **Susan Rush**, widow of
_____ **Peters**. Susan died in 1831 and Philip married (3) **Maria Magdalena "Polly"
Moser**, daughter of **Daniel** and **Polly Moser**, widow of **Daniel Condo**. They had no
children. After her death, Philip married for the last time, **Susan Miller**, daughter of
Christian Miller and Anna Maria Moser, widow of **David Oswald**. During his
lifetime, Philip operated a farm and a sawmill. He was a large man and had been well
educated in the German language. He died Nov 1871 and is buried in Heckmans
Cemetery. Children of Philip and Hannah Moser:
1. **Marianna Moser**
   b. 9 Oct 1814, Gregg Twp., Centre Co., Pa.
   bp. 30 Oct 1814, Penn Creek Church
   Sponsors: Michael and Catharina Wallborn
2. **Elisabeth Moser**
   b. 26 Aug 1816, Gregg Twp., Centre Co., Pa.
   bp. 29 Sep 1816, Penn Creek Church
   sponsors: Philip and Elisabeth Moser
   m. **Jacob Condo**, who was a wagonmaker
   Children of Jacob and Elisabeth Condo:
      George Condo, b. 1842, Pa.
      Charles Condo, b. 1844, Pa.
      Benjamin Condo, b. 1846, Pa.
      Joseph Condo, b. 1848, Pa.
   They went to Illinois after the 1850 census.

3. **Rebecca Moser**
   b. 29 Sep 1818, Gregg Twp., Centre Co., Pa.
   bp. 11 Oct 1818, Penn Creek Church
   Sponsors: Daniel and Rebecca Moser
   m. **Charles Hennich**
   They lived at Penn Hall, Pa.

Susah Rush Moser was the mother of four children, but only the following are known:

4. **John Moser**, b. 1824, Pa. (died young)
5. **George Moser**, b. 1827, Pa. (died young)
6. **D. J. Moser**, b. 1829, Centre Co., Pa.
   m. 1849 **Catherine Rearick** (b. 1827, Haines Twp., Centre Co., Pa., dau of **William** and **Friene Rearick**.)
   Children of D.J. and Catherine Moser:
   Alice R. Moser m. **John Swarm**
   John P. Moser, died young
   Mary A. Moser
   Charles A. Moser (1854-1896)
      had a son, **Wallace Moser**
   William H. Moser, stayed in Penn Twp.
   Cornelius Moser, went to Miles Twp.
   Melancthon Moser, went to Potter Twp.
   There should be five more children.

2c. Daniel Moser

Daniel Moser, son of **Philip Moser** and **Elisabeth Oswald**, was born 1 Oct 1792 in Lynn, Northampton County, Pennsylvania. He was married to his second cousin, **Susanna Everett** on 29 Jun 1819 in Warren, Trumbull County, Ohio. They soon purchased a farm in Liberty Township, Trumbull County and farmed there all their lives. Susan died 9 Jun 1857 and Daniel died 10 Dec 1872. They are buried in the Girard Cemetery, located in Girard, Mahoning County, Ohio. Children of Daniel and Susan Moser:

1. **Samuel E. Moser**
   b. 1818, Trumbull Co., Oh.
   m. 23 Nov 1854 Trumbull Co., Oh. **Helen Mosher**
   d. after 1860
   known children:
   Marcus Moser (b. 1855)
      In 1880, Marcus, a painter, was living in Girard, with Alice C (21), Clara M (16) and Ida (14).
   Alesei Moser (b. 1857)
   Rebecca Moser (b. 1859)
   Living with them in 1860 was **Alesei Mosher**, age 16, born NY, probably a younger sister of Helen.

2. **Phoebe Moser**
   b. 1821, Trumbull Co., Oh.
   m. 1 May 1851, Trumbull Co., Oh. **John Hawkins**
   d. after 1860
   known sons: **W.H. Hawkins** (b. 1852)
               J. J. Hawkins (b. 1854)

3. **Mary Barbara Moser**
   b. 1826, Trumbull Co., Oh.
   m. 13 May 1847, Trumbull Co., Oh. **James H. Bard**
   d. 9 May 1892
   They lived in Liberty Twp. and raised eight children.

4. **Charles E. Moser**
>   b. 1828, Trumbull Co., Oh.
>   m. 30 Nov 1849, Trumbull Co., Oh. **Margaret Von Wine**
5. **Sarah Moser**
>>   b. abt.1831, Trumbull Co., Oh.
>>   m. 30 Nov 1849 Trumbull Co., Oh. **William Douglas**
6. **Henrietta Moser** b. 4 Dec 1832, Trumbull Co., Oh.
7. **Angelinus Moser** b. abt. 1833, Trumbull Co., Oh.
8. **Slyvanus S. Moser** b. abt. 1837, Trumbull Co., Oh.
9. **Horace Moser** b. abt. 1840, Trumbull, Oh.
>   (He is called Harrison in later records.)
10. **P. N. Moser (male)** b. 1841, Trumbull Co., Oh.

2f. Lydia Moser Riehm

Lydia Moser, sixth child of **Philip Moser** and **Elisabeth Oswald**, was born
8 Nov. 1807 in Centre County, Pennsylvania and baptized 5 Dec 1807 at Penn Creek
Church. Sponsors at her baptism were Philip and Elisabeth Moser. She married
Michael Riehm about 1828. Only one child is know at this time:
>   **Johannes Benjamin Riehm**
>>   b. 29 Nov 1829, Centre Co., Pa.
>>   bp. 1 Jan 1830, Penn Creek Church
>>>   Sponsors were the parents
Either they left the area or Lydia died and Michael remarried. No other children were
baptized at Penn Creek Church for this couple.

4. Anna Maria Moser Miller

Anna Maria Moser, daughter of **Johann Burkhard Moser** and **Maria Agatha
Lichtenwallner**, was born 14 Oct 1769 in Centre County, Pennsylvania. She married
(1) 29 Jan 1799 in Milford Township, Northampton County, Pennsylvania **Christian
Miller**. Anna Maria died 18 Apr 1842 and is buried in Christ Lutheran Cemetery,
Schoenersville Township, Lehigh County, Pennsylvania. Only two children are known:
>   **Elisabeth Miller**
>>   b. 22 Jun 1803, Centre Co., Pa.
>>   bp. 24 Jun 1803, Penn Creek Church
>>>   Sponsors: Sebastian Moser and Anna Maria (Miller) Moser
>   **Susan Miller**
>>   m. **Philip Moser** (son of **Philip Moser** and
>>>   **Elisabeth Oswald**) as his fourth wife.
>>   They had no children.

3. Michael Moser

Michael Moser, son of **Johann Burchard Moser** and **Maria Agatha Lichtenwallner**,
was born in 1762, probably in Lynn, Northampton County, Pennsylvania. There are
several speculations as to his date of birth, but this one seems most likely. He and
Maria Margaretha Weber were married on 4 Apr 1801 by Rev. Johannes Helffrich.
The family settled in Centre County, Pennsylvania and had several children baptized at
the Penn Creek Church in Gregg Township.

There is speculation that Michael had another wife, possibly named **Catharina Elisabetha Wasser**. To this date, no marriage or death records have been located for this wife. She is believed to be the mother of the first two sons.

    a. Michael Moser
        Records not found
        m. **Hannah** _____
    b. Philip Moser
        b. Mar 1801, Lowhill, Northampton Co., Pa.
        (date from Ohio death records, bp records not found)
        m. **Elisabeth Snobel**
        d. 27 Feb 1873 Warren, Trumbull Co., Ohio

Michael and Maria Margaretha are buried in Heckmans Cemetery, Haines Township, Centre County, Pennsylvania. Margaretha's stones have no dates, but Michael's says he died in 1853. Known children of Michael and Maria Margaretha:

    c. Jonas Moser
        b. 1801*
        bp. (no date listed) Penn Creek Church Sponsor: Philip Moser
        d. 1853*
        m. **Maria A. Pollock**
        buried Heckmans, Haines Twp., Centre Co.
        (*dates on grave marker)
    d. Georg Moser
        b. 7 Jul 1804, Centre Co., Pa.
        bp. 29 Jul 1804, Penn Creek Church
            Sponsors: Georg and Magdalena Lilly
        m. (1) **Maria Elisabeth Moser**, dau.**Philip B. Moser** and
            Elisabeth Ilgen
        d. 1846, buried Heckmans Cemetery, Haines Twp.
    e. Maria Magdalena "Molly" Moser
        b. 24 Dec 1804, Centre Co., Pa.
        bp. (no date listed) Penn Creek Church
        sponsors: Philip Moser and Susan Miller
        m. abt 1831 **John Adam Confer**
    f. Jonathan (Johannes) Moser
        b. 1 Nov 1807, Centre Co., Pa.
        bp. (no date listed) Penn Creek Church
        Sponsors: Johannes and Catharina Moser
        m. **Anna Maria Durst** (d. 1841, buried Brethern Church, Harmony,
            Frederick Co., Md.)
        d. 1855, Gentryville, Gentry Co., Mo.
        Children of Jonathan and Maria Moser:
            Eli Moser, d. 1883, Polk City, Iowa
            Johan Harrison Moser, d. 1894, age 73. married twice.
            Aaron Moser, went to Des Moines, Iowa in 1857
            Betsey Moser, m. **Andrew Snyder**, went to Warren Co., Iowa
            Rebecca Moser, m. **William Higbee**
            Maria Margaretha "Betsy" Moser
                b. abt 1804, Pa.
                m. **Georg Haring/Hering**

3a. Michael Moser

Michael Moser is the oldest son of **Michael Moser** and (probably) **Catharina Elisabeth Wasser**. He married **Hannah** _____. No other records have been found on this couple, other than the birth of the following three children:
Michael Moser
bp 10 Sep 1820, Penn Creek Church, Gregg Twp.
Magdalena Moser
b. 26 Mar 1823, Centre Co., Pa.
bp. 20 Apr 1823, Penn Creek Church, Gregg Twp.
Johannes Moser
b. 19 Jun 1825, Centre Co., Pa.
bp. 31 Jul 1825, Penn Creek Church, Gregg Twp.
Sponsors: Philip and Elisabeth Moser
Michael and Hannah probably left the area after 1825.

3c. Jonas Moser

Jonas Moser, third son of **Michael Moser**, first recorded child of **Anna Margaretha Weber**, is listed as baptized at Penn Creek Church, Gregg Township, Centre County, Pennsylvania but no dates are given. Dated records at this church began in November of 1801. Sponsor at his baptism is listed as Philip Moser.

Jonas married **Maria A. Pollock** in Centre County, about 1827. Many sources claim she was Maria Durst, but unless there were two by that name, Maria Durst was married to his brother, Johathan. Seven children were baptized at Penn Creek Church prior to 1841. Jonas and Maria acted as sponsors for all of their own children.

Sources claim that Jonas and Maria went to Richland County, Ohio. However, Jonas and Maria have been found in Stephenson County, Illinois records, where their last two children were born, and they are both buried in Heckman's Cemetery, Penn Valley, Pennsylvania. Known children of Jonas and Maria Moser:
Georg Moser
b. 20 Oct 1828, Centre Co., Pa.
bp. 23 Nov 1828, Penn Creek Church
m. **Susan Condo**, dau of Daniel Condo and Magdalena Moser
Maria Margaretha Moser
b. 10 Nov 1831, Centre Co., Pa.
bp. 14 Jan 1832, Penn Creek Church
Johannes Moser
b. 18 Mar 1833, Centre Co., Pa.
bp. 8 Apr 1833, Penn Creek Church
Peter Michael Moser
b. 10 Nov 1834, Centre Co., Pa.
bp. 11 Jan 1835, Penn Creek Church
m. **Sarah Wohlford**
Daniel Moser
b. 26 Oct 1836, Centre Co. Pa.
bp. 4 Dec 1836, Penn Creek Church
Wilhelm Moser
b. 24 Feb 1839, Centre Co., Pa.
bp. 28 Apr 1839, Penn Creek Church

Benjamin Moser
    b. 15 Jan 1841, Centre Co., Pa.
    bp. 18 Jul 1841, Penn Creek Church
James Moser
    b. abt. 1844, Stephenson Co., Ill
    m. **Kate Zimmerman**
Charles Moser
    b. abt. 1846, Stephenson Co., Ill.
    m. **Mary Pollock**

3d. George Moser

George Moser, son of **Michael Moser** and **Anna Margaretha Weber**, was born 7 Jul 1804 in Centre County, Pennsylvania and baptized 29 Jul 1804 at Penn Creek Church. He married about 1830 **Maria Elisabeth Moser**, daughter of **Philip B. Moser** and **Elisabeth Ilgen**. Maria was born 10 Oct 1811 in Centre County, Pennsylvania, probably in Gregg Township as her brothers and sisters were born there and she was baptized there on 3 Nov 1811. If you want to get out your calculators, they were either third cousins, or first cousins twice removed. Maria died in 1833, either in childbirth or shortly thereafter. Children of George and Maria Elisabeth:

Elias Moser
    b. 1832, Centre Co., Pa.
    m. **Elisabeth** _____
    d. 1888, Gregg Township, Centre Co., Pa.
Rosetta Moser
    b. about 1833
    m. **John W. Krumrine**

George then married **Elisabeth Ilgen** (a relative of Maria's mother), who died in 1899. George died 1846. They are buried in Heckmans Cemetery, Haines Township, Centre County, Pennsylvania. Children of George and Elisabeth Moser:

Emanuel Moser
    b. 1 Jun 1834, Centre Co., Pa.
    bp. 22 Jun 1834, Penn Creek Church (name on record is Immanuel)
    m. **Katharine Bottorf**
Anna Margaretha Moser
    b. 24 Feb 1836, Centre Co., Pa.
    bp. 7 Apr 1836 Penn Creek Church
Maria Katherina Moser
    b. 28 Mar 1838, Centre Co., Pa.
    bp. 15 Apr 1838 Penn Creek Church
    m. **Henry Gramley**
    They went to Iowa.
Georg Michael
    b. 14 Oct 1840,Centre Co., Pa.
    bp. 18 Jul 1841, Penn Creek Church
    died in childhood
William H. H. Moser
    b. about 1842
    bp. record not found
Elisabeth Moser
    b. about 1844, Pa.
    m. **Isaac Gates**
    They went to Illinois.
Rebecca Moser
    b. about 1845, Pa.
    m. _____ **Wolf**
    d. 1883, Pa.

3e. Maria Magdalena "Molly" Moser Confer

Maria Magdalena "Molly" Moser, daughter of **Michael Moser** and **Anna Margaretha Weber,** was born in Centre County, Pennsylvania on 24 Dec 1805 and baptized 19 Jan 1806 at Penn Creek Church in Gregg Township. Sponsors at her baptism were Philip Moser and Susana Miller, both single. She married about 1831 **John Adam Confer,** son of **Adam** and **Margaretha Confer.** He was born 30 Jul 1809 and baptized 10 Sep 1809 at Penn Creek Church. His sponsors were Johannes and Magdalena Blattner. Known children of John and Molly Confer:

Henrietta Catharina Confer
>b. 30 Sep 1832, Centre Co., Pa.
>bp. Penn Creek Church, date not given

Israel Confer
>b. 6 Nov 1833, Centre Co., Pa.
>bp. 8 Dec 1833, Penn Creek Church

Johan Michael Confer
>b. 27 Jan 1836, Centre Co., Pa.
>bp. 28 Feb 1836, Penn Creek Church

Jakob Benjamin Confer
>b. 26 Aug 1837, Centre Co., Pa.
>bp. 8 Oct 1837, Penn Creek Church

3g. Maria Margaretha "Betsy" Moser Hering

Maria Margaretha "Betsy" Moser, daughter of **Michael Moser** and **Anna Margaretha Weber,** was born about 1805 (baptism records not found) in Centre County, Pennsylvania. She acted as sponsor for Magdalena Moser, daughter of her brother, Michael, in April 1823, along with **George Hering,** whom she later married. George was born in 1801, and is probably a son of the **Jacob** and **Eva Hering** who were busy sponsoring at baptisms between 1819 and 1825 at Penn Creek Church. Jacob Hering was born 3 Apr 1781, baptized 3 May 1781 at Jerusalem Lutheran Church in Berks Co., Pennsylvania. Sponsors at his baptism were Freiderich Kampf and Sabina Hering. Maria and George were living in Gregg Township, Centre County, Pennsylvania at the time of the 1850 Federal Census. According to the Census, Maria was born in 1804. Known children of Maria and George Hering:

George Hering
>b. 14 Dec 1830, Centre Co., Pa.
>bp. 9 Jan 1831, Penn Creek Church
>(Not listed with parents in 1850 census)

Samuel Jacob Hering
>b. 17 Dec 1828, Centre Co., Pa.
>bp. 11 Jan 1829, Penn Creek Church

John George Hering
>b. 15 Mar 1833, Centre Co., Pa.
>bp. 31 Mar 1833, Penn Creek Church
>(Not listed with parents in 1850 census)

Elisa Fronica Hering
>b. 22 Dec 1838, Centre Co., Pa.
>bp. 16 Feb 1839, Penn Creek Church

Carolina Hering b. about 1840
James Hering b. about 1845

5. Jacob Moser

Jacob Moser, son of Johann Burkhard Moser and Maria Agatha Lichtenwallner, was born in Pennsylvania 29 Apr 1772. He married (1) _____ Oswald.
Children of Jacob and _____ Moser:

    a. Jacob Moser
        b. 13 Dec 1799, Pa.
        m. abt. 1829 **Susanna Peter** (dau of Jacob Peter and **Margaretha**
            Moser, b. 1 Jun 1805, Heidelberg, Pa)
        d. 26 Mar 1885
        bur. Ebeneezer Cemetery
    b. Michael Moser
        b. abt. 1792, Pa.
        m. **Elisabeth** _____
    c. John Moser
        b. abt. 1794, Pa.
        m. **Catharine** _____
    d. David Moser
        b. abt. 1796, Pa.
    e. Molly Moser
        b. abt. 1798, Pa.
        m. **James Neff**
        d. 1883, Slatington, Pa.
    f. Lydia Moser (twin)
        b. 13 Apr 1810, Pa.
        m. 1 Jun 1833 **Elias Neff**
        d. 29 Nov 1888, New Tripoli, Pa.
    g. Leah Moser (twin)
        b. 13 Apr 1810, Pa.
        m. 4 Jun 1832 **Jacob Martz/Mentz**
        d. 28 Mar 1895, Carbon, Pa.

Jacob married (2) **Susanna Hunsicker** (b. 12 Jul 1775). During the 1850 census, he was a shopkeeper in Lynn, Lehigh County, Pa., living with his daughters, Regina and Sally Ann. Since Susanna is not listed with them, she may have died before 1850.
Children of Jacob and Susanna Moser:

    h. Nathan Moser m. **Mariann** _____
    i. Samuel Moser
    j. Nettie Moser m. **Nathan Snyder**
    k. Abbie Moser m. **Jacob Weaver**
    i. Regina Moser
        b. abt. 1828, Pa.
        m. **Frank Hausman**
    j. Sally Ann Moser
        b. abt. 1831, Pa.
        m. **Adam Benninger**

Children of Jacob and Susanna Moser:
1. **Catherine Moser**, b. 1821 m. **Michael Werley**
2. **Leah Moser**, b. 1825 m. **Jeremiah Klingerman**
3. **Mary Ann Moser**
   b. 20 Aug 1829, New Tripoli, Pa.
   m. **John Kistler**
   (son of **David Kistler & Catherine Whetstone**)
   d. 9 Jul 1907, Andover, Pa.
   Children of John and Mary Ann Kistler:
   Mary Emma Kistler
   Louisa Kistler
   Owen Kistler
   Wilson Alfred Kistler m. **Savannah Sittler**
   Sarah Alice Kistler m. **Charles S. Kistler**
   Ada Moser Kistler
   John Wesley Kistler m. **Savina Gerber**
   Grant M. Kistler m. **Rosie Heintzleman**
   Jennie Kistler
   Edward Daniel Kistler m. **Clara Behler**
4. **Elisabeth Moser**
   b. about 1832, Pa.
   m. **Daniel Snyder**
5. **Jacob Moser**
   b. about 1833, Pa.
   m. **Abbie Hunsicker**
   Known child of Jacob and Abbie Moser:
   Osville Jacob Moser
   b. 7 Feb 1866
   m. **Lizzie Victoria Weaver** (dau. of **Rhuben**
   Weaver and Rebecca Brobst)
6. **Betsy Ann Moser**, b. about 1835, Pa.
7. **Sally Moser**
   b. about 1836, Pa.
   m. **Noah Kistler**
8. **Lidia Moser**
   b. 21 Oct 1837, Pa.
   d. 10 Mar 1917
9. **Carolina Moser**
   b. about 1841, Pa.
   m. **Alfred Dorward**
10. **Levi Moser**
   b. 23 Sep 1844, Pa.
   m. (1) 26 Dec 1868 **Polly Kistler** (d. 20 Mar 1906)
   (2) **Kate Kistler**
   Children of Levi and Polly Moser:
   Edwin Jacob Moser, b. 16 Nov 1870
   m. **Hertha Rubens**
   They had two children.
   Mary Moser, b. 1869
   m. _____ **Longacre**

Living with them at the time of the 1850 census was **Elisabeth Klause**, age 4. Another reported daughter is **Judith Moser**, (b. 1835 m. **Aaron Peter**). However, she does not appear in the 1850 census when she would have been age 15.

5e. Molly Moser Neff

Molly Moser, daughter of **Jacob Moser** and _____ **Oswald**, was born in Pennsylvania about 1798. She married **James Neff** (born about 1799 in Pennsylvania) who was a gunsmith. In 1850, they were living in Heidelberg, Lehigh County, Pennsylvania with the following children:

    Mariann Neff, b. about 1831
    James Neff, b. about 1833
    Adam Neff, b. about 1834
    Joseph Neff, b. about 1836

5f. Lydia Moser Neff

Lydia Moser, daughter of **Jacob Moser** and _____ **Oswald**, was born 13 Apr 1810 in Lehigh County, Pennsylvania and died 29 Nov. 1888 in Franklin, Pennsylvania. She married **Elias Neff**, a farmer who was born in 1811 in Pennsylvania. In 1850, they were farming in Lynn, Lehigh County, Pennsylvania and had the following children:

    Madina Neff, b. about 1838
    Owen Neff, b. about 1839
    Dianna Neff, b. about 1841

5i. Samuel Moser

Samuel Moser, son of **Jacob Moser** and **Susanna Hunsicker** cannot be the Samuel as thought by other researchers. That Samuel is the father of Elisabeth (b. 1800), Joseph (b. 1802), Jacob (b. 1804), Samuel (b. 1806), Catherine (b. 1808), John (b. 1810) Michael (b. 1811) and Abraham (b. 1814). Since Jacob's daughter, Lydia, (by his first wife) was born in 1810, Samuel, a son of Jacob's second wife, could not have been having children in 1800. In truth, Jacob's oldest son, Jacob, was only ten years old when the other Samuel was having these children. More research needs to be done on these two families.

c. Jacob Moser

Jacob Moser, son of **David Moser** and **Catharine Oswald**, was born 29 Jan 1798 in Mosserville, Northampton County, Pennsylvania. He married **Salome Kistler** (b. abt 1799) and moved to Trexlerville, Lehigh County, Pennsylvania in 1829. By 1849 the family was in Allentown, where Jacob was working as a tanner. At the time of the 1850 census, **Eliza Jane Mertz** was living with the family. Jacob died in 1877. Children of Jacob and Salome Moser:

    c1. Catherine Moser
        b. 9 Mar 1823
        bp. Upper Milford Church, Zionsville, Lehigh Co., Pa.
        m. **Samuel Albright**
    c2. William K. Moser
        b. abt 1822
        m. aft. 1850, **Lucy Fisher**
        They had three children.

2. John Adam Mosser, Jr.

John Adam, Mosser Jr., son of **Hans Adam Mosser** and his wife, **Eva**, was born about 1736 and is found on the tax lists by 1756. He married **Anna Maria** _____, and was one of the two Moser boys shot by indians in 1758. His father, along with either his second wife or the young widow, provided surety for the settlement of the estate. In Orphans Court Records of Lancaster County, **Isaac Meyer** (founder of Myerstown, Pa.) is appointed as the guardian of minor son, John. No other minor children are mentioned. Anna Maria married second **John Brown** in 1760, when she was listed as the widow of Adam Mosser, Jr. by the Rev. Stoever. Known children of John Adam & Anna Maria:

a. **John Adam Moser**, b. 28 Nov 1745
   confirmed 25 Dec. 1760
   died unmarried in 1804
   John's will was probated 1 May 1804 in Reading,
   Lancaster County, Pa. The abstract is faint and hard to
   read, but mentions the following siblings who are most
   likely to be surnamed Brown:
b. **Michael (Brown?)**
   This Michael has a son, also named Michael,
   who is to get his uncle John's horse. It is doubtful that
   he would be an older brother, as it is usually the
   firstborn son who becomes the namesake. He is probably John's
   half-brother, surnamed Brown.
c. **Eva (Brown?)** m. **Philip Heckman (?)**
   (The husband's surname is very faint.)
d. **Catharine (Brown?)** m. **Jacob Young**

3. Johann Nicholas Mosser

Johann Nicholas Mosser, thought to be the second son of **Hans Adam**, was born in 1738 in Pennsylvania. He married (1) **Catherine Ley**, daughter of the **Christian Ley** who arrived on the *Loyal Judith* in 1732, and (2) **Margaret Hahn Ruth**, (b. 20 Jul 1747, d. 10 Jul 1818) daughter of **Peter Johann Hahn**. This Nicholas is found on tax lists in 1771, 1772, 1773 and 1782. He served in the Rev. War and was the father of eleven daughters and one son. He died 19 Apr 1824. They are all buried in the Tulpenhocken Cemetery. Nicholas is registered with the DAR. Known children of Nicholas and Catherine Mosser:

a. **Anna Maria Mosser**
   b. 1763 m. **J. Nicholas Albert**
   d. 1835
b. **Michael Mosser**
   b. 1764 m. **Margaret Ann Copenhaver**
c. **Christena Mosser**
   b. 1773 m. 1790 **William Siebert**
   at Tulpehocken (Trinity) Church
d. **Elisabeth Mosser**
   b. 1778 m. 1799 **Thomas Batdorff**
   at Tulpehocken (Trinity) Church

e. **Eva Mosser**
>> m. 1796 **Philip Tice** (son of **Mathias Tice &**
>> **Regina Copenhaver**) (Mathias Tice arrived on the
>> *Thistle* in 1730. Regina is a daughter of **Thomas**
>> **Copenhaver** who arrived in 1728 on the *Goodwill* with
>> Hans Adam and Hans Martin Mosser.)

Only known child of Nicholas and Margaret Mosser:

f. **Margaret Mosser**
>> bp. 1788 at Tulpehocken Church

Three other daughters have been identfied in a letter found in the Myerstown Library (mother unknown). They are as follows:

g. **Mrs. Frederick Seibert**
h. **Mrs. Batdorff** (possibly Elisabeth, see d above)
i. **Barbara (Mrs. David Tice)**

The identities of the other two daughters are not known at this time.

a. Anna Maria Moser Albert

Anna Maria Moser, daughter of **Johann Nicholas Moser** and **Catherine Ley**, was born in 1763 and confirmed in 1777 at Trinity (Tulpehocken) Church in Millardsville, Lebanon County, Pennsylvania. At the same church in 1786 she married **J. Nicholas Albert** (b. 1765). She had one known daughter:

Anna Maria Albert
>> b. 1795, Pa.
>> m. **Christian Decker** (1784-1869)
>> d. 1867
>> buried at Host Church with her husband

Anna Maria died in 1835 and is buried with her husband, who died in 1831, in Klopp's Cemetery in Hamlin (now Lebanon County), Pennsylvania.

b. Michael Moser

Michael Moser, son of **Johann Nicholas Moser** and **Catherine Ley**, was born and baptized in 1764 at the Trinity Lutheran Church. He married **Margaret Ann Copenhaver** (b. 1766), daughter of **Henry Copenhaver** and **Christena Reed**. Michael served as an ensign during the Rev. War. By 1813 he had acquired land in Myerstown, Lebanon County, Pennsylvania. Michael died in 1843 and is buried with his wife (died 1842) in Frieden's Evangelical Lutheran Cemetery in Myerstown. Children of Michael & Margaret Ann Moser:

b1. **Elizabeth Moser**
>> b. 1794, Pa.
>> bp. Tulpenhocken (Trinity) Church
>> m. **John Groff**
>> Known children of Elizabeth & John Groff:
>>> **Isaac Groff**
>>> **Elizabeth Groff**

b2. **William Moser**
>> b. 1796, Pa., died young
>> bp. Tulpenhocken (Trinity) Church

b3. John Moser
    b. 1799, Pa.
    bp. Tulpenhocken (Trinity) Church
    m. (1) **Sarah (Salome) Shutz** (1799-1876)
    d. 1871, buried at Union Cemetery
    He was one of the founders of Meyerstown Accademy.
    Known children of John & Sarah Moser:
        Susanna Moser, b. 1822
        Maria Moser, b. 1824
        Sarah Moser, b. 1827
        Aaron Moser, b. 1829
            m. **Maria** _____ and
            had a son, **William Penn Moser**, b. 1855
        Lavina Moser, b. 1832
        Elizabeth Moser, b. 1837
        (female) Moser

b4. Daniel Moser
    b. 1805, Pa.
    bp. Tulpenhocken (Trinity) Church
    m. 1826 **Magdalena Holstein** (1807-1875)
    (dau. of **Leonard Holstein & Elizabeth Mohr**)
    d. 1877, Pa.
    buried in Union Cemetery.
    They had a total of seven children.
    Known children of Daniel and Magdalena Moser:
        Maria Moser, b. 1827, Pa.
        Cyrus Moser, b. 1829, Pa.
            m. **Mary Ann Kelly**
            (They had a son named **William**)
        John Moser, b. 1833, Pa.
        Rev. Henry Moser. b. 1837, Pa.
            m. **(1) Catherine Schoch** (d. 1871)
            (dau of **Jacob Schoch & Elisabeth Illig**)
            (2) Sarah Powers
           d. 1910
           Rev. Henry was a graduate of Myerstown Academy
           and served as pastor of the First Baptist Church
           in Reading, Pa.
           Children of Rev. Henry & Catherine:
                Lizzie Moser
                Maggie Moser
                Clara Moser
                Samuel Moser
                Rachel Moser
                Charles Moser
           Daughter of Rev. Henry & Sarah:
                Mary W. Moser
    Amanda Moser
        b. 1840, Pa.
        m. 1880, **Capt. J. H. Bassler** as his
        second wife
        d. 1919, Myerstown, Lebanon Co., Pa.
        They had one son, **Professor Harvey Bassler**
        of John Hopkins University.

4. Henry Mosser

Henry Mosser, son of **Hans Adam Mosser** and **Eva**, was also mentioned in his father's will. He may be the one who married **Elisabeth** _____ and had two daughters baptized at Trinity Lutheran Church in Millardsville, Pennsylvania:
Christina Mosser b. 1767
Elisabeth Mosser b. 1769
There are three wills mentioned in the index of the "Collections of the Genealogical Society of Pennsylvania," Vol. 24, for a Henry Mosser. Wills #58, 671 and 738 have been abstracted and printed in the volume.

5. Anna Mary Mosser Ruth

Anna Mary Mosser, daughter of **Hans Adam Mosser**, was born in 1735. Anna Mary married **Michael Ruth/Ruhr** and is mentioned in her father's will. She died in 1804 and was the mother of nine children. Michael Ruth was born 1725, the oldest son of **Johann Peter Ruth** and **Anna Sophia Lauer**. He served as a Court Martial Official in the 7th Co., Berks County Militia in 1771. They lived in Heidelberg, Pennsylvania. Michael died in 1803 and Anna in 1804. They are buried in Haines Cemetery.
Children of Anna Mary and Michael Ruth:
a. Michael Ruth
had son, **Leonard Ruth** (1795-1852, m. **Elizabeth Weinhold** and had 10 children.
b. Catherine Ruth m. **Nicholas Haag**
c. John Adam Ruth (1752-1821)
bp. Haines Church
m. **Anna Catherine Filsmeyer** (1760-1839)
Buried together in Haines Cemetery, Berks Co., Pa.
John served in John Spohn's Co. during the Rev. War.
Children of John Adam & Anna Catherine Ruth:
Catherine Ruth (1778-1813)
Anna Margaret Ruth (1781-1847)
Maria Barbara Ruth (1783-1826)
Michael Ruth (1787-1815)
Christina Ruth (1793-1820)
Anna Ruth (1796-1815)
John Adam Ruth (1790-1843)
m. **Anna Maria Hain** (dau. of **George Hain**
& **Mary Magdalena Ruth**
They had 5 sons and 5 daughters
d. Christian Ruth (1758-1823)
m. 1786 **Barbara Bollman** (d. 1811)
Both buried at Haines Cemetery, Berks Co., Pa.
Children of Christian and Barbara Ruth:
Catherine Ruth (1787-1826)
m. 1811, **Henry Miller** (1792-1864)
Both buried at Haines Cemetery,
Berks Co., Pa.
They had 2 sons and one daughter
Anna Maria Ruth (1789-1803)
Buried at Haines Cemetery, Berks, Pa.
Susanna Ruth b. 1791
Leonhard Ruth b. 1793
Isaac Ruth (1797-1813) buried at Haines Cemetery

e. Margaret Ruth (1761-1808)
> bp. at Haines Reformed Church, Berks Co., Pa.
> Sponsor: Weyerly Moser
> m. **Daniel Graff** (1749-1808)
> Daniel was born in Kirchberg, Germany and served
> in the Rev. War. Both are buried at Zion Lutheran
> Reformed Cemetery, Womelsdorf, Pa.

f. Maria Barbara Ruth (1763-1818)
> m. 1785 **David Hain** (1759-1823), son of
> **John Casper Hain & Catherine Laucks**
> They owned a 240 acre farm in Bern Township,
> Berks Co., Pa. David served in the Rev. War.
> They are buried in Epler's Cemetery.
> Children of Maria Barbara and David Hain:
>> **William Hain** (1786-1845)
>>> m. **Catherine Epler** (1794-1881)
>>> dau. of **Jacob & Margaret Epler**
>>> Both buried in Epler's Cemetery.
>>> They had 8 sons and 6 daughters
>> **Maria Margaret Hain**, b. 1788
>> **John Hain** (1791-1858)
>>> m. **Sarah Goetz** (1797-1864)
>>> dau. of **Nicholas Goetz**
>>> Both buried in Epler's Cemetery
>>> They had 2 sons and 3 daughters
>> **George Hain**, b. 1795
>> **Isaac Hain**, b. 1797
>> **Michael Hain**, b. 1799

g. Magdalena Ruth (1768-1831)
> m. **Peter Hain** (1761-1811)
> (brother of David Hain, above)
> They owned 360 acres in Dauphin County, Pa.
> Peter served under **Capt. Conrad Kershner**
> during the Rev. War.
> Children of Magdalena and Peter Hain:
>> **Catherine Hain** (1788-1848)
>>> m. **Michael Fisher**
>>> Both buried in Haines Cemetery, Berks Co., Pa.
>>> They had 2 sons and 6 daughters
>> **Michael Hain** (1790-1857)
>>> m. (1) **Elizabeth Wenrich** (1791-1825, (dau. of
>>> **Matthias Wenrich**).
>>> They had 4 children.
>>> m. (2) **Rebecca Wenrich**
>>> (1807-1833, Elizabeth's sister)
>>> They had 2 sons, 1 daughter
>>> m. (3) **Mary Keith** (1808-1864, dau. of
>>> **Michael** and **Elizabeth Keith**)
>>> They had 9 children.
>>> After his third marriage, he purchased a 204 acre
>>> farm at Swatara, Lebanon Co., Pa. Michael is buried
>>> in Klopp's Cemetery, Hamlin, Lebanon Co., Pa. with
>>> his third wife, Mary.

Maria Barbara Hain
    b. 1793
    m. **Richard Adam**
    Both are buried in Haines Cemetery, Berks Co., Pa.
Susanna Hain (1795-1799)
George Hain (1798-1885)
    m. **Eve Fisher** (1799-1886
      dau. of **Daniel Fisher & Catherine Moyer**)
    George was a blacksmith and a gunsmith.
    Both are buried in Haines Cemetery, Berks Co., Pa.
    They had 8 children.
Elizabeth Hain (1800-1870)
    m. **David Eirich** (1800-1879, son of
      John Eirich & Elizabeth Werheim)
    He was the first postmaster and R. R. agent
    at Wernersville, Pa. They had 3 sons and
    7 daughters. Both are buried in Haines
    Cemetery, Berks Co., Pa.
Peter Hain (1803-1860)
    m. **Anna Tobias** (1810-1889 of Bern Twp.
    They built the first two story residence
    in Wernersville, Pa. Both are buried in
    Haines Cemetery, Berks Co., Pa.
Anna Hain (1809-1884)
    Buried at Haines Cemetery
    She never married.
Samuel Hain (1809-1884)
    m. **Margaret Kintzel** (1813-1887, dau. of
      Jacob Kintzel & Margaret Fitzenberger)
    They had 5 children. They are buried at the
    Charles Evans Cemetery in Reading, Pa.
Ellen Hain (1812-1888)
    m. **Dr. Edward B. Livingood** (1807-1851,
      son of **John Livingood & Elizabeth Bricker**)
    He was the first physician in Wernersville,
    Pa. They went to Farmersville, Montgomery
    Co., Ohio, and are buried in the United
    Brethern Cemetery there. They had 4 sons
    and 3 daughters.

6. Catharine Mosser Bickel

Catharine Mosser Bickel is mentioned in the will of **Hans Adam Mosser** as one of his daughters. Catharine married **Tobias Bickel/Pickell**.

Tobias Bickel and Catharine sold two tracts of land in Heidelberg Township on 9 Sep 1768 to **John Weaver** of Heidelberg. The largest tract was located on the Tulpehocken Creek and adjoined the lands of **Adam Moser** and **Simon Copenheffer**, and had been purchased from **Casper Wistar** in 1737. By 1 May 1771, John Weaver had paid only half of the money, so Tobias assigned the debt over to Simon Coppenhever of Lancaster County and deeded him the land. (Please note the various spellings of 'Coppenhaven'. They are noted here the way they appear on the documents.) The deed was witnessed in Lancaster County in 1769 but not recorded until 1794, after the area had become Dauphin County.

The other tract of land in Heidelberg Township was sold to Simon Koppenhoffer on 13 Jun 1768. Tobias' name is spelled "Bichell' on this deed. This tract adjoined one belonging to Catharine's brother, **Nicholas Mosser**.

Tobias and Catharine settled in Penn Township, Northumberland County, Pennsylvania, where he is listed on the tax lists of 1771. Catharine preceeded Tobias in death, and he took a second wife. All three are buried in Row's Cemetery.

Children of Tobias and Catharine Bickel are unknown at this time.

7. Peter Mosser

Peter Mosser was also mentioned as a son of **Hans Adam Mosser** in his will, dated 1770. Peter lived in Derry Township, Berks County, Pennsylvania. He married **Catherine Snider**, daughter of **Nicholas Snider**. He served in the Hanover Rifle Battalion under **Capt. Thomas Koppenhoffer** during the Rev. War.

A Peter Moser made his will in 1844 in Wythe County, Virginia. This will mentions his brothers **John & Adam Moser**, his brothers-in-law **Michael Steffy, Lorenz Wolf & Henry Pickle** (who were probably married to Catherine's sisters, as they were also heirs of Nicholas Snider), and his nephew **John Adam Moser**, son of his brother John. Peter gave his wife, Catharine a negro boy named **Reuben** who was to be set free either at her death or in the event of her remarriage. The will does not mention any children.

The only known evidence indicating that the Peter, son of Hans Adam, is the same Peter who died in Virginia, is the fact that he and his father-in-law both named the three above mentioned heirs in their wills.

8. Jacob Mosser

Jacob Mosser, son of **Hans Adam** and **Eva Mosser**, married **Maria Hostettler**, daughter of the **Oswald Hostettler** who came to Philadelpyhia on the *Samuel* in 1732.

Jacob was listed on the 1756 tax list for Hanover Township as having fled the area. He is found again on the tax list for Coalbrookdale (now part of Tamaqua) in 1779 and 1780. It is unlikely that his father would have included Jacob in his will of 1770 if he were no longer living. Therefore, he could not be the Jacob Moser whose estate was settled in 1766 (and who is thought to have been killed by indians). Known children of Jacob and Mary Moser:

    a. Christina Moser
        20 Mar 1749 at Swatara
        m. **John Wallner**
        (son of **Johannes & Christina Walmer**)
    b. Catherine Moser
        m. **Capt. Thomas Coppenhaver**
    c. Rachel/Regina Moser
        m. **Adam Gutman**
    d. Elisabeth Moser
    e. Jacob Moser, Jr.
        b. 1757
    f. Eva Moser
        m. _____ **Weirick**

There is another **Jacob Moser** who arrived in Philadelphia on the *Restoration* with **Peter Moser** and **Peter Moser, Jr.** in 1757. Since the two Peters settled in Virginia, it seems plausable that this Jacob did also. He is more likely to be the Jacob who died intestate in 1766, leaving minor children. His estate was settled in Orphans Court in 1772. His children were identified as:

        Catherine Moser (oldest)
        Rachel Moser
        Christine Moser
        Elisabeth Moser
        Jacob Moser, Jr.

Although the names are similar, it is doubtful that he is the same man as our Jacob.

9. Daniel Moser

Daniel Moser was a son of **Hans Adam Mosser**, according to his father's will. He appeared on the tax list of 1756 in Hanover Township, Berks County, Pennsylvania, but fled during the French and Indian War to safer territory.

He married **Anna Maria** _____. They had two children baptized at Swatara Reformed Church in Jonesville, Berks County, Pennsylvania.

        John Henry Moser, bp. 1771
        Magdalena Moser, bp. 1775

1. Weyerly Moser

Weyerly Moser, the last child mentioned in **Hans Adam Mosser's** will, married **Margaret Epler** in Cocalico Township, Lancaster (now Berks) County, Pennsylvania. He was born 16 Mar 1733 and baptized 17 Sep 1733 at Cocalico. Like his brothers, Weyerly served in the Rev. War. He and Margaretha are buried in Epler's Cemetery, located in Schulykill Co, Pennsylvania. Weyerly's will was filed in Reading, Lancaster County, Pennsylvania in 1811. Although he and Margaretha became the parents of five sons and four daughters, only the following are mentioned in his will:

 a. Anna Maria Moser
  m. **William Albrecht**
  They went to North Carolina
 b. Barbara Moser
 c. Catherine Moser
  (Is she the Catherine who married **John Reber**?)
 d. John Moser
  m. **Elisabeth Lamm**
 e. Valentine Moser
  b. 1759, Pa.
  m. **Rosina Fischer**
  d. 1833 in Berks County, Pa.

e. Valentine Moser

Valentine Moser, son of **Weyerly Moser** and **Margaret Epler**, was born in 1759 in Lancaster (now Berks) County, Pennsylvania. He married about 1780 **Rosina Fischer**. Valentine died in 1822 and is buried in Epler Cemetery, Leesport, Berks County, Pennsylvania. Children of Valentine & Rosina Moser:

 John Moser, b. 1782, Berks Co., Pa.
  m. **Elisabeth Reber**
 Catharine Moser, bp. 1784, Bern Reformed Church, Pa.
  m. **Abraham Herbein**
 (male) Moser, b. 1786, Berks Co., Pa.
 Weirli Moser, b. 1788, Berks Co., Pa.
  m. **Elisabeth Yost/Jost**
 (male) Moser, b. 1790, Berks Co., Pa.
 Anna Maria Moser, bp. 1793 by Rev. Schwartzwald
 Daniel Moser, bp. 1794, Trinity Lutheran, Reading, Pa.
 (female) Moser, b. 1795
 (female) Moser, b. 1797
 Samuel Moser
  b. 1801, Pa.
  m. **Maria Bode**
  d. 1862

A. Michael Moser

Michael Moser/Musser, son of **Hans Paul** and **Elisabeth Mosser**, was born
11 Apr 1739 in New Hanover Township, Northampton County, Pennsylvania, where he
was confirmed in 1752 at age 14. He married (1) **Elisabeth** _____ and (2) **Maria**
_____, who is referred to as both **Anna Maria** and **Anna Barbara** in Trinity Church
records of Lancaster County. These records state that he was one of the three sons of
Paul Moser who went to Lancaster County and changed their name to **"Musser"**.

In the 1790 census of Lancaster County, Michael had a household of six males over
sixteen, two males under sixteen, six females, one other free person and two slaves.
Michael made his will 5 Jun 1814, and it is recorded in Book K., Vol. 1, page 554.
Children of Michael and Maria Moser:

1. **William Moser**
   b. 23 Jan 1764
   bp. Trinity Lutheran Church, Lancaster, So., Pa.
   d. 31 Jul 1803, Lancaster Co., Pa.
2. **Elisabeth Moser**
   b. 7 Oct 1765
   d. young
3. **Frederich Moser**
   b. 14 Jul 1769
   d. 21 Jan 1785
4. **Elisabeth Moser**
   b. 24 Nov 1771
5. **John Moser**
   b. 2 Nov 1774
   m. 11 May 1802 **Mary Catharine Muhlenberg**
   d. 1813
6. **Anna Maria Moser**
   b. 26 Jul 1778, Lancaster Co., Pa.
7. **Catharine Moser**
   b. 1 Apr 1781, Lancaster Co., Pa.
8. **Rebecca Moser**
   b. 14 May 1784
   d. 9 Aug 1787

No children are known to have been born to Michael and his first wife.

A5 John Moser/Musser

John Moser, son of **Michael Moser** and (2) **Maria Moser/Musser**, was born
2 Nov 1774 in Lancaster County, Pennsylvania. He married 11 May 1802 **Mary
Catharine Muhlenberg** (b. 2 Sep 1776), daughter of **Gotthelf Henry Ernest
Muhlenberg** and Mary Catharine Hall. John died in 1813 in Lancaster County and
Mary Catharine died in 1843. Children of John and Mary Moser/Musser:

a. **Mary Catharine Moser**
   b. 6 May 1803, Pa.
   d. 6 Jun 1856, Pa.
   She never married
b. **Henrietta Augusta Moser**
   b. 29 Sep 1804, Pa.
   m. 20 Dec 1832 **Zephniah McLenegan**
   d. 5 Jun 1856

c. **Henry Muhlenberg Moser**
    b. 6 Jan 1807, Pa.
    d. 1855
d. **Caroline Amelia Moser**, twin
    b. 28 Dec 1808, Lancaster Co., Pa.
    m. 5 Jul 1848 **John Philip Hiester, M.D.**
    d. 1875
e. **Selma Matilda Moser**, twin
    b. 28 Dec 1808, Pa.
    m. 1 May 1827 **George Bowman Withers** (1798-1860)
    d. 7 Dec 1880
f. **Susan Ann Moser**
    b. 22 Feb 1811, Pa.
    m. 21 Mar 1843 **John George Hoffman**
    d. 15 Oct 1853
g. **John Perry Moser**
    b. 20 Nov 1813, Pa.
    d. 1814

A5b Henrietta Augusta Moser McLenegan

Henrietta Augusta Moser, daughter of **John Moser** and **Mary Catharine Muhlenberg**, was born 29 Sep 1804 in Pennsylvania. She married 20 Dec 1832 **Zephaniah McLenegan**, who was born 7 Mar 1801 and died 13 Jan 1842. Henrietta died 6 Jun 1856. Children of Henrietta and Zephaniah McLenegan:

1. **Edward McLenegan**
    b. 19 Feb 1833
    m. **Mary L. Dunn**
    d. 13 Jun 1863
    Children of Edward and Mary McLenegan:
        James Lorraine McLenegan
        b. 2 Oct 1862
        m. **Emily L. Fichthorn**
        d. 27 Apr 1889
        They had one known son:
            James Lorraine McLenegan, Jr.
            b. 1 Apr 1889

2. **Henry Hall McLenegan**
    b. 24 Nov 1835
    m. 26 Feb 1857 **Sarah F. Reigart**
    d. 15 Sep 1905
3. **Charles McLenegan**
    b. 3 Oct 1837
    d. Nov. 1859
4. **John Archibald McLenegan**
    b. 2 Feb 1841
    m. 25 Feb 1864 **Mary Ann McKnight**
    d. 10 Jun 1906

A.5b2 Henry Hall McLenegan

Henry Hall McLenegan, son of Zephaniah McLenegan and Henrietta Augusta Moser, was born 24 Nov 1835. He married 26 Feb 1857 **Sarah F. Reigart**, who was born 12 Feb 1836. Henry died 15 Sep 1905. Children of Edward and Sarah:

a. **Charles Edward McLenegan**
   b. 23 Jan 1858
   m. 22 Jul 1886 **Clara Rogers** (b. 22 Jul 1861)
   Son: **David Wallace McLenegan**
      b. 30 Jun 1900
b. **Samuel Bowman McLenegan**
   b. 23 Feb 1861
   m. 1 Mar 1887 **Carrie Harrison Cutler**
   Two children:
      Arthur Sturgis McLenegan b. 2 Feb 1888
      Edith Marion McLenegan b. 7 Nov 1896
c. **Augusta McLenegan**
   b. 17 Sep 1866
   d. 1866
d. **Archibald Reigart McLenegan**
   b. 7 Aug 1868
   m. 3 Aug 1892 **Julia Richardson** (b. 3 Dec 1871)
   Son: **Henry Richardson McLenegan**
      b. 11 Jul 1899
e. **Anna Susanna McLenegan**
   b. 12 Apr 1875

A.5b4 John Archibald McLenegan

John Archibald McLenegan, son of **Zephaniah McLenegan** and **Henrietta Augusta Moser**, was born 3 Oct 1841. He married 25 Feb 1864 **Mary Ann McKnight** who was born 13 Dec 1839 and died 10 Oct 1895. John died 10 Jun 1906. Children of John and Mary Ann McLenegan:

a. **Elizabeth Heister McLenegan**
   b. 3 Jan 1865
   She was a librarian in Reading, Pa.
b. **Selina Withers McLenegan**
   b. 6 Apr 1866
   m. 23 Sep 1889 **Frederick Estabrooke Yorke**
   Dau: **Dorothy McLenegan Yorke**
      b. 2 Feb 1891
c. **Henry McLenegan** (twin)
   b. 21 Nov 1867
   d. 7 May 1880
d. **William McLenegan** (twin)
   b. 21 Nov 1867
   m. **Elisabeth Holmes**
   d. 11 Nov 1935
e. **John McLenegan**
   b. 1 Jan 1873
   d. 5 Jan 1874
f. **Robert Wallace McLenegan**
   b. 5 Jan 1877
g. **Frederick Augustus McLenegan**
   b. 22 Feb 1880

A.5d Caroline Amelia Moser Hiester

Caroline Amelia Moser, daughter of **John Moser** and **Mary Catharine Muhlenberg**, was born 28 Dec 1808 in Pennsylvania. She married 5 Jul 1848 **John Philip Hiester, M.D.**, who was born 9 Jun 1803 and died 15 Sep 1854. Caroline died in 1875. Children of Caroline and Dr. John Hiester:

1. **Caroline Elizabeth Hiester**
   b. 29 Mar 1851
   She became a Roman Catholic Nun and
   lived in the Canary Islands
2. **John Louis Hiester**
   b. 2 Sep 1849
   d. 20 Apr 1851
3. **Mary Augusta Hiester**
   b. 10 Apr 1854
   m. 13 May 1885 **George A. Reid** (artist)
   d. Sept. 1921

A5f Susan Ann Moser Hoffman

Susan Ann Moser, daughter of **John Moser** and **Mary Catharine Muhlenberg**, was born 22 Feb 1811 in Pennsylvania and died 15 Oct 1853. She married 21 Mar 1843 **James George Hoffman** and had the following children:

1. **Ann Muhlenberg Hoffman**
   b. 4 Jul 1844
   d. 3 Nov 1844
2. **Frederick Max Hoffman**
   b. 29 Nov 1845
   m. 26 Jun 1868 **Pusha A. Teed**
   Children of Frederick and Pusha Hoffman:
   a. **Ida Caroline Hoffman**
      b. 26 Mar 1869
      m. 28 Oct 1891 **Edward Stevens**
   b. **Frank Ellis Hoffman**, b. 18 Jan 1873
   c. **Rose Selina Hoffman**, b. 27 Jul 1874
   d. **Oscar Frederick Hoffman**, b. 19 May 1877
   e. **Ernest Benjamin Hoffman**, b. 17 Nov 1885
3. **Efiginia Craig Hoffman**
   b. 8 Jun 1847
   d. 1 Jun 1855
4. **John Andrew Hoffman**
   b. 16 Jun 1848
   m. 21 Jan 1871 **Caroline S. Lind**
   Children of John and Caroline Hoffman:
   a. **George William Hoffman**, b. 7 Sep 1873
   b. **Louise Watson Hoffman**, b. 9 Sep 1875
   c. **Carrie Selina Hoffman**, b. 18 Aug 1877
   d. **Andrew John Hoffman**, b. 7 Aug 1879
   e. **Francis Max Hoffman**, b. 18 Aug 1881, d. 16 Sep 1882
   f. **Arthur James Hoffman**, b. 1 Jul 1883
   g. **Charles Millard Hoffman**, b. 12 Sep 1885
   h. **Henry Maxwell Hoffman**, b. 10 Aug 1887
   i. **Edward Benjamin Hoffman**, b. 10 May 1889
   j. **Mabel Irene Hoffman**, b. 4 Oct 1891
5. **(Male) Hoffman**, b. 4 Nov 1849, d. 7 Nov 1849

B. George Moser

George Moser, son of **Hans Paul** and **Elisabeth Moser**, was born 27 Mar 1741 and confirmed at age 13 at the New Hanover Lutheran Church, Lancaster County, Pennsylvania. He married 16 Jul 1765 **Christina Young/Jung** who was born 11 Sep 1748. They lived in Lancaster County where they were known as **'Musser'**. George served in the Revolutionary War as a captain in the 1st Lancaster Co. Bn. under Col. Ross. According to the records of the Trinity Lutheran Church in Lancaster County, Pennsylvania, he died on either 12 Jul 1804 or 14 Jul 1806. His will is recorded in Book J, Vol. 1, page 185. Christina died 31 Mar 1828 and is buried with her husband in the Trinity Lutheran Cemetery. Children of George and Christina Moser:

1. Rebecca Moser
    b. 5 Aug 1766, Pa.
    bp. Trinity Lutheran Church
    m. **Henry Dering**

2. John Moser
    b. 25 Sep 1768, Pa.
    bp. Trinity Lutheran Church
    d. 7 May 1773

3. Anna Maria Moser
    b. 8 Apr 1771, Pa.
    bp. Trinity Lutheran Church
    m. 6 Mar 1793 **John Singer**
    d. 20 Jan 1827/8

4. Elisabeth Moser
    b. 29 Mar 1773, Pa.
    bp. Trinity Lutheran Church

5. Salome Moser
    b. 9 Jul 1774, Pa.
    bp. Trinity Lutheran Church
    d. 15 Oct 1854

6. John Moser
    b. 10 May 1775, Pa.
    bp. Trinity Lutheran Church
    d. young

7. George Moser
    b. 11 Jul 1777, Pa.
    bp. Trinity Lutheran Church
    m. (1) **Mary Graff**
       (2) **Sarah Graff**
    d. 26 May 1868

8. Jacob Moser
    b. 16 Oct 1779, Pa.
    bp. Trinity Lutheran Church
    d. young

9. Catharine Moser
    b. 30 Jan 1781, Pa.
    bp. Trinity Lutheran Church
    m. 1803 **William Haverstick, Jr.**

10. Jacob Moser
    b. 31 May 1783, Pa.
    bp. Trinity Lutheran Church
    d. young

11. **Matthias Moser**
    b. 2 Apr 1785, Pa.
    bp. Trinity Lutheran Church
    m. **Ann Haverstick**
12. **John Adam Moser**
    b. 3 Apr 1787, Pa.
    bp. Trinity Lutheran Church
    m. **Margaret Schaum**
13. **William Moser**
    b. 11 Aug 1789, Pa.
    bp. Trinity Lutheran Church
    m. **Susan Elisabeth Greiner**
        30 Mar 1815, Philadelphia, Pa.
    d. 17 May 1881
14. **Henry Moser**
    b. 11 Mar 1791, Pa.
    bp. Trinity Lutheran Church
    d. 26 Jul 1822, Augusta, Georgia
15. **Abraham Moser**
    b. 15 May 1793, Pa.
    bp. Trinity Lutheran Church
    m. **Maria Dutchman**
    d. 11 Nov 1828
16. **Henrietta Moser**
    b. 27 Nov 1794, Pa.
    bp. Trinity Lutheran Church
    m. (1) **William Glenn**
       (2) **John William Kane**
    d. 18 Dec 1886

B1 Rebecca Moser Dering

Rebecca Moser, daughter of **George Moser** and **Christina Young/Jung** was born 5 Aug 1846 and baptized at the Trinity Lutheran Church in Lancaster, Pennsylvania. She married **Henry Dering** (b. 1760), a Revolutionary War Veteran. Rebecca died in 1846. Children of Rebecca and Henry Dering:

a. **George Small Dering** m. **Nancy McNeely**
    Children of George and Nancy Dering:
        Henry Dering
        Mary Ann Dering (1814-1890)
            m. **Edwin W. Tower** (1810-1869)
            Child of Mary and Edwin Tower:
                Anna Littleton Tower
                    b. Morgantown, W. Va.
                    m. 1870 **James Calvin Darrington**
        Rebecca Dering
        Harriet Dering
        Sarah Dering
b. **Maria Christina Dering** m. **Raleigh Evans**
    Children of Maria Christina and Raleigh Evans:
        George Dering Evans m. **Julia Dorsey**
            Child of George and Julia Evans:
                Mary Evans, b. Va., m. **Benjamin Franklin Smith**
        Henry Evans

William Musser Evans (1812-1903)
 m. 1839 **Martha Ann Worner** (1816-1903)
 Children of William and Martha Evans:
 Julia Anne Evans, b. 1840 Morgantown, W. Va.
  m. 1859 **Charles Rust Hopkins** (1834-1903)
 Ann Evans m. _____ **Chadwick**
 Ellen Evans m. _____ **Mills**
 Laura G. m. _____ **Peckenpaugh**
 Harriet L. Evans

c. **Harriet Dering** m. _____ **Lowry**
 Children of Harriet Dering Lowry:
 Julia Rebecca Lowry
 Delia Maria Lowry m. _____ **Allen**
 Jane Sophia Lowry m. _____ **Hazens**
 Harriet Elizabeth Lowry (twin) m. _____ **Chadwick**
 Martha Ann Lowry (twin)

d. **Henry Young Dering**
e. **William Musser Dering**
f. **Sophia Dering**
g. **John Franklin Dering**
h. **Franklin Augustus Dering**
 Children of Franklin Dering:
 Mary Dering m. _____ **Lorentz**
 William W. Dering
 Ellie E. Dering
 M. Augusta Dering
 H. Ray Dering
 D. Lida Dering m. 1859 **Charles Rust Hopkins** (1834-1868)

B3 Anna Maria Moser Singer

Anna Maria Moser, daughter of **George Moser** and **Christina Young/Jung** was born 8 Apr 1771 and baptized at the Trinity Lutheran Church in Lancaster County, Pennsylvania. She married 6 Mar 1793 **John Singer** (born 11 Mar 1763 in Lancaster). John served as a drummer boy during the Revolutionary War and was held prisoner on one of the British prison ships in New York Harbor. He later served as a private in Col. Shee's Batalion during the Whiskey Insurrection. Anna Maria died 20 Jan 1827. Only known child of Anna Maria and John Singer:

 Sarah Singer
  b. 15 Nov 1798
  m. 28 Jul 1829 **John Charles Capp**
  (John was dean of the Philadelphia Stock Exchange)
  d. 19 Apr 1876
  Children of Sarah and John Capp:
   Charles Singer Capp
   b. 19 Oct 1831
   m. 6 Aug 1889 **Lillian F. Stillwell** (b. 1864)
   Children of Charles and Lillian Capp:
    Lillian Capp, b. 20 May 1890
    Miriam Capp, b. 4 Dec 1891
     m. 1915 **Rev. Clifton Alden Douglas**
    Charles Capp, b. 7 Dec 1893

2. **John Singer Capp**
　　b. 29 Apr 1833
　　m. 22 Nov 1860 **Mary Michener**
　　d. 10 Jan 1882
　　He served as a Lieutenant during the Civil War.
　　Child of John and Mary Capp:
　　Sarah Emma Capp
　　　　b. 21 Dec 1882
　　　　m. **Traff Haverstick** (son of
　　　　Rev. Alexander Haverstick)
3. **Allen Capp**
4. **Samuel Capp** (died young)
5. **Samuel M. Capp**
　　b. 3 Mar 1836
　　d. 1908 in California
6. **Rev. Edward Payson Capp**
　　b. 11 Sep 1837
　　m. 17 Feb 1882 in Tung Chow, China
　　Margaret Brown
　　d. 26 Oct 1873
　　bur. Yokohama, Japan
　　He was the co-founder of a university and the
　　Presbyterian Church at Tung Chow, China.
7. **Alfred Capp**
　　b. 13 Feb 1840
　　d. 2 Apr 1852
8. **Dr. William Musser Capp**
　　b. 20 Nov 1842
　　m. 4 Mar 1868 **Ida Estelle Stitt**
　　(b. 28 Nov. 1845, dau. **Seth Bunker** and **Sarah**
　　Wilkinson Stitt)
　　Children of Dr. William and Ida Capp:
　　a. **Estelle Capp**
　　　　m. 3 Nov 1902
　　　　Frederick Jost (1870-1908)
　　b. **William Edgar Capp**
　　　　b. 19 Aug 1872
　　　　d. 30 Sep 1891
　　c. **Louise Thayer Capp** (died young)
　　d. **Seth Bunker Capp** b. 23 May 1875

B7 George Moser/Musser

George Moser/Musser, son of **George Moser** and **Christina Young/Jung** was
11 Jul 1777 and baptized at the Trinity Lutheran Church in Lancaster, Pennsylvania.
He married (1) **Mary Graff** (b. 25 Mar 1783), daughter of **Sebastian Graff**. Children
of George and Mary Moser:
　a. **William Musser**
　　　b. 5 Mar 1808
　　　m. 19 Aug 1834 **Sarah Ann Henderson**
　　　d. 16 Jun 1891
　b. **Sebastian Graff Musser**
　　　b. 24 Aug 1810, d. Apr. 1861
　c. **Christina Catharine Musser**
　　　b. 8 Sep 1812, d. 1 Nov 1894
　d. **Mary Eleanor Musser**, b. 2 Aug 1814

Mary died 31 Aug 1816. On 17 Oct 1817, George married (2) **Sarah Graff** (b. 10 Jul 1775, d. 17 Aug 1854), possibly an older sister of his first wife. George died 26 May 1868. Children of George and Sarah Graff:

    e. **George Musser**, b. 31 Aug 1818, d. 25 Jan 1884
    f. **Jacob Graff Musser**, b. 3 Sep 1819
    g. **Sarah Elizabeth Musser**, b. Nov. 1820
    h. **Susanna Musser**, b. 27 Jan 1823
        m. **Robert Philip Gibson** (1819-1890)
        d. 1902
    i. **Anna Maria Musser**, b. 27 Mar 1824, d. Feb 1894
    j. **Henry Young Musser**, b. 14 Feb 1826, d. Dec 1831
    k. **Margaretta Schaum Musser**, b. 26 Feb 1833, d. 5 Jan 1877

B11 Mathias Musser

Mathias Musser, son of **George Moser** and **Christina Young/Jung** was born 17 Nov 1774 and baptized at the Trinity Lutheran Church in Lancaster, Pennsylvania. He married **Ann Haverstick** (b. 1786). He died 22 Feb 1833. Only known child of Mathias and Ann Musser:

    Christina E. Musser (d. 1875) m. **Peter Ellmaker Lightner** (d. 1862)
        Only child of Christina and Peter Lightner:
        Emma Musser Lightner b. 1842 m. **Tunis John Hellings**
            Only child of Emma and Tunis Hellings:
            Laura Hellings m. 1886 **George Flagg**
            They had a daughter, **Adelaide Bordon Flagg**
            born in Philadelphia, Pa.

B.7a William Musser

William Musser, son of **George Moser** and **Mary Graff**, was born Mar 1808. He married (1) 19 Aug 1834 **Sarah Anne Henderson**, daughter of **James** and **Sarah Henderson**, who was born 5 Nov 1813. Sarah Anne died 23 Sep 1855, after which he married (2) 10 Mar 1857 **Maria Catharine Cromwell**, daughter of **William** and **Sarah Cromwell**. Maria Catharine died on 12 Jun 1860. William died 16 Jun 1891. Children of William and Sarah Anne Musser:

    1. **George James Musser**
        b. 28 Sep 1835, Montgomery Co., Md.
        m. 17 Apr 1859 in Washington, D.C.
        Sarah E. Hutchinson
        d. 17 Mar 1891
        Children of George and Sarah Musser:
            a. **Annie Catharine Musser**
                b. 19 May 1861
            b. **Eliza May Musser**
                b. 16 Mar 1863
            c. **William Musser**
                b. Dec 1866
            d. **Sarah Elizabeth Musser**
                b. 30 Oct 1869
                m. 12 Nov 1894 **Walter B. Randal**
    2. **Sarah Marie Musser**
        b. 30 Jul 1837, Montgomery Co., Md.

3. **Flavel Augustus Musser**
   b. 31 Jul 1839, Montgomery Co., Md.
   m. 2 Apr 1862 **Martha Ann Culbertson**
   (b. 9 Oct 1839, d. 12 Nov 1917)
   dau. of **Hugh Culbertson** and **Jane M. McClellene**
   Child of Flavel and Martha Musser:
   M. Jennie Musser
   b. 12 Oct 1867
   m. 6 Feb 1895 **Raymond C. Drum**
   (b. 13 Dec 1842, d. 10 Jan 1915)
   Child of Jennie and Raymond Drum:
   Emma Dorothy Drum
   b. 21 Oct 1899
   m. 23 Aug 1924
   Herbert F. Davis
   (b. 1 Feb 1890)
   d. 11 Mar 1949
   Child of Emma and Herbert:
   Redmond Stewart Davis
   (SAR #5412)
   b. 24 Feb 1926
   m. 20 Jul 1946
   Bertha Adeline Peltz
   (b. 5 Sep 1927)

4. **Christina Catharine Musser**
   b. 10 Oct 1841
   d. 5 Nov 1908
5. **Susan Jane Musser**
   b. 4 Aug 1843
   d. 9 May 1918
6. **William Henderson Musser**
   b. 8 Aug 1845
   m. 30 May 1883 **Mary Jane Fairfax** (b. 1 Apr 1858)
   d. 26 May 1899
   Children of William and Mary Jane Musser:
   a. **Minnie Palmer Musser**
   b. 30 Mar 1884
   m. 21 Jun 1909 at Rochelle
   Edward Mack Curtis Hawkins
   b. **Annie Laurie Musser**
   b. 21 Aug 1885
   m. 6 Sep 1912 at London
   Neill Graham Stevens
   c. **Sarah Fairfax Musser**
   b. 5 Jan 1889
   m. 3 Jul 1907 at Fort Smith, Ark.
   Harrison Burall
   d. **Ida Cary Musser**
   b. 20 Apr 1891
   e. **Mary Jett Musser**
   b. 27 Jan 1899
   d. 16 Aug 1909
7. **Caroline Beall Musser**
   b. 8 Aug 1847
   m. 19 Dec 1893 **James William Graff**
   d. 26 Jun 1924

8. **Mary Ellen Musser**
   b. 17 Oct 1850
   Lived Germantown, Md.
9. **Henry Martyn Musser**
   b. 17 Oct 1850
   m. Oct 1882 **Mary E. Burdette**
   d. 30 Sep 1894
   Children of Henry and Mary Musser:
   Frances E. Musser b. 6 Feb 1888
   Henry Marcellus Musser b. 26 Jan 1891
   Jessie Musser b. 12 May 1895

C. John Adam Moser

John Adam Moser, son of **Hans Paul** and **Elisabeth Moser**, was born 28 Nov 1746
and baptized 31 Dec 1746 at the New Hanover Church, Goshenhoppen, Philadelphia
County, Pennsylvania. His sponsor was **George Peck**. He was confirmed on
25 Dec 1760 at Falkner Swamp at age 14. He married **Christina Prunner** (born
5 Nov 1752). They settled in Reamstown, Cocalico Township, Lancaster County,
Pennsylvania where he became a tanner and an inn keeper. In 1782 he signed a petition
requesting relief from paying his taxes on account of bad weather. John Adam died in
Cocalico 26 Jun 1823. His will is located in Book N, Vol. 1, page 276 in Lancaster
County records. Christina died 5 Nov 1823. Children of John Adam and Christina:

1. **George Moser**
   b. 14 Dec 1774, Pa.
   bp. Trinity Lutheran Church
   m. 1798 **Elisabeth Montelius**
   d. 21 Jan 1853
2. **Christina Moser**
   b. 15 Jan 1776, Pa.
   bp. Trinity Lutheran Church
   m. **Samuel Ream**
   d. 1860
   Children of Christina and Samuel Ream:
   Elisabeth Ream m. **John Redding**
   Susanna Ream
   Christina Ream m. **Abraham Myers**
3. **Elisabeth Moser**
   b. 5 Nov 1777, Pa.
   bp. Trinity Lutheran Church
   m. 11 Sep 1798 **Christian Harter**
   d. bef. 1823
4. **Adam Moser**
   b. 4 Oct 1779, Lancaster Co., Pa.
   m. **Catharine** _____
5. **Susanna Moser**
   b. 3 Aug 1781
   m. 2 Dec 1825 **John Hocker (?)**
6. **Sarah Moser**
   b. 9 Aug 1783, Pa.
   bp. Trinity Lutheran Church
   m. 2 Dec 1825 **John Hocker**
7. **Rebecca Moser**
   b. 25 Nov 1785, Pa.
   bp. Trinity Lutheran Church
   m. **John Ruth**

8. **Henry Moser**
   b. 10 Jul 1787, Pa.
9. **William Moser**
   b. 13 Jun 1790, Pa.
   bp. Trinity Lutheran Church
   m. **Elizabeth Schweitzer**
10. **Mary Moser**
    b. 20 Nov 1792, Pa.
    d. bef. 1796

11. **John Moser**
    b. 28 May 1794, Pa.
    bp. Trinity Lutheran Church
    m. **Catharine** _____
12. **Mary Moser**
    b. 26 Sep 1796, Pa.

C1. George Moser/Musser

George Moser, son of **John Adam Moser** and **Christina Prunner**, was born 14 Dec 1774 and baptized at the Trinity Lutheran Church in Lancaster, Pennsylvania. He married **Elizabeth Montelius**, daughter of **Marcus Montelius** and **Christina Bartholme**. She was born 18 Jul 1779 and died 21 May 1833. George died 21 Jan 1853. Children of George and Elizabeth:
   a. **Charles Musser**, b. 11 Apr 1800
   b. **George Musser**, b. 14 Nov 1802, d. 17 Feb 1841, Philadelphia, Pa.
   c. **Christina Musser**, b. 20 May 1804
   d. **John Musser**, b. 10 Jul 1806, d. 20 Aug 1806
   e. **William Musser**, b. 10 Aug 1808, d. 17 May 1860
      m. 12 Dec 1833 **Susan Ream**
      Children of William and Susan Musser:
         Henry Moser, b. 19 Jan 1835
            Went to Akron, Summit Co., Oh.
         Caroline Moser, b. 15 Apr 1836, d. 23 Dec 1836
         George Moser, b. 1 Jul 1837, m. **Margaret Nixdorf**
         Edwin Moser, b. 1 Dec 1838
            m. 18 Jan 1864 **Susan Elizabeth Becker**
               (dau of **George Becker** and **Elizabeth Gross**)
            He served as a Lieutenant in the Union Army during the Civil War. Children of Edwin and Susan:
            Susan Elizabeth Moser
               b. 27 Oct 1864, d. 16 Feb 1871
            George William Moser
               b. 16 Mar 1866, d. 18 Feb 1871
            Horace Moser
               b. 5 Sep 1867, d. 22 Dec 1868
            Henry Moser
               b. 28 Dec 1868, d. 26 Jul 1914
               m. **Etta Susan Becker**
               child of Henry and Etta:
               Henry Edwin Moser
                  m. **Miriam Bixler**, dau of
                     Stephen & Laura Bixler
                  They went to Lincoln, Pa.
            Albert Moser
               b. 21 Dec 1870. d. 25 Feb 1872

f.. **Charles Moser**
  b. 28 Jul 1872, d. Aug 1951
  m. **Florence Amelia Bucher**, dau of
  Rev. John Bucher. They had no children.
g. **Edward Moser**
  b. 22 Oct 1874, d. 13 Sep 1875
h. **Martin Moser**
  b. 12 Aug 1876, d. 24 Jan 1944
  m. **Katherine Beiji** of New York
  Child of Martin and Katherine:
      Mildred Moser m. **George R. Dell**
      They went to California.
i. **Sarah Emma Moser**
  b. 22 Aug 1878, d. Lincoln, Pa.
j. **Rev. James B. Moser**
  b. 22 Feb 1881, d. 28 Jul 1946
  m. **Mary Ellen Long**, dau. of **Rueben Long**
k. **Clara Amanda Moser**
  b. 4 Feb 1883, d. 5 Oct 1935
l. **Mary Harriet Moser**
  b. 28 Mar 1887, d. 16 May 1887
m. **John Marcus Moser**
  b. 18 May 1892, d. Jun 1918 during WWI
  m. **Beulah S. Brubaker**, dau. of **Simon
      Brubaker** and **Emma Stohler**
  bur. National Cemetery, Somme Sector, France
  Children of John and Beulah:
      Marguerite Moser
      b. 10 Nov 1913
      m. **(1) Israel Weidman** (d. 1935)
          (2) Alvin S. Mease, son of **Henry P.
          Mease** and **Lizzie Schultz**
          Child of Alvin and Marguerite:
          Anna Grace Mease,b. 25 Aug 1949
      H. Richard Moser
      b. 31 Mar 1915
          m. **Anna Margaret Pottieger** dau. of
              Freeman & Esther Pottieger
          Child of Richard and Anna:
              Richard Stuart Moser
                  b. 1 Feb 1951
F. Adam Musser, b. 19 Feb 1817

C3. Elizabeth Moser Harter

Elizabeth Moser, daughter of **John Adam Moser** and **Christina Prunner**, was born
5 Nov 1777 and baptized at the Trinity Lutheran Church in Lancaster, Pennsylvania.
She married 11 Sep 1798 **Christian Harter**. Elizabeth died before her father wrote his
will in 1823. Children of Elizabeth and Christian Harter:
  a. **William Harter**, b. 31 Jan 1801, d. 19 Dec 1878
      m. **(1) Hannah Crouse**
          (2) Mary Rudisell
          (3) 15 Jun 1857, Richland Co., Ohio **Nancy Billings**, widow of
              _____ **McCullough**
  b. **Christina Harter**, b. 11 May 1802,
      bp. Emanuel Lutheran Church, Tusseyville, Pa.

c. **Christian Harter**, b. 10 May 1805, d. 21 Jan 1849, Caldwell, Mo.
   m. **Catharine Crouse**
d. **Susanna Harter**, b. 31 Mar 1811, Tusseyville, Pa.
e. **John Adam Harter**, b. 12 Mar 1812, Tusseyville, Pa.
   bp. Emanuel Lutheran Church, d. 16 Apr 1871, Cameron, Mo.
   m. 20 Jul 1840 in Richland Co., Ohio **Elizabeth Tinkey**, dau of
   Frederick Tinkey. Children of John Adam and Elizabeth:
    1. Amanda Harter
      b. 9 Aug 1841, Mansfield, Oh.
      m. **Joseph Wirt**
      d. 1927, Cameron, Mo.
    2. Elizabeth Harter
      b. 25 May 1843, Richland Co., Oh.
      m. **Willis E. Gilbert**
      d. 1927, Kansas City, Mo.
      They had no children.
    3. Margaret Ann Harter
      b. 10 May 1845, Cameron, Mo.
      m. **Samuel Bangs**
      d. 19 Jan 1886
      Children of Margaret & Samuel Bangs:
        Benjamin Ernest Bangs
        Birdie Bangs
        Abi Bangs
        William Luther Bangs
        Margaret Bangs
        Camille Bangs
        Samuel Bangs
        Edward Bangs
    4. Sarah Jane Harter
      b. 22 Dec 1847, Mo.
      m. **Mathew L. Wrigley**
        b. 9 Aug 1841, Conn., d. 20 Nov 1915 Kansas City, Mo
      d. 3 Aug 1908, Excelsior Springs, Mo.
    5. Frederick Harter, b. 16 Jan 1849, Cameron, Mo.
      m. **Elizabeth Sudsbury**
      Children of Frederick and Elizabeth Harter:
        Elmer Harter
        Milton Harter
        Jessie Harter
    6. Christian Harter, b. 22 Apr 1851, Cameron, Mo.
      m. **(1) Flo Sophia Scoville**
        (2) Emma Hunt
      Children of Christian and Flo Harter:
        Elotus Harter
        Ruby Harter
    7. William Harter, b. 28 Mar 1853, Mo.
    8. Mary Susan Harter, b. 21 Apr 1855, Mo.
      m. **Rade Hardin**
      d. Sep 1950
    9. Melissa Harter, b. 6 Feb 1847, Mo.
      m. **Freddy Ossman**
      d. 19 Nov 1929, Cameron, Mo.
      Children of Melissa and Freddy Ossman:
        Gertrude Ossman
        Minnie Ossman

10. John Adam Harter, b. 29 Mar 1859, Mo.
    m. **Nellie Puskett**
    d. 1927, Kansas City, Mo.
    Children of John Adam and Nellie Harter:
        Nellie Harter
        Muda Harter
11. Missouri Harter (female)
    b. 13 Dec 1860, Mo., d. 31 Dec 1860

4. Sarah Jane Harter Wrigley

Sarah Jane Harter, daughter of **John Adam Harter** and **Elizabeth Tinkey**, was born 22 Dec 1847 in Missouri and died 3 Aug 1908 in Excelsior Springs, Missouri. She married **Mathew L. Wrigley** who was born 9 Aug 1841 in Connecticut and died 20 Nov 1915 in Kansas City, Missouri. Children of Mathew and Sarah Wrigley:
  a. **Grace Elizabeth Wrigley**, b. 20 Mar 1869, Winston, Mo.
        m. **Charles Hudson Cutler**
        d. 1963, Kansas City, Mo.
  b. **Susan Amanda Wrigley**, b. 15 Apr 1871, Winston, Mo.
        m. **James Franklin Mott** (b. 16 Jun 1872, New Market, Mo.,
                d. 26 Jun 1910, Kansas City, Mo.)
        d. 24 Dec 1955, Omaha, Neb.
    Both are buried in Elmwood Cemetery, Kansas City, Mo.
    Children of Sarah and James Mott:
        1. **Susie Alda Mott**, b. 8 Apr 1899, Alvaretta Woods, Ok.
            m. **William Henry Perkins**
        2. **Donnis Irene Mott**, b. 18 Aug 1901, Hillsdale, Ok.
            m. 2 Dec 1919, Kansas City, Mo.
            Ferman Edward Borchers (b. 21 May 1896)
            Children of Donnis and Ferman Borchers:
            a. **Maggie Lee Borchers**
                b. 20 May 1924, Kansas City
                m. 7 Sep 1940, LaGrange, Ill.
                Kenneth Edward Konig
                Children of Maggie and Kenneth Konig:
                Sherrill Lee Konig,
                    b. 16 Mar 1942, Milwaukee, Wisc.
                    m. **Joel R. Jensen**
                    Children of Sherrill and Joel Jensen:
                        Scott Jensen
                        Karl Jensen
                Kenneth Edward Konig, Jr.
                    b. 3 Jan 1945, Beaver Dam, Wisc.
                    m. **Marsham Yotka**
                    Children of Kenneth and Marsham:
                        Kenneth Edward Konig, III
                        Michelle Konig
                Patricia Lynn Konig
                    b. 4 Oct 1938, Milwaukee, Wisc.
                    m. Oakbrook, Ill., **William Lee Shafer**
            b. **Wallace Edward Borchers**
                b. 4 Apr 1923, Kansas City, Mo.
                m. 3 Dec 1949 Coalinga, Ca., **Edna Devine**
                Children of Wallace and Edna Borchers:
                    Mary Elizabeth Borchers b. 23 Mar 1951
                    Kathleen Cecilia Borchers b. 13 Feb 1955
                    James Edward Borchers b. 23 Mar 1958
                    Margaret Adlyn Borchers b. 17 Dec 1963

  c. **Sarah Jane Borchers**
   b. 25 Nov 1929, Kansas City, Mo.
   m. 19 Oct 1951, Burlingame, Ca.
   Roger Malcolm Quinn
   Children of Sarah and Roger Quinn:
    Kathleen Quinn b. 1952
    Kevin Michael Quinn b. 1953
  3. **Ella Lees Mott**
   b. 20 Jan 1902, Carmen, Woods Co., Ok.
   m. **John Gardett Strader**
 c. **Sarah Josephine Wrigley**, b. 10 Jun 1873, Winston, Mo., d. young
 d. **Alvaretta Wrigley**, b. 5 Dec 1875, Winston, Mo., d. 1972, California
 e. **Matthew Frank Wrigley**, b. 27 Sep 1877, Winston, Mo., d. 18 Apr 1879, Mo.

4. Adam Moser

Adam Moser, son of **John Adam Moser** and **Christina Prunner**, was born 4 Oct 1779 in Lancaster Co., Pennsylvania. He had a wife named **Catharine** and lived in Potter Township, Centre County, Pennsylvania. Children of Adam and Catharine:
 John Moser
  b. 1804, Potter Twp., Centre Co., Pa.
 Adam Moser
  b. 10 Aug 1806
  bp. Aaronsburg Lutheran Church, Centre Co., Pa.
 Lida Moser
  b. 1811, Potter Twp., Centre Co., Pa.

6. Sarah Moser Hocker

Sarah Moser, daughter of **John Adam Moser** and **Christina Prunner**, was born 9 Aug 1783 and baptized at the Trinity Lutheran Church in Lancaster, Pennsylvania. She married **John Hocker** (who was possibly married first to her suster, Susanna) on 2 Dec 1825. Children of Sarah and John Hocker:
 George Hocker
 Lydia Hocker
 John Hocker
All three children are listed as over fourteen years of age in the Lancaster Court Records of 2 Dec. 1825.

9. William Moser

William Moser, son of **John Adam Moser** and **Christina Prunner**, was born 13 Jun 1790 and baptized at the Trinity LUtheran Church in Lancaster, Pennsylvania. He married **Elizabeth Schweitzer**, daughter iof **Ludwig** and **Rosina Schweitzer**, who died 26 Jul 1838. William died 15 Sep 1847. Children of William and Elizabeth:
 Edward Moser
  bp. 4 Dec 1823, Muddy Creek, Lancaster Co., Pa.
 Caroline Moser
  bp. Oct 1825, Muddy Creek, Lancaster Co., Pa.
  d. 15 Aug 1848
 William Henry Moser
  bp. 11 Sep 1828, Muddy Creek, Lancaster Co., Pa.
  d. Jun 1891

D. Andrew Moser

Andrew Moser, son of **Hans Paul** and **Elisabeth Moser**, m. 6 Sep 1774 in Easton, Pennsylvania. **Magdalena Bign** (b. 6 Jun 1754, d. 1 May 1820), daughter of **Jacob** and **Anna Maria Bign** of Easton, Pennsylvania. They lived in Williams Township, Northampton County, Pennsylvania. Children of Andrew and Magdalena Moser:

1. Anna Maria Moser
    b. 2 Feb 1776, Easton, Northampton Co., Pa.
    bp. 9 Mar 1776, German Lutheran Church, Easton, Pa.
    Sponsors: **Mathias** and **Anna Maria Pfeiffer**

2. John Jacob Moser
    b. 24 Feb 1778, Pa.
    m. **Elisabeth Nickom** (b. 1781, d. 3 Aug 1850)
    d. 4 Mar 1852, age 73

3. Andreas Moser
    b. 24 Sep 1780, Easton, Northampton Co., Pa.
    m. **Catharine Nickom**
    He had a son, **Andrew Moser, Jr.**

4. Frederick Moser
    b. 20 Mar 1783, Pa.
    m. 26 Mar 1806 **Rosina Lattig**
    d. 12 Oct 1830
    This couple had no children. He owned 28 acres in
    Williams Twp., Pa. in 1811.

5. Maria Moser
    b. 8 Sep 1785, Williams Twp., Northampton Co., Pa.
    bp. 7 Nov 1785, German Lutheran Church, Easton, Pa.
    Sponsors: **George** and **Charlotte Ehret**

6. George Moser
    b.1789, Pa.
    m. 20 Mar 1812 **Maria Seiffert**

7. Margaret Moser
    b. 23 Apr 1791, Pa.

8. Paul Moser
    m. **Maria Deily**

2. John Jacob Moser

John Jacob Moser, son of **Andrew Moser** and **Maria Magdalena Bign**, was born 24 Feb 1778 and baptized 22 Mar 1778 in Pennsylvania. Sponsors at his baptism were **Jacob Bign** and **Christina Meyer** who were both single. He married **Elizabeth Nickom** (born 10 May 1850), daughter of **Thomas** and **Elizabeth Nickom**. She died 3 Aug 1850. Jacob died 4 Mar 1852 at the age of 73. They are buried in Section H, Lot #163, Easton, Pa. Cemetery. Children of John Jacob and Elizabeth (all baptized at German Lutheran Church, Easton, Northampton Co., Pa.):

a. Carl Moser, b. 24 Sep 1801, Pa.
    bp. 6 Dec 1801, sponsors: **Andreas** and **Magdalena Moser**

b. David Moser, b. 28 Aug 1804, Pa.
    bp. 18 Nov 1804, sponsors: **Henrich** and **Anna Megenfus**

c. Jacob Moser, b. 14 Aug 1806, Pa.
    bp. 19 Oct 1806, sponsors: **Frederich** and **Susana Pfeister**

d. Anna Moser, b. 25 Oct 1808, Pa.
    bp. 25 Dec 1808, sponsors: **George Jacob** and **Margareth Moser**

e. Rosina Moser. b. 28 Oct 1810
    bp. 13 Jan 1811, sponsors: **Frederich** and **Rosina Moser**

f. Elizabeth Moser, b. 11 Mar 1814, Pa.
    bp. 22 May 1814, sponsors: **Thomas** and **Elizabeth Nickom**

8. Paul Moser

Ⅹ **Paul Moser**, son of **Andrew Moser** and **Maria Magdalena Bign**, married **Maria Deily** on 20 Mar 1812 and moved to Plainfield Township, Northampton County, Pennsylvania. Children of Paul and Maria Moser (all baptized at First Reformed Church, Easton, Pa.):

Ⅹ a. **Paul Moser**, b. 5 Sep 1808, Pa.
bp. 13 Nov 1808, sponsors: **Frans Stocker** and **Susan Deily**
Ⅹ b. **Valentine Moser**, b. 2 Nov 1810, Pa.
bp. 15 Aug 1814, sponsors: **George Meyer** and **Susanna Breitinger**
Ⅹ c. **William Moser** (twin), b. 17 Sep 1816, Pa.
bp. 17 Nov 1816, sponsors **William** and **Margaret Heitzman**
Ⅹ d. **Anna Maria Moser** (twin), b. 17 Sep 1816, Pa.
bp. 17 Nov 1816, sponsors: **Philip** and **Anna Maria Deily**
Ⅹ e. **Leah Moser**, b. 6 Mar 1819, Pa.
bp. 6 Jun 1819, sponsors: **Philip** and **Anna Maria Deily**
Ⅹ f. **Louisa Moser**, b. 6 Mar 1821, Pa.
bp. 9 Sep 1821, sponsors: **Philip** and **Anna Maria Deily**

E. Jacob Moser

Jacob Moser, son of **Hans Paul** and **Elisabeth Moser**, had a wife named **Margaret**, who is mentioned 29 May 1815 on a release deed (A-4-426). They were living in Waynesburg Township, Green County, Pennsylvania but moved to Tyler (now Pleasants) County, West Virginia where he died. When his estate was settled in 1830, his lands were divided into five parts, omitting the daughter Margaret. Children of Jacob and Margaret Moser:

1. **George Moser/Musser**
   b. 3 Nov 1790, Green Co., Pa.
   m. 12 Aug 1819 **Mary Hanlin** (1800-1869)
   d. 3 Dec 1869, Tyler Co., W. Va.
2. **Mary "Polly" Moser/Musser**
   m. 5 Nov 1820 **Felix Hanlin**
   They lived in Jackson Co., W. Va.
3. **Catharine Moser/Musser**
   b. 1792, Green Co., Pa.
   m. **Christopher Wagner** (1791-1862)
   d. aft. 1850, Tyler Co., W. Va.
4. **John Moser/Musser**
   m. 13 Jul 1845 **Lucinda Mike**
5. **David Moser/Musser**
   m. **Elizabeth** _____
6. **Margaret Moser/Musser**

3. Catharine Moser Wagner

Catharine Moser, daughter of **Jacob** and **Margaret Moser**, was born in Green Co., Pa. in 1792. She married **Christopher Wagner** (1792-1862) and moved to Tyler Co., West Virginia. Children of Catharine and Christopher Wagner:

a. **Joseph Wagner**, b. 22 Dec 1810, Green Co., Pa.
   m. 22 Dec 1832, Tyler Co., W. Va., **Nancy Williamson**
   (b. 4 Oct 1812, d. 12 May 1889, dau of **James Williamson** and **Margaret Ball**)
   d. 25 May 1910, Sugar Valley, Pleasants Co., W. Va.
   Both are buried in Shawnee Cemetery, Sugar Valley, W. Va.

b. Margaret Wagner, b. 8 Oct 1812, Green Co., Pa.
    m. 3 Jan 1833, Tyler Co., W. Va., **John J. Williamson**
      (b. 12 Jul 1810, brother of Nancy above.)
    d. 27 Aug 1872, buried Beech Run, Pleasants Co., W. Va.
    Child of Margaret and John Williamson:
        Chester K. Williamson, b. 7 Feb 1856
          m. 20 Jan 1876, **Eliza Ellen Gorrell**
          d. 13 Mar 1906, Sugar Valley, W. Va.
c. Maria Wagner, b. 1814, Green Co., Pa.
    m. 1 Jan 1835 **Isaac Williamson** (brother to Nancy and John)
    d. abt 1891, Pleasants Co., W. Va.
d. David W. Wagner, b. 6 May 1817, Green Co., Pa.
    m. 26 Mar 1840 **Margaret Williamson** (Sister to Nancy, John
      and Isaac, b. 28 May 1819, d. 15 Jan 1900)
    d. 24 Aug 1889, Sugar Valley, Pleasants Co., W. Va.
    Both buried Hebron Methodist Church Cemetery
    Children of David and Margaret Wagner:
      1. Isaac Wagner, b. 7 Aug 1841, Sugar Valley
        m. 2 Nov 1871 **Samantha Jane Flesher** (dau of
          Granville Cheyney Flesher and **Martha**
          Bryson Morgan, b. 12 May 1851, d. 20 May 1902
        d. 1 Apr 1898, Hebron, Pleasants Co., W. Va.
        both buried Hebron Methodist Cemetery. Isaac served
        in Co. F., 14th W. Va. during the Civil War.
        Children of Isaac and Samantha Wagner:
          Addie Wagner, b. 28 Oct 1872, Hebron, W. Va.
            m. **Henry Barker**
            d. 1931, Houston, Texas
            Children of Addie and Henry Barker:
              Mamie Barker
              Nellie Barker m. **Charles Grey**
              Mildred Esta Barker m. _____ **Fleming**
          Ella Louise Wagner, b. 18 Jun 1876, Hebron W. Va.
            m. 23 Dec 1901 **William Halleck Cunningham**
              (b. 17 Oct 1871, d. 8 Feb 1942)
            d. 29 Jul 1925, Belpre, Ohio
            Both buried Rose Hill Cemetery, Tulsa, Ok.
            Children of Ella and William Cunningham:
              Norris Haswell Cunningham
                m. **Dorothy Boughton**
                had son, **William Cunningham**
              Paul Kermit Cunningham
                m. **Altha Harrison**
                They had no children
              Donald Wagner Cunningham
                m. **Lucille Cooper**
                had dau **Donna Lou Cunningham**
              William Halleck Cunningham
                m. (1) **Opal Gray**
                  (2) **Odessa Howard**
              Betty Jean Cunningham
                m. (1) **Lt. Duval West, III**
                  had dau **Susan Jane West**
                (2) **John Taylor Hamner, Jr.**
                  had dau **Nancy Ann Hamner**

George Bryson Wagner b. 10 Oct 1874, Hebron
m. **Loretta Moore**
d. abt 1950, Belpre, Ohio
Children of George and Loretta Wagner:
 Herman B. Wagner
 Esta Betty Wagner m. **Robert Petty**
Mary Olive Wagner b. 9 Mar 1878 Hebron, W. Va.
 m. **Aubrey Crum**
 Child of Mary and Aubrey Crum:
  Merton Crum
Ora Blaine Wagner b. 31 Jan 1881, Hebron, W. Va.
 d. unmarried, 9 Jul 1898
Esta M. Wagner b. 11 Apr 1889 Hebron, W. Va.
 m. 19 Sep 1906 **William Pontefract Shepherd**
 (of Harrisburg, Tx., b. 3 Sep 1883)
 d. 16 Feb 1962, San Antonio, Tx.
Hollie Wagner b. Jun 1891, d. Jun 1891

e. **Rachel Wagner**, b. 20 Aug 1820, Tyler Co., W. Va.
 m. 17 Sep 1849 **Ralph Correll** (b. 4 Jan 1819, d. 26 Mar 1882)
 d. 1890, both buried Beech Run Methodist Church Cemetery
f. **John W. Wagner**, b. 1826, Tyler Co., W. Va.
 m. 3 Nov 1846 **Elizabeth Smith** (b. 1827, d. 4 Aug 1881)
 d. 4 May 1894, Pleasants Co., W. Va.

F. John Paul Moser

John Paul Moser, son of **Hans Paul Moser** and **Eva Maria Becholt**, was born
1 Feb 1756 and baptized 7 Mar 1756 at New Hanover Lutheran Church, New Hanover,
Northampton County, Pennsylvania. Sponsors at his baptism were **Magdalena** and
Eva Barbara Krumreiss. He married **Maria Magdalena Heiter** about 1791.
Paul served four tours of duty during the Revolutionary War and received a pension
(National Archives #S5797) for his service. On 13 Sep 1834, Paul signed an affidavit,
stating that was unable to appear in court due to infirmities. At that time, he lived in
Rye Township, Perry County, Pennsylvania with his wife and a widowed daughter.
Paul made his last will and testament 1 Jan 1842, which was proved 5 Apr 1842 in Rye
Township. Children of John Paul and Maria Moser:
1. **(female) Moser** m. **Joseph Swartz**
 Children:
  Betsy Swartz
  Leah Swartz
 (These two granddaughters were the exeturors of Paul's will.)
2. **Elizabeth Moser**, b. 4 Aug 1792, Pa.
 bp. 5 Aug 1792, Sponsors: **Peter** and **Catherine Moser**
 m. **John Miller**
3. **Susanna Moser**, b. 25 Oct 1794
 bp. 7 Oct 1794, Sponsors: **Peter** and **Catherine Moser**
 d. bef. 1842
4. **Joseph Moser**, b. 27 Nov 1794, Pa.
 bp. 7 Dec 1794, Lower Saucon, Pa.
 Sponsors: **Adam** and **Elizabeth Moser**
 (Parents listed as Paul and Maria!)
5. **William Moser**
6. **Isaac Moser**

G. Tobias Moser

XTobias Moser, son of **Hans Paul Moser** and **Eva Maria Becholt**, was born 26 Feb 1763 and baptized 11 Apr 1763 at the New Hanover Church, New Hanover, Northampton County, Pennsylvania. Sponsors at his baptism were **Tobias Scholl** and his wife. He married **Christina** _____ (b. 21 Dec 1771). They lived in Bethlehem, Northampton County, Pennsylvania and had their children baptized at the Dryland Church. Tobias died after 1811 when he signed a deed. Christina died 24 Dec 1816 and is buried in the Dryland Cemetery. Children of Tobias and Christina Moser:

1. **John Moser**, b. 21 Nov 1789, Pa.
   - bp. 27 Dec 1789, Dryland Church
     - Sponsors: **John Moser** and **Catharine Theobold**
2. **Elizabeth Moser**, b. 12 Sep 1791, Pa.
   - bp. 12 Sep 1791, Dryland Church
     - Sponsors: **Daniel Sherer** and **Margaret Schepply**
   - m. 31 Mar 1812, **Jonas Derr** (d. 5 Jan 1880)
     - Child of Elizabeth and Jonas Derr:
       - **Susan Derr**, b. abt 1832
         - m. (1) 1 Jan 1852 **Nathan Brown**
           - (2) 24 Jun 1860 **Stephen Smith**
3. **Jacob Moser**
4. **John George Moser**, b. 11 Dec 1797, Pa.
   - bp. 17 Oct 1798, Dryland Church
     - Sponsors: **George Hertzel** and wife
5. **Tobias Moser**, b. 15 Aug 1802, Pa.
   - bp. 21 May 1804, Dryland Church
     - Sponsors: the parents
6. **Rebecca Moser**, b. 14 Aug 1804, Pa.
   - bp. 15 Sep 1805, Dryland Church
     - Sponsors: **John** and **Margaret Osterstock**
7. **Daniel Moser**, b. 20 Mar 1807, Pa.
   - bp. 13 Nov 1807, Dryland Church
     - Sponsors: **Daniel** and **Dorothea Claus**

H. John Peter Moser

XJohn Peter Moser, son of **Hans Paul Moser** and **Eva Maria Becholt**, was born 14 Feb 1767 in Easton, Pennsylvania, and baptized 19 Nov 1769. He married **Elizabeth Catharine Miller** (born 9 Mar 1767), daughter of **Henry Miller**. Elizabeth died in 1806. John Peter died in Lower Saucon Township, Northampton Co., Pa. in 1841. Children of John Peter and Catharina Moser:

1. **Michael Moser**, b. 25 Jun 1792, Pa.
   - bp. 2 Jul 1792 Lower Saucon Reformed Church
     - Sponsors: **Paul** and **Magdalena Moser**
   - m. **Elisabeth Schick** (b. 1804)
2. **Susanna Moser**, b. 25 Oct 1794, Pa.
   - bp. 7 Dec 1794 Lower Saucon Reformed Church
     - Sponsor: **Elisabeth Acker**
3. **Maria Eva Moser**, b. 5 Mar 1802, Pa.
4. **Peter Moser**, m. 20 Oct 1822, **Magdalena Horlacher**
5. **Henry Moser**, b. 1806, Pa.
   - bp. German Lutheran Church, Easton, Pa.
6. **William Moser**
   - He was a bricklayer and moved to northwestern Pa.

1. Michael Moser

Michael Moser, son of **John Peter Moser** and **Elizabeth Catharine Miller**, was born 5 Jun 1792 in Pennsylvania and baptized at the Lower Saucon Reformed Church in Northampton County. He married **Elizabeth Schick** and emigrated to Muskingham County, Ohio, where he worked as a mechanic. During the War of 1812, he served in Capt. George Hess's Vol. Rifle Co., attached to the 1st Regiment of Pa. Rifle Vol. He moved to Pike County, Ohio before 1850 and worked as a brick mason. He received a military pension on 1 Mar 1851. The family then moved back to Muskingum County, Ohio, where he died in 1864. Elizabeth took her children to Monroe County, Iowa where she died in 1871 at the age of 71. Children of Michael and Elizabeth:

- **a. Samuel Moser**
- **b. Henry Moser**
- **c. Mary Ann Moser**
- **d. David Moser**
  - b. 24 Mar 1827, Muskingum Co., Ohio
  - m. Apr 1857 **Rachel A. Brill** (dau of **Henry** and **Catherine Brill**
    - b. 1828, Guernsey Co., Oh.)
  - They settled in Philo Twp., Champaign Co., Ill.
- **e. Peter Musser**
- **f. Michael Musser**
  - b. 1833, Oh.
- **g. Elizabeth Musser**
  - b. 1835, Oh. m. **Philip Baker**
- **h. George Musser**
  - b. 1838, Oh, m. **Charlotte Gordon** (dau of **John V. Gordon** and
    - **Maria Bechamp**)
  - d. 1898
- **i. John Musser**
  - b. 1841, Oh.
  - m. **Lavina Gordon** (half-sister of Charlotte, dau of **John V. Gordon** and _____ **Keller**)

4. Peter Musser

Peter Musser, son of **John Peter Moser** and **Elizabeth Catharine Miller**, was born in Pennsylvania. He married 21 Oct 1822 **Magdalena Horlacher**. They lived in Northampton County, Pennsylvania until about 1840, when they went to Marion Township, Pike County, Ohio. Known children of Peter and Magdalena:

- **a. Owen Joseph Moser** (twin)
  - b. 27 Jul 1823, Pa.
  - bp. 7 Sep 1823, Lower Saucon Church, Northampton Co, Pa.
  - Sponsors: **Joseph** and **Rosina Weber**
- **b. Josiah Anthony Moser** (twin)
  - b. 27 Jul 1823, Pa.
  - bp. 7 Sep 1823, Lower Saucon Church, Northampton Co., Pa.
  - Sponsors: **Anthony** and **Rebecca Oberly**
- **c. Hannah Louise Moser**
  - b. 9 Jul 1829, Pa.
  - bp. 25 Oct 1829, Lower Saucon Church, Northampton Co., Pa.
  - Sponsors: the parents
- **d. Adam Moser**
  - b. 13 Dec 1833, Pa.
  - bp. 5 Jan 1834, Lower Saucon Church, Northampton Co., Pa.
  - Sponsors: **Adam Miller** and **Elizabeth Heberling**

e. **Samuel Moser**, b. 1835, Pa.
f. **George A. Moser**, b. 1837, Pa.
g. **Mary M. Moser**, b. 1842, Oh.
h. **Jacob L. Moser**, b. 1844, Oh.

I. Catharine Moser Reiser

Catharine Moser, daughter of **Hans Paul Moser** and **Eva Maria Becholt**, married **Conrad Reiser**. They lived in Bethel Township, Northampton County, Pennsylvania. Only one possible son has been found:

 Conrad Reiser
  m. 2 Jul 1808 **Christina Hartendorf**
  Only known child: **Thomas Reiser**
   b. 18 Jan 1815, Easton, Pa.
   bp. 19 Apr 1815, First Reformed Church
   Sponsors: **Peter** and **Catharine Koechline**

J. Johannes Moser

Johannes Moser, son of **Hans Paul Moser** and **Eva Maria Becholt,** was born 16 Jul 1771 and baptized 3 Aug 1771 at the Dryland Reformed Church, Northampton County, Pennsylvania. His sponsors were **George Evereth** and **Eve Sewen**. On 14 Jan 1794 he married **Anna Maria Nickom** at the St. John's Lutheran Church in Easton, Pennsylvania. She was born 26 Apr 1773, daughter of **Thomas** and **Elizabeth Nickom**, and died 23 Aug 1843 of consumption. Her obituary stated that she was the mother of eight sons and three daughters, twenty-five grandchildren and two great-grand children. Five children preceeded her in death.

The release deed of Johannes Moser, dated 29 May 1811 in Forks Township, Northampton County, Pennsylvania identifies five of their children:

1. **Susanna Moser**, b. 1797, Pa.
  m. 15 Oct 1819 **Joseph Troxell**
  d. 14 Feb 1881, Newark, New Jersey
  buried Easton Cemetery
2. **Paul Moser**, b. 4 Oct 1799, Easton, Northampton Co., Pa.
  bp. 9 Oct 1799, German Lutheran Church
  m. 10 Sep 1820 **Sarah Gross**
3. **Andreas Moser**, b. 5 Mar 1805, Easton, Northampton Co., Pa.
  bp. 15 Mar 1805, German Lutheran Church
  sponsors: **Andreas** and **Magdalena Moser**
  m. **Elisabeth _____**
  Had son, **Jacob Moser** confirmed 10 Apr 1846
  at the German Lutheran Church.
4. **Peter Moser**, b. 8 Feb 1818, Williams Township, Pa.
  bp. 8 Oct 1818, sponsors: **Henry** and **Anna Ziegenfuss**
5. **Hannah Moser**, b. 2 Sep 1813, Pa.
  bp. 7 Sep 1813, German Lutheran Church
  Sponsors: **Thomas** and **Elisabeth Nickom**

The following two children are probably also the children of Johannes and Anna:

6. **Joseph Moser**, b. 1802, d. 22 Aug 1839
  buried German Lutheran Church
 Maria Susana Moser, b. 26 Feb 1810
  bp. 3 Apr 1810, German Lutheran Church
  Sponsors: **Heinrich** and **Maria Susana Yeager**

J1. Susanna Moser Troxell

Susanna Moser, daughter of **Johannes Moser** and **Anna Maria Nickom**, was born in Pennsylvania about 1797. She married Oct 1819 at St. John's Lutheran Church in Easton, Northampton County, Pennsylvania **Joseph Troxell**, son of **John Nicholas Troxell** and **Margaret Becker**. Susanna died 14 Feb 1881 while visiting in Newark, New Jersey, and is buried in Easton Cemetery, Easton, Pennsylvania. Children of Susanna and Joseph Troxell:

a. **William Henry Troxell**
   b. 22 Jun 1820, Easton, Northampton Co., Pa.
   m. 16 Feb 1843, **Caroline Maria Weygandt**
   d. 19 Feb 1884
b. **Alexander Troxell**
   b. 18 Oct 1822, Easton, Northampton Co., Pa.
   bp. 2 Mar 1823, sponsors: **Jacob** and **Margaret Nichols**
   d. 13 Jul 1853
c. **Abraham Troxell**
   b. 1825, Pa., d. 7 Sep 1852
d. **Maria Sabina Troxell**
   b. 4 Sep 1829, Easton, Northampton Co., Pa.
   bp. 12 Aug 1830, sponsor: **Eva Schmidt**
   m. **Joseph Davenport**
   They moved to Minnesota.
e. **Bejnamin Troxell**
   b. 1831, Pa., d. 26 Jun 1893
   He served in the Civil War, Co. E., 41st Pa. Volunteers.
f. **Louisa Troxell**
   b. 22 Jun 1835
   bp. 21 Nov 1837, sponsor: **Louise Trittenboch**.
   m. **Napoleon Patier**, son of the French confectioneer,
      Augustus Patier and **Elizabeth _____**.
   In 1860, they had the following children in Easton, Pa.:
      Elizabeth Patier, b. 1854
      Mary Patier, b. 1856
      William Patier, b. 1857
      Emalie Patier, b. 1859
g. **Margaret Troxell**
   b. 13 Aug 1837, Pa.
   m. abu 1858, **Barnet Van Fossen**
   d. 23 Aug 1861
   buried St. John's Cemetery, Easton, Northampton Co., Pa.
   Only child of Barnet and Margaret Van Fossen:
      Maria Elizabeth Van Fossen, b. 1859
h. **Joseph Troxell**
   b. Jul 1841, Pa.
   bur. 28 Oct 1892, Easton Cemetery, Northampton Co., Pa.

J.1a William Henry Troxell

William Henry Troxell, son of **Joseph Troxell** and **Sus**'
22 Jun 1820 in Easton, Northampton County, Pennsylva'
Plainfield Reformed Lutheran Church on July 30. Spor
and **Anna Maria Deily**. William married 16 Feb 184'
the St. John's Lutheran Church in Easton. She was b(
daughter of **Peter** and **Barbara Weygandt** and died ∠∪
19 Feb 1884 in the Lehigh County Alms House. They are bu∪∖
in Bethlehem, Lehigh County, Pennsylvania. His obituary listed surviv∖_
Charles A. and Robert of South Bethlehem and George and Oscar of Tiffin, Un∖
sister, Mrs. Joseph Davenport of Minnesota and two brothers also survived him.
Children of William and Caroline Troxell:

1. **Emma Troxell**
   b. 22 Jul 1843, Pa.
   bp. 14 Nov 1843, St. John's Lutheran, Easton, Lehigh, Pa.
   m. 21 Nov 1863 **John Charles Bright**
   (son of **John Bright** and **Maria Trumbauer**
   b. 17 Jun 1841 Bucks Co., Pa., d. 9 Apr 1890)
   d. 26 Jun 1880, Pa.
   bur. Union Cemetery, Bethlehem, Lehigh, Pa.
   Children of Emma and John Bright:
   a. **Laura Bright**, b. 17 Oct 1864, W. Bethlehem, Pa.
      m. 11 Nov 1889 **Morris Schick**
      (son of **Henry Schick** and **Sarah Ziegler**)
      d. 10 Feb 1948
      Children of Laura and Morris Schick:
      1. **Charles Johnson Schick**
         b. 6 Sep 1893
         m. **Rachel Hicks** (divorced)
         d. 26 Apr 1941
         No children.
      2. **Lillian Mae Schick**
         b. 29 Jul 1898
         m. 8 Aug 1925 **Raymond Porter Webb**
         (divorced) No children.
   b. **Lillie Bright**
      b. 20 Nov 1866
      d. 10 Feb 1948
   c. **Ira Bright**
      b. 21 Aug 1868
      d. 21 Aug 1868
   d. **Infant daughter**
      b. 24 Jun 1869
      d. 24 Jun 1869
   e. **John Charles Bright**
      b. 25 Jul 1870
      d. 18 Sep 1872
   f. **Nina May Bright**
      b. 20 Aug 1872, Bethlehem, Pa.
      m. 24 Apr 1893, Philadelphia, Pa.
         Osville Clinton Weaver (son of **Davis Butler Weaver** and **Amanda C. Ziegler**
         b. 10 May 1871, Allentown, Pa.
         d. 20 Jun 1950 Placerville, Ca.)
      d. 10 Nov 1949, Placerville, Ca.
      bur. Memorial Park Cemeter, Oroville, Ca.

Children of Nina and Osville Weaver:
1. **Lloyd P. Weaver**
>> b. 6 Feb 1894, Philadelphia, Pa.
>> m. 14 Mar 1916
>>> **(1) Doris Eileen Beaver**
>>>> (b. 11 Feb 1899,
>>>> d. 7 Jun 1921)
>>> Child of Lloyd and Doris:
>>>> **Watt Thomas Weaver**
>>>> b. 29 Mar 1918, Oroville, Ca.
>> m. **(2) Marie Stafford Baker**
>>> (b. 9 Aug 1901, Blade of Crasse, Ky.,
>> d. 9 Jul 1959, Placerville)
>> Child of Lloyd and Marie:
>>> **Rachel Marie Weaver**
>>> b. 2 May 1934, Albany, Ca.
>>> m. **George Sareeram**
>>> d. 17 Jan 1969
>>> Children:
>>> **Christeen Marie Sareeam**
>>> **Michele Alyne Sareeam**
>>> **George B. Sareeam**

2. **Ruth Weaver**
>> b. 25 Oct 1905 Bucks Co., Pa.
>> m. **William Henry Anderman** (son of
>> **Henry Anderman** and **Mirna Mueller**
>>> (b. 4 Sep 1905, Kauaii, Hawaii)
>> Children of Ruth and William Anderman:
>>> a. **Elaine Leilani Anderman**
>>>> b. 20 Jul 1932 Hollywood, Ca.
>>>> m. **(1)** _____
>>>> had son, **Charles** _____
>>>>> b. 1 Feb 1957, Pasadena, Ca.
>>>>> **(2)** 28 Nov 1957, **Edward**
>>>>> **Neal Mansell** (son of
>>>>> **Elmer Vincent**
>>>>> **Mansell** and **Harriet**
>>>>> **Lechert**, b. 6 Sep 1930)
>>>> Children of Elaine and Edward:
>>>>> **Scott Allen Mansell**
>>>>> **Todd Edward Mansell**
>>>>> **Cynthia Elaine Mansell**
>>> b. **William Henry Anderman**
>>>> b. 29 Sep 1934, Berkeley, Ca.
>>>> m. 20 Jun 1959 **Jean Alice**
>>>> **Massey** (dau. of **Charles**
>>>> **Walden Massey**)
>>>> Children of William and Jean:
>>>>> **Gregory Alan Anderman**
>>>>> **Kristi Lynn Anderman**
>>>>> **Glen Edward Anderman**
>>> c. **Roger Craig Anderman**
>>>> b. 7 Sep 1944, Altadena, Ca.
>>>> m. 18 Jun 1966
>>>>> **Janice Elisabeth Jones**
>>>>> (dau. of **Alan Russel Jones**)

Children of Roger and Janice:
Mark Alan Anderman
Elizabeth Anderman
Katharine Anderman
3. **Laura Helen Weaver**
b. 13 May 1909 Hatfield,Montgomery Co., Pa.
m. 25 Mar 1934, Lodi, Ca. **Truman Ladd Gould**
(son of **Arthur Truman Gould** and **Viola Bella Corbett** b. 3 May 1910)
Child of Helen & Truman Gould:
Robert Weaver Gould
b. 13 May 1935, Berkeley, Ca.
unmarried
4. **Margaret Weaver**
b. 15 Jan 1911, Oroville, Ca.
m. 26 Jan 1936 **David S. Galvin**
Children of Margaret and David Galvin:
a. **David John** m. **Rachelle Louise** ____
(Their three daughters were adopted by Rachelle's 2nd husband in 1974.)
b. **Alexander Clinton**
m. **(1) Diana Kay Peck**
They had two daughters.
g. **Ira Bright**, b. 9 Jan 1875,   d. 9 May 1875
h. **May Bright**, b. 10 Mar 1876, d. 10 Oct 1877
i. **Infant son**, b. 10 Dec 1877, d. 10 Dec 1877
j. **Daisy Bright**, b. 2 Aug 1879, d. 9 Nov 1880
2. **Edward/Edwin Troxell**
b. 9 Mar 1845
bp. 27 Jul 1848, St. John's Lutheran, Easton, Pa.
bur. 20 Jul 1865, Easton
3. **William Henry Troxell**
b. 10 Jul 1847
bp. 27 Jul 1848, St. John's Lutheran, Easton, Pa.
m. **Clara** _____
bur. 10 Feb 1870
Child of William and Clara Troxell:
William Henry Troxell, b. 3 May 1870
4. **Charles A. Troxell**, b. 1850
m. _____
d. 10 May 1918, Bethlehem, Pa. the first mail carrier in Bethlehem, Pa.
Children of Charles Troxell:
a. **Minnie Troxell**, b. 1871, Bethlehem, Pa.
m. **Harvey Acker**
d. aft. 1955
b. **Eva Troxell**, b. 1874, Bethlehem, Pa.
m. _____ **Hendricks**
d. aft. 1956
c. **Emma Troxell**
5. **James F. Troxell**, b. 17 Nov 1852, Lower Saucon, Pa., d. 22 Nov. 1858
6. **Sethos Alonzo Troxell**, b. 5 Apr 1854, d. 14 May 1858
7. **Joseph Troxell**, b. abt. 1858, Pa.
8. **George Troxell**, b. abt. 1859, Pa.
9. **Oscar Troxell**
10. **Robert Troxell**

Philip Moser

Philip Moser, believed to be the son of **Michael Moser** and **Catharine** _____, was born in March, 1801 in Lowhill, Lehigh County, Pennsylvania, according to information given at the time of his death. The first written record located of this Philip is the christening of his son, Gideon, which took place at Heidelberg Union Church on 12 Feb. 1821. This record gives the mother's name as **Elisabeth Schnobel,** who was born 9 Feb 1804, according to her tombstone. An Elizabeth born on that date to **Andrew Schnable** and **Catharine Mutard(t)** and christened in St. Paul's Catholic Church in Bally, Berks County, Pennsylvania may be our Elizabeth .

Elisabeth Schnobel and Philip Moser were married about 1820 and made a home in Heidelberg, Lehigh County, Pennsylvania, where the three oldest children were christened. The family went south to Lowhill, then moved to Allentown, before heading west with a wagon train led by Rev. Paltsgraff around 1835.

Philip purchased a large tract of land in Warren Township, Trumbull County, Ohio, which was located partly in what is now Braceville, with the larger part in Leavittsburg. Their last four children were born on the farm. In 1850, there was an **Elisabeth Moser,** age 14, living in the household, along with their unmarried children, John (24), Fiern Anna (11), Rebecca (7), and Susannah (3). It is not know how she is related to the family. It is possible that the daughter, Elisabeth, who was christened at Heidelberg Union in 1830 died young and the family gave another daughter the name.

Elisabeth (Snobel) died on 10 October 1857, after which time Philip moved to a boarding house, run by **Lewis Hoyt,** in Warren, Ohio (the same boarding house where two of their sons were living in 1850). Philip was struck by a railroad car while crossing the tracks and died on 27 Feb 1873. The records of the Atlantic & Great Western Railroad state that he was run over when Train #38 (conductor, Russell and engineer, Swan) was backing out of a switch in the Leavittsburg yard. They called to him, but he did not hear them or the train whistle as he was quite deaf.

Philip and Elizabeth are buried in the old Paltzgraff Cemetery, Hewitt-Gifford Road, Lordstown, Trumbull County, Ohio. Children of Philip and Elisabeth Moser:
A. Gideon Moser
    b. 3 Dec 1820, Pa.
    chr. 12 Feb 1821, Heidelberg Union, Lehigh Co., Pa.
    m. 8 Jan 1846 **Susan Hower** Trumbull Co., Oh.
    d. 7 Jan 1891, Ovid, Lockwood Co., Mi.
    buried in Union Cemetery in Ovid.
B. Catharina Moser
    b. 15 Apr 1822, Heidelberg, Lehigh Co., Pa.
    m. 1 Feb 1842 **Paul Reigert** Trumbull Co., Oh.
C. John Moser
    b. 23 Oct 1824, Heidelberg, Lehigh Co., Pa.
    chr. 5 Dec 1824, Heidelberg Union, Lehigh Co., Pa.
    m. 25 Sep 1855 **Catharine Weaver** Trumbull Co., Oh.
    d. 22 Sep 1897 Trumbull Co., Oh
    buried Paltzgraff Cemetery, Lordstown, Oh.
D. David S. Moser
    b. 15 Sep 1826, Lowhill, Lehigh Co., Pa.
    m. 30 Oct 1851 **Johanna Hofflinger** Warren,
        Trumbull, Oh.
    d. 4 Feb 1900 Leavittsburg, Trumbull Co., Oh.
    buried Oakwood Cemetery, Warren, Oh.

E. Owen Moser
  b. 10 Mar 1827, Allentown, Lehigh Co., Pa.
  m. 28 Jul 1850 **Laura Lane** Canfield, Mahoning Co., Oh.
  d. 28 Apr 1904, Warren, Trumbull, Oh.
  buried Oakwood Cemetery, Warren, Oh.
F. Elisabeth Moser
  b. 9 Nov 1829, Pa.
  chr. 24 Jan 1830, Heidelberg Union, Lehigh Co., Pa.
  m. 1850 **Adam Schwab**
G. Lydia Moser
  b. 3 Apr 1836, Warren Twp., Trumbull, Oh.
  m. **(1) Jackson Rowe** Mar 1858, Trumbull Co.
    (2) Isaac Brobst
  d. 30 Apr 1918 Trumbull Co., Oh.
  buried Oakwood Cemetery, Warren, Oh.
H. Fiern Anna Moser
  b. 31 Mar 1839, Warren Twp., Trumbull, Oh.
  m. **Emery Hower** 10 Dec 1863, Branch Co., Mi.
  d. 19 Jul 1911, Trumbull Co., Oh.
  buried Oakwood Cemetery, Warren, Oh.
I. Rebecca Moser
  b. 16 Sep 1842, Trumbull Co., Oh
  m. **Henry Lapham**
  d. 5 Jan 1895, Oh.
  buried Oakwood Cemetery, Warren, Oh.
  Rebecca is buried alone. In 1880, she was still single,
  working as a servant for the Adams family at
  254 Mahoning Ave., Warren, Oh.
J. Susannah Moser
  b. 1843, Warren Twp., Trumbull, Oh.
  d. 28 Feb 1921, Trumbull Co., Oh.
  buried Oakwood Cemetery, Warren, Oh.
  Susannah never married. In 1880, Susie was working as a
  servant for the Warren Packard family, at 269 Mahoning
  Ave., Warren.

A. Gideon Moser

Gideon Moser, oldest son of **Philip Moser** and **Elisabeth Schnobel**, was born on
3 Dec 1820 in Pennsylvania and baptized on 12 Feb 1821 at Heidelberg Union
Reformed Church in Lehigh County. Sponsors at his baptism were **David** and
Magdalene (Seiss) Moser. Gideon married **Susan Hower** on 8 Jan 1846 in Trumbull
County, Ohio, when their marriage is listed under "Moses". She was born 8 Jun 1827
in Juniata Township, Perry County, Pennsylvania, daughter of **Jacob Hower** and
Hannah Kimmel (m. 5 Oct 1826, Carlisle, Cumberland Co., Pa.) and granddaughter of
Anthony Kimmel of Rye Township, Perry County, Pennsylvania.

The family lived in Lordstown, Trumbull County, Ohio until 1862 when they moved to
Coldwater, Branch County, Michigan. Susan died on 23 Jun 1886 and Gideon
following her on 7 Jan 1891. They are buried in Union Cemetery, Ovid Township,
Branch County, Michigan. Children of Gideon and Susan Moser:
  1. **Margaret J. Moser**
    b. 8 Apr 1846 in Trumbull Co., Oh
    m. (1) **Noah Batterson**
      (2) **George W. Reed** (no issue)
      (3) **William Woodard** (no issue)
    d. 12 Jun 1930

2. **John Moser**
   - b. 2 Oct 1848, Lordstown, Trumbull Co., Oh
   - m. (1) 13 Mar 1869, **Betsey A. Spencer** (d. 1 Aug 1876)
   - (2) 30 Jul 1877, **Francelia Hall** (d. 10 Mar 1916)
   - d. 3 Mar 1916, Branch Co., Mi
3. **Samuel Franklin Moser**
   - b. 9 Mar 1850, Lordstown, Trumbull Co., Oh
   - m. (1) 24 Feb 1876 **Cora Green**
     - in Bethel, Branch Co., Mi.
   - (2) 29 Oct 1892 **Cora Barnes**
   - d. Jun 1891, Benzonia Twp., Benzie Co., Mi.
   - Buried Benzonia Cemetery
4. **Henry A. Moser**
   - b. 26 Oct 1851, Lordstown, Trumbull Co., Oh
   - m. (1) 24 Dec 1874, **Eva Sibley**
   - (2) **Sophia M. "Loby" Parson**
   - (3) 12 Oct 1895, **Louise Gage Ball**
5. **Hannah Elizabeth Moser**
   - b. 20 Dec 1853, Lordstown, Trumbull Co., Oh
   - m. **Lafayette Hyster**
   - d. 1884
6. **Seymour A. Moser**
   - b. 20 Mar 1856, Lordstown, Trumbull Co., Oh
   - m. 8 Aug 1893 **Maude E. Mitchell** in Mi
   - d. 29 Apr 1919
7. **Lilliam M. "Lucy" Moser**
   - b. 6 Jul 1858, Lordstown, Trumbull Co., Oh
   - m. (1) **John Dubendorff**
   - (2) **Clarence H. Carpenter**
   - d. 10 Jan 1928
8. **Owen L. C. Moser**
   - b. 6 Apr 1863, Coldwater, Branch Co., Mi
   - m. 17 May 1885, **Lunettie "Hattie" Lozier**
   - d. 1942
9. **William Moser**
   - b. 30 May 1865, Coldwater, Branch Co., Mi
   - m. **Sylvia Beebe**

A1. Margaret J. Moser

Margaret J. Moser, daughter of **Gideon Moser** and **Susan Hower**, was born 8 Apr 1846 in Trumbull County, Ohio. Margaret was married three times, first to **Noah Batterson**, by whom she had five children. She married second, **George W. Reed** and third, **William Woodard**. Margaret died 12 Jun 1930. Children of Noah and Margaret:
   a. **Edith D. Batterson** (no issue)
   b. **Susan D. Batterson** (no issue)
   c. **Carl Batterson**
   d. **Nelson Batterson** who was the father of:
      1. **Reginald Batterson**
      2. **Wilbern Batterson**
   e. **Golden Batterson**
      - m. (1) _____ **Lewis**
      - (2) _____ **Hardy**
      - She had one child:
         - **Belle Lewis** m. **Charles Deeds**

A2. John Moser

John Moser ,son of **Gideon Moser** and **Susan Hower**, was born on 2 Oct 1848 in Lordstown, Trumbull County, Ohio. He married (1) **Betty Spencer** on 28 Mar 1869 in Branch County, Michigan. Betty died before they had any children. John married second **Francelia Hall**, by whom he had two children. John died in Branch County, Michigan on 2 Mar 1916. Children of John and Francelia Moser:

- a. **Dane F. Moser**
  - b. 5 May 1878
  - m. **Ina Brooks**
  - d. 1930
  - Children of Dane & Ina Moser:
    1. **Louise Moser**
       - m. 2 Feb 1913 **Bill Landis**
    2. **Margaret Moser**
       - m 3 Aug 1921 **Bob Starkweather**
    3. **Esther Ann**
       - m 25 Feb 1921 **"Doc"** _____
- b. **Harry J. Moser**
  - b. 8 Apr 1882
  - m. 30 Aug 1904, Branch Co., Mi., **Orpha Alger**
  - d. 9 Oct 1973, buried in Oak Grove Cemetery

A3. Samuel Franklin Moser

Samuel Franklin Moser, son of **Gideon Moser** and **Susan Hower**, was born on 9 Mar 1850 in Lordstown, Trumbull County, Ohio. He married (1) **Cora Green** on 24 Dec 1876 in Branch County, Michigan, by whom he had one daughter:

- a. **Bertha B. Moser**, b. abt. 1880

Samuel then married **Cora Barnes**, daughter of **Alfred W. Barnes** and **Sarilda Lease** on 29 Oct 1892. Samuel died on 4 Dec 1917 and is buried in Benzonia Cemetery, Benzie County, Michigan. Children of Samuel & Cora (Barnes) Moser:

- b. **Smith LeRoy Moser**
  - b. 5 Nov. 1893, Mi.
  - m. 11 Nov 1914, Wauseon, Fulton Co., Oh.
    - **Ruie Jane Daniels**
  - d. 11 Dec 1976, Wauseon, Fulton Co., Oh.
  - buried Greenlawn Cemetery, Delta, Fulton Co., Oh.
- c. **Dorothy A. Moser**, b. 5 Nov 1897, Mi.
  - m. 27 Dec. 1919 **Louis Alexander Mallion**
- d. **Beulah Moser**, b. 24 Jan 1906, Mi.
  - m. **Bert Wise**
- e. **B. F. "Pete" Moser**, b. 14 Jul 1911, Mi.
  - m. 1938, **Ella Cox**
  - d. 2 Mar 1976

A3b. Smith LeRoy Moser

Smith LeRoy Moser, son of **Samuel Franklin Moser** and his second wife, **Cora M. Barnes**, was born 5 Nov. 1893 in Batavia, Branch County, Michigan. He married 11 Nov. 1914 in Wauseon, Fulton County, Ohio, **Ruie Jane Daniels**, daughter of **Royal H. Daniels** and **Frances Ann Thomas**, who was born on 3 Sep 1893. He died 11 Dec 1976 in Wauseon and is buried in Greenlawn Cemetery in Delta, Fulton County, Ohio. Ruie died on 29 Jan 1989 and is buried with her husband.

Children of Smith LeRoy and Ruie Moser:
  3b1. Grace Peggy Lucille Moser
    b. 4 Mar 1917, Benzonia Twp., Benzie Co., Mi.
    m. **Perry Shaw**
    d. 29 Jun 1979
  3b2. Ruby Jane Moser
    b. 31 Mar 1917, Mi.
    m. 10 Oct 1938 **Robert Hosimer**
    Children of Robert & Ruby Hosimer:
      Sandy Kay Hosimer
      Mary Lynne Hosimer
  3b4. Helen Maria Moser
    b. 2 Mar 1920, Beulah, Benzie Co., Mi.
    m. 17 Sep 1938, Angola, Steuben Co., In.
    Marvin Montgomery Morr
    (son of **Howard Earl Morr** and **Helen**
    Kear Montgomery)
    d. 7 Sep 1992, Wauseon, Fulton Co., Oh.
    Children of Marvin & Helen Morr:
      Carl Moser Morr
        b. 1 Jul 1934
        m. 24 Oct 1972, Bunker Hill, Ingham
        Co., Mi. **Margaret Ann Brady** (b. 23 Dec 1937)
      Daryl Eugene Morr
        b. 22 Jul 1940
        m. 4 Jul 1964 Detroit, Wayne Co., Mi.
        Judith Jayne Wilmot (b. 27 Oct 1941)
        They have a daughter, **Lisa Jane Morr**
          b. 2 Jun 1971, Reed City, Osceola, Mi.
      Janice Sue Morr, b. 5 Jul 1942
        m. 6 Jun 1964, Delta, Fulton Co., Oh
        Gary Lee Friess (b. 8 Jun 1943)
        Children of Gary and Janice Friess:
          Carryl Jean Friess
            b. 22 Aug 1965
            Toledo, Lancaster, Oh.
          Scott Alan Friess
            b. 29 May 1968
            Wauseon, Fulton, Oh.
          Trace Earl Friess
            b. 18 Jun 1970
            Toledo, Lancaster, Oh.
          Kristen Leigh Friess
            b. 13 May 1971
            Toledo, Lancaster, Oh.
      Philip Leroy Morr, b. 30 Jul 1943
        m. 5 Aug 1972 Chicago, Cook Co., Ill.
        Dianne Margaret Cahill
  3b5. Lois Jayne Moser
    b. 6 May 1922, Beulah, Benzie Co., Mi.
    m. **Walter Ficklin**
    d. 23 Nov 1984, Battle Creek, Calhoun Co., Mi.
    Children of Walter & Lois Ficklin:
      Gary Lee Ficklin
      Linda Leigh Ficklin

3b6. Dorothy Jean Moser
    b. 14 Mar 1924, McBain, Missaukee, Mi.
    m. 11 Sep 1942 **Ira Leon Evans**
    Children of Dorothy & Ira Evans:
        Judith Evans
        Edward Evans
        Rosei Evans

3b7. Smith Moser, Jr.
    b. 7 Dec 1925, McBain, Missaukee Co., Mi
    m. 30 May 1946, Van Wert, Van Wert Co., Oh.
    Virginia R. McGhee
    d. 18 Dec 1989, Delta, Fulton Co., Oh.
    Children of Smith & Virginia Moser:
        Vickie Sue Moser
        Lorell Jean Moser

A4. Henry A. Moser

Henry A. Moser, son of **Gideon Moser** and **Susan Hower**, was born on Christmas Day of 1851, in Lordstown, Trumbull County, Ohio. He married first, **Eva Sibley**, 25 Dec. 1874, by whom he had a son, **Otis Moser** in 1875. His second wife was **Loby Parson**. They had a son in 1885 named **Morris Moser**, who died young. The last wife of Henry A. Moser was a widow, **Louise Gage Ball**, whom he married 12 Oct 1895 in Branch County, Michigan. They had a son **Charley Moser** who was born the following year.

A5. Hannah Elizabeth Moser Hyster

Hanna Elizabeth Moser, daughter of **Gideon Moser** and **Susan Hower** was born in Lordstown, Trumbull County, Ohio on 20 Dec 1853. She married **Lafayette Hyster** and was the mother of four children:
    Arthur Hyster
    Edward Hyster
    Nina Hyster
    Gideon Hyster

A6. Seymore A. Moser

Seymore A. Moser, a son of **Gideon Moser** and **Susan Hower** was born in Lordstown, Trumbull County, Ohio 20 Mar 1856. The name of his first wife is unknown at this time. They had a daughter, **Edith Moser** (who married _____ **Hearst**). Children of Edith Moser Hearst:
    Madeline Hearst m. **Glen McPherson**
    Gerald Hearst
    Katherine Hearst
    Robert Hearst
Seymore married (2) **Maude E. Mitchell** 9 Aug 1893 in Branch County, Michigan. They were the parents of two daughters:
    Della D. Moser, b. 21 Sep 1894 in Mi.
    Maude Moser, b. abt. 1895

A7. "Lucy" Lillian Moser Carpenter

Lillian Moser (called Lucy), daughter of **Gideon Moser** and **Susan Hower**, was born in Lordstown, Trumbull County, Ohio 6 Jul 1858. She married (1) **John Dubendorff** 7 Feb. 1883. After his death, she married (2) **C. H. Carpenter** in Branch County, Michigan 9 Jan 1899. The Carpenters adopted **Lydia Jucket**, who married _____ **Frisinger** and was the mother of two children. Lucy died on 17 Jan 1923.

A8. Owen L. C. Moser

Owen L. C. Moser, son of **Gideon Moser** and **Susan Hower**, was born 6 Apr 1863, probably in Lordstown, Ohio. He married **Lunettie Lozier** (called **Hattie** in some records) on 17 May 1885. Lunettie was born in May 1868 and died in 1929. Owen died in 1942 in Branch County, Michigan. The couple is buried in Matteson Cemetery, located in Branch County. Children of Owen & Lunettie Moser:

Hollie Moser, b. 27 Jan 1886
Hazel Moser, b. 8 Apr 1888
   m. **Claude Smith**
   Children of Hazel and Claude Smith:
      Harlan Smith
      Doris Smith
      Kenneth Smith
      Lucille Smith
Walter Moser, b. 3 Jul 1891, d. 1956, buried in Matteson Cemetery
Rolland Ford Moser, b. 28 May 1893
Maggie Murl Moser, b. 20 Mar 1896
   m. **Earl Young**
   Children of Maggie & Earl Young:
      Pauline Young
      Dorothea Young
      Owen Young
      Ruth Young
      Max Young
Howard Moser, b. 10 Jan 1898
   m. **Minnie Low**
   d. Dec. 1970, San Antonio, Texas
Willis Moser, b. 13 May 1903
   m. **Edna Low**
   d. Mar 1984, Wayne Co., Mi.
Mildred Moser, b. 4 Jul 1906, d. 21 May 1910, buried Matteson Cemetery

B. Catharina Moser Reigert

Catharina Moser, daughter of **Philip Moser** and **Elisabeth Schnobel**, was born in Heidelberg, Lehigh Co., Pa. 15 Apr 1822. She married **Paul Reigert** (b. 1811 in Germany) before 1843 in Ohio. In 1850, the family was farming in Thompson Township, Geauga County, Ohio. Living with them at that time were **John** (age 40) and **Louisa** (age 50) **Reigert**, who were probably siblings of Paul. Known children of Paul and Catharina Reigert:

Mary Reigert, b. 1843, Oh. (probably died young)
John Reigert, b. 1845. Oh.
Louise Reigert, b. 1845, Oh.
Charles Reigert, b. 1847, Oh.
Sarah E. Reigert, b. 1849, Oh.
Dave "Guy" Reigert
Lydia Reigert

C. John Moser

John Moser, son of **Philip Moser** and **Elisabeth Schnobel**, was born 23 Oct 1823 in Heidelberg, Lehigh County, Pennsylvania. He was baptized 5 Dec 1824 at Heidelberg Union Church by Rev. Helffrich. His sponsors were **Jonathan** and **Maria Lang**. At the time of the 1850 census, John was still single and living with his parents in Lordstown, Trumbull County, Ohio. On 22 Sep 1855 he married **Catharine Weaver** in Warren, Trumbull County, Ohio. Catharine, whose parents were born in Germany, was born 25 Jul 1839 and died 18 Jun 1917. In 1860, the couple lived in Lordstown on the farm next to his brother, Gideon. John died 21 Sep 1897. They are buried in Paltzgraff Cemetery with his parents. Known children of John & Catharine Moser:

1. **Loui E. Moser**
   b. 3 Jan 1868, Lordstown, Trumbull, Oh.
   d. 8 Sep 1869 buried Paltzgraff Cemetery
2. **George M. Moser**
   b. 28 Sep 1859, Lordstown, Trumbull, Oh.
   m. **Ida McCorkle**
   George was a farmer in Lordstown, Trumbull Co., Oh. and served his community as township turstee from 1893 to 1896. He was treasurer of the Lordstown Farmer's Mutual Insurance Company.
   Known children of George & Ida Moser:
   a. **Olive Edna Moser**, b. 15 Feb 1889, Southington, Trumbull, Oh
   b. **Ida May Moser**, b. 9 Jul 1893, Lordstown, Trumbull, Oh.
3. **Alice E. Moser**
   m. **Wallace Hoffman**
   Note: An Alice E. Moser married 4 Mar 1885 **George Coser** and on 7 Mar 1887, an Alice E. Moser married **Jacob H. Hoffman**.
4. **Frances E. Moser**, b. 1865
5. **Olive C. Moser**
   b. 1872
   d. 1950
   bur. Paltzgraff with parents.
   Olive was a talented and successful teacher. She never married.

D. David S. Moser

David S. Moser, son of **Philip Moser** and **Elisabeth Schnobel**, was born 15 Sep 1826 in Lowhill, Lehigh County, Pennsylvania, according to his statement in '*Trumbull County Atlas and Directory, 1899*". His christening record has not been located in Pennsylvania. By 1850, David and his brother, Owen, were living in a boarding house, operated by **Lewis** and **Sarah Hoyt**, at 684 South Street, in Warren, Trumbull County, Ohio. They were listed as laborers, and worked on the railroad. Also living in the boarding house was **Johanna Hoeflinger**, widow of **Christian Kibler**, who would become David's wife. Johanna, daughter of **Johannes Christian** and **Johanna J. Hoefflinger**, was born in Marksburg, Germany in May of 1821. Her family came to America between 1825 and 1830, living in Alleghney County, Pennsylvania before moving to Ohio. Johanna married 12 Jan 1842 in Trumbull County, Ohio, **Christian Kibler** (b. 9 Sep 1816 in Wurtemberg, Germany, d. 1849), son of **Johannes Kubler** and **Catharina Kubler**. They were the parents of **Martin Kibler**, whose son, **Charles Kibler**, was living in Indiana when Johanna made her will in 1900. There are also two girls, one of whom was named **Hannah**, who were possibly daughters of Johanna, although they are not mentioned in her will. These children, who were not living with their mother in the boarding house, have not been located in census records, and were not raised in the household of Johanna and David Moser. Photos of the three children were among the effects left by Hannah.

Johanna had at least one sister, **Louisa Hoefflinger** (who married Christian's brother, **Jacob Kibler**) and two brothers, **Jamie Hoefflinger** (who married **Catherine** _____) and **Daniel Hoefflinger** (b. 4 Jul 1824, d. 4 Jul 1909, m. **Catherine Brobst** (b. 1826, d. 1888). The Hoefflingers are buried in Paltzgraff Cemetery, Lordstown, Trumbull County, Ohio.

David Moser owned a large farm, located in Warren Township (now Leavittsburg), Trumbull County, Ohio. He and Johanna Hoefflinger Kibler were married on 30 Oct 1851 before Rev. F. C. Becker, in Warren. His brother Owen signed the marriage certificate as witness. David died in Leavittsburg on 3 Feb 1900 at the age of 73. Johanna followed him a year later, on 31 May 1901. They are buried together in Oakwood Cemetery, Warren, Trumbull County, Ohio. Children of David and Johanna:

1. **Comfort B. Moser**,
   b. 9 Jun 1852, Leavittsburg, Trumbull, Oh
   m. **Pauline Sanzenbacher**, 14 Apr 1878, Southington, Oh.
   d. 17 Jun 1890, Trumbull Co., Oh
   buried Oakwood Cemetery, Warren, Oh
2. **Owen Nelson Moser**
   b. 4 May 1854, Leavittsburg, Trumbull, Oh
   m. (1) **Lucy Manda Long** 7 Sep 1887
   (2) **Effie Elosia Beegle**
   d. 12 Aug 1893, Warren, Trumbull, Oh
   buried Oakwood Cemetery, Warren, Oh
3. **Edward D. Moser**
   b. 23 Aug 1867, Leavittsburg, Trumbull, Oh
   d. 12 Jan 1886, Warren, Trumbull, Oh
   buried Oakwood Cemetery, Warren, Oh

D1. Comfort B. Moser

Comfort B. Moser, son of **David S. Moser** and **Johanna Hoefflinger**, was born 20 Jun 1852 in Leavittsburg, Trumbull County, Ohio. He married **Pauline Sanzenbacher** (b. 2 Jun 1859, d. 29 Dec 1920) on 11 Apr 1878 in Southington, Trumbull County, Ohio before Rev. L. A. Schmidt, Lutheran. She was the daughter of **Jacob Sanzenbacher** and **Caroline Holyworth**. In 1880, they lived on the farm next door to his father. Comfort worked his farm, but also worked as a laborer on the railroad. He died 13 Jun 1890 from injuries suffered in a railroad accident. They are buried with their son, Harmon B., in Oakwood Cemetery in Warren, Ohio. Children of Comfort and Pauline, all born in Trumbull County:

a. **Harmon B. Moser**
   b. 16 May 1880, Warren, Oh
   d. 13 Apr 1928
   buried Oakwood Cemetery
b. **Minnie E. Moser**
   b. 30 Jan 1887, Warren, Oh
   m. **Ben Philips**
   d. Dec 1974, Lordstown, Oh
c. **Edward David Jacob Moser**
   b. 22 Jul 1890, Leavittsburg, Oh
   m. 19 Apr 1911 **Lillian May Smith**
d. **Elmer Noble Moser**
   b. 1 Sep 1881, Warren Twp., Oh
   m. **Della Luetta Dorland**
   d. 19 Feb 1970, Warren, Oh

D1d. Elmer Noble Moser

Elmer Noble Moser, son of **Comfort B. Moser** and **Pauline Sanzenbacher**, was born 1 Sep 1881 in Warren Township, Trumbull County, Ohio. He married **Della Luetta Dorland**, b. 27 Apr 1888, who had a two year old daughter, **Lucille Dorland**. Elmer adopted her in 1920, at which time her name was changed to **Lucille Moser**.

Della and Elmer had a farm in Braceville, Trumbull County, Ohio. Della died in 1958 and Elmer died 19 Feb 1970 in Warren, Ohio. Children of Elmer and Della Moser:
1. **Lucille (Doreland) Moser**, b. 1918
2. **Clarence Alfred Moser**
    b. Sep 1923, Braceville, Trumbull Co., Oh
    m. 1947 **Margaret Cross**
    Children of Clarence and Margaret Moser:
      a. **Sandra Jean Moser**, b. 2 Aug 1948, d. 3 Aug 1948
      b. **Alan C. Moser**
        b. 10 Feb 1950, Warren, Trumbull Co., Oh
        m. (1) 18 Mar 1969 **Karen Bailes**
        Child of Alan and Karen Moser:
          Jeffery Alan Moser
            b. 6 Nov 1970, Warren, Oh
        m. (2) 12 Feb 1972 Newton Falls, Trumbull, Oh
        Glenna Lou Hilty (b. 4 Jun 1951, Niles, Oh.,
          m. (1) **George Paulley**
        son of Glenna and George Paulley:
          George Paulley, b. 8 Dec 1969
        Child of Allan and Glenna Moser:
          Ronald Dean Moser
            b. 16 Jan 1974, Warren, Oh
      c. **Margaret Ann Moser**
        b. 19 Sep 1951, Trumbull Co., Oh
        m. 24 Aug 1969 **James Edward Brooks**
        Children of Margaret and James Brooks:
          James Clarence Brooks, b. 2 Mar 1970
          Kevin Alan Brooks, b. 24 Aug 1971
          Sandra Jane Brooks, b. 16 May 1973
            m. 15 Oct 1994 **Kevin Allen Hellock**
            Child of Sandra and Kevin Hellock:
              Ryan Allen Hellock
                b. 18 May 1995
      d. **John Alfred Moser**
        b. 24 Jul 1954, Trumbull Co., Oh
        m. 11 Apr 1981 **Diana Horseley**
        Children of John and Diana Moser:
          Robert John Moser, b. 22 May 1984
          Thomas Dean Moser, b. 10 Jan 1987
      e. **Donald Paul Moser**
        b. 11 Dec 1956, Trumbull Co., Oh
        m. 1 Nov 1980 **Pamela Grayem**
        Children of Donald and Pamela Moser:
          Gregory Scott Moser, b. 3 Dec 1984
          Jessica Linn Moser, b. 30 Aug 1988
          Brian Mitchell Moser, b. 27 Aug 1993
3. **David Moser**, b. 1921, Warren Township, Trumbull Co., Oh
4. **Paul Moser**, b. Feb 1926, Braceville, Trumbull Co., Oh
5. **Pauline Moser**, b. Feb 1928, Braceville, Trumbull Co., Oh

D2. Owen Nelson Moser

Owen "Nils" Nelson Moser, son of David S. Moser and Johanna Hoefflinger, was born 4 May 1854 in Leavittsburg, Trumbull County, Ohio. He was a farmer, but like his father and uncle Owen, he also worked on the railroad for many years, receiving a gold watch for his service. His first wife, Lucy Manda Long, was working as a servant to David's mother prior to their marriage in Leavittsburg on 7 Sep 1887. She was born 10 Aug 1862 in Southington, Trumbull County, Ohio to Lewis W. Long and Rebecca Shoop. Lucy died of ungentine fever in Leavittsburg on 23 Nov 1899, while nursing her children back to health. Children of Owen and Lucy Moser:

    a. **Ethel Pearl Moser**, b. 29 Dec 1887, Braceville, Trumbull Co., Oh
       m. 16 Sep 1906 **Charles W. Allen**
    b. **Mary Ida Moser**, b. 4 Jan 1891, Leavittsburg, Trumbull Co., Oh
       m. 11 Apr 1914 **Walter Lee McClellan**
    c. **Morris Milton Moser**, b. 7 Apr 1893, Leavittsburg, Trumbull Co., Oh
       m. 10 Jun 1915, Warren, Oh, **Evelyn "Lina" Mae Mann**
    d. **Lewis Dewey Moser**, b. 15 Apr 1898, Leavittsburg, Trumbull Co., Oh
       m. 7 Aug 1918 **Vena Rose Swab**

Owen hired **Effie Eloisa Beegle** to care for his motherless children after Lucy's death. Effie was born 9 Oct 1867 in Holmes County, Ohio, daughter of **Joseph Beegle** and **Martha Korns**. Effie and Owen were married on Morris' seventh birthday, 7 Apr 1900. They were the parents of one daughter:

    e. **Helen Clara Moser**, b. 11 Jun 1904, Leavittsburg, Trumbull Co., Oh
       m. 1 Sep 1923 **Lawrence Edwin Eaton** (b. 11 Jan 1901, d. 10 Jun 1992)

Owen died 12 Aug 1915 in Warren City Hospital (now Trumbull Memorial Hospital) from complications following surgery, and is buried in Braceville Cemetery. Effie then married **Warren William Strock** and moved to 278 Dickey Ave., Warren, Ohio, where she died 15 Mar 1941. Helen and Larry lived in the house (located across the street from her half-brother, Morris Moser) until their deaths. Effie and Waren Strock are buried together in North Jackson Cemetery.

D2a. Ethel Pearl Moser Allen

Ethel Pearl Moser, daughter of **Owen Nelson Moser** and **Lucy Manda Long**, was born 29 Dec 1857 on the family farm in Braceville, Trumbull County, Ohio. She married **Charles W. Allen** on 16 Sep 1906 in Trumbull County, Ohio. They made their home in Windham Township, Portage County, Ohio and were the parents of seven children. Ethel died on 15 Apr 1941. Children of Charles and Ethel Allen:

    1. **Lucy Allen**
       b. 18 Mar 1907, Windham Twp., Portage Co., Oh.
       d. 22 Sep 1909, Portage Co., Oh.
    2. **Walter Allen**
       b. 20 Apr 1908, Windham Twp., Portage Co., Oh.
       m. 4 Sep 1929 **Melda Eucher** (b. Jan. 1908)
       d. 30 Oct 1955, Geneva, Ashtabula Co., Oh.
       Children of Walter and Melda Allen:
          a. **Lynn Richard Allen**, b. 18 Apr 1936
          b. **Gary Ross Allen**, b. 15 Apr 1941
          c. **Margaret Louise Allen**, b. 20 Aug 1944
    3. **Mildred Allen**
       b. 15 Dec 1909, Windham Twp., Portage Co., Oh.
       m. 29 Jun 1933 **Elmer Johnson**
       Children of Mildred and Elmer Johnson:
          a. **Donna Lou Johnson**, b. 17 Feb 1938
             m. 16 Apr 1960 **Daniel L. Stickler**

Children of Donna and Daniel Stickler:
>> **Dwight L. Stickler**
>>> b. 11 Oct 1961, Dwight, Ill.
>> **Dwayne Lee Stickler**
>>> b. 19 Feb 1963, W. Richfield
>> **Douglas Lynne Stickler**
>>> b. 31 Jan 1964, Amarilla, Texas
> b. **Patricia Ann Johnson**
>> b. 15 Oct 1939
>> m. **Robert Waller**
>> Children of Patricia and Robert Waller:
>>> **Lou Ann Waller**, b. 10 Jan 1961
>>> **Brian Lynn Waller**, b. 14 Mar 1962
> c. **Judith Lee Johnson**
>> b. 1 Sep 1942
>> m. 7 Aug 1965 **Jim Capirano**

4. **George Newton Allen**
   b. 15 Mar 1913, Windham Twp., Portage Co., Oh.
   m. **Pauline Rising**
   d. 10 Apr 1966
   Children of George and Pauline Allen:
   >> **Fred Allen**
   >> **Marion Allen**
   >> **George Allen**
   >> **Robert Allen**
5. **Marion Moser Allen**
   b. 16 Jun 1916, Windham Twp., Portage Co., Oh.
   m. **Gladys Phillips**
6. **Charles Fredrick Allen**
   b. 23 Sep 1921, Windham Twp., Portage Co., Oh.
   d. 7 Nov 1923, Portage Co., Oh.
7. **Robert Edward Allen**
   b. 7 Oct 1931, Fairview, Michigan
   m. **Doris Knapp**

D2b. Mary Ida Moser McClellan

Mary Ida Moser, second child of **Owen Nelson Moser** and **Lucy Manda Long**, was born 4 Jan 1891 in Leavittsburg, Trumbull County, Ohio. On 11 Apr 1914, she married **Walter Lee McClellan**, born 28 Aug 1890. Children of Mary Ida and Walter:

a. **Eleanor Mary McClellan**
   b. 8 Jan 1914
   m. 3 Nov 1939 **Russell Lewis**
   both died before 1996
   Children of Eleanor and Russell Lewis:
   >> **Rosalyn Lewis**, b. 22 Nov 1942, d. bcf. 1996
   >> **Beverly Lewis**, b. 28 Apr 1946
   >> **James Lewis**, b. 9 May 1948
b. **Harold Lee McClellan**
   b. 1 Feb 1920
   m. 8 Jun 1943 **Mary Howk** (d. 29 Jan 1994)
   Children of Harold and Mary McClellan:
   >> **Terry McClellan**, b. 2 Jun 1945
   >> **Janet McClellan**, b. 5 Dec 1948
   >> **Mary Jane McClellan**, b. 23 Dec 1954213

D3. Morris Milton Moser

Morris Milton Moser, third child of **Owen Nelson Moser** and **Lucy Manda Long**, was born 7 Apr 1893 on the farm in Leavittsburg, Trumbull County, Ohio. He grieved for his mother (who died when he was only six years old) all of his life. He tried to shift his affection to the housekeeper, **Effie Eloisa Beegle**, but was devastated when his father married her. As a result, he never quite accepted his half-sister, **Helen Moser**, eleven years his junior, until a few years prior to his death.

School was very important to Morris. For six years he attended the little one room school house in Leavittsburg where his brother **Dewey Moser** and **Irene Darrow** were also students. Although the teacher tried to convince Owen to send him on for a teaching degree, Owen felt that he needed Morris more on the farm. Irene was more fortunate, and became teacher at Dickey Avenue School in Warren, Ohio for many years. Among her students were **Dorothy Evelyn Moser**, daughter of Morris, and two of her daughters, **Anita** and **Donna Tilton**.

Morris worked on the railroad and as a streetcar conductor prior to his marriage to **Evelyn Mae Mann**. She was born 24 Nov 1889 **Lina Mae Mann**, daughter of **George W. Mann** and **Elizabeth Fox**, but "adopted" the name of "Evelyn" during her teenage years. Evelyn was born and raised on a large farm in Bazetta, Trumbull County, Ohio, moving to Dickey Avenue, Warren, Ohio when her parents separated. Morris and Evelyn were married in a double ceremony with Evelyn's sister, **Bessie Mann** and **Arthur Harper** in Warren.

Morris took his bride to the house he had built for her at 281 Dickey Avenue and went to work as a drill press operator at Taylor Winfield Company in Warren. His love for farming led him to plant many fruit trees around his property as well as a large vegetable garden. The young couple also raised chickens and sold the eggs to their neighbors. Both Morris and Evelyn built several houses on the west side of Warren, which they rented out for many years.

Morris purchased several acres of land on Palmyra Road in Warren, and maintained a truck farm there for many years. (When he sold it during the 1970's, he stipulated that it could not be divided for one hundred years. As a result, in 1998, it was the only undeveloped land in an area surrounded by housing developments!) He planted a very large garden and sold fresh produce to his neighbors during World War II. He kept three or four head of milk cows on the farm, and loved to head off after a hard day at the factory to do his farming chores.

Morris died of a heart condition on 9 Aug 1968 in Warren and is buried in Oakwood Cemetery. Evelyn lived on in the home he built for her until entering a nursing home a few months prior to her death in Warren on 18 Feb 1987 at the age of 98. She had lived nearly twenty years as a widow, and outlived her only daughter by eleven years. Only child of Morris and Evelyn Moser:

> **Dorothy Evelyn Moser**
> b. 26 Jul 1917 at 281 Dickey Avenue, Warren, Trumbull Co., Oh.
> m. (1) 23 Apr 1936 **Howard Mills Tilton**
> (2) 8 Mar 1946 **Thomas Hill Groves**
> d. 6 Dec 1976 at Trumbull Memorial Hospital in Warren
> bur. Oakwood Cemetery

Dorothy Evelyn Moser Tilton Groves

Dorothy Evelyn Moser, only child of **Morris Milton Moser** and **Evelyn Mae Mann**, was born 26 Jul 1917 at her parents home, located at 281 Dickey Avenue, Trumbull County, Warren, Ohio. She attended Dickey Avenue School, where she was instructed by **Irene Darrow**, who had been a classmate of her father. She then attend West Junior High School, Warren G. Harding Senior High School, and Warren Business School. While Dorothy was in highschool, the family of **William Harley Tilton** and **Tuwanda Belle Mills** moved across the street from her. The first time she met **Howard Mills Tilton**, their oldest son, she was hanging upside down on the monkey bars at Dickey Avenue School. Since their other son, **Robert Victor**, was in the same highschool class, the two families soon became friends. The parents would gather at each other's homes for an evening of cards, while Howard kept Dorothy entertained with his music.

Although Howard had never had any formal musical training, his natural talent at the piano led him to dreams of playing professionally. He formed a band and they were able to get hired at a few clubs. However, they were never able to become busy enough to support themselves, and they soon all drifted into the steel mills.

Dorothy was usually a very obedient, well-behaved daughter, always ready to help her mother around the house. She spent most of her time with her studies, practicing on the piano and working around the house. However, on 23 Apr 1936, she and Howard eloped to New Cumberland, West Virginia. Fear set in on the trip home, so that they newly weds returned to their parent's homes, only getting up the courage to tell their families what they had done three months later. The young people then moved into a small house on York Street that was owned by her mother and set up housekeeping. Howard took a job at Republic Steel, a few blocks from their home. After the initial shock wore off, her parents decided to build her a new house on property they owned at the corner of Ward Street and Ohio Avenue. By the time it was finished enough to move in, two daughters had been born to Dorothy and Howard:
1. **Anita Louise Tilton**
    b. 19 Oct 1937, Warren, Trumbull Co., Oh.
2. **Donna Jean Tilton**
    b. 27 Nov. 1938, Warren, Trumbull Co., Oh.
At the time of Anita's birth, Dorothy's hospital roommate was **Mildred Lucille Rogers**, wife of **Willis Alfred Mott**, who gave birth to her second son, **Willis Lloyd Mott**, 21 Oct 1937. As the two men shared many interests in common, the two families became instant friends.

On 4 Jul 1941, Howard, his parents, Dorothy and daughter Anita set off in Howard's brand new Oldsmobile for South Olive, Noble County, Ohio to attend his cousin's wedding. As they were about to leave, Dorothy noticed the bathroom light was still on. Being thrifty by nature, she went back to turn it off. In her absence, Tuwanda moved to the other side of the car so that Dorothy would not have to crawl over her to get back in. They got as far as North Jackson, Trumbull County, Ohio when an oncoming driver went thru the red light at the intersection of Rt. 5. In the panic and confusion, Howard stepped on the gas instead of the brake and a terrible crash occured. Howard was killed instantly, while his mother (seated behind him) died a few hours later in Warren City (now Trumbull Memorial) Hospital. The others were hospitalized for many days with serious injuries. A regular visitor to the hospital rooms of both Dorothy and Anita was Willis Alfred Mott, whose wife was on another floor with her new baby daughter. He brought a doll and much comfort to a frightened three year old girl, who couldn't understand what was happening to her.

When she finally recovered from her injuries, Dorothy worked at the YMCA in Warren. She joined the red cross, and rolled bandages during World War II. She tried her hand at knitting mittens for the troups, but was not successful learning that skill. When the war ended, **Thomas Hill Groves**, son of **Joel Hill Groves** and **Ethel Totterdale**, returned home after serving in the Marine Corp. Joel maintained a steam bath and massage business on Parkman Road in Warren for many years. Dorothy often accompanied her father when he visited the business to ease his aching muscles. Tom was painting the sign out front when they drove up. He soon climbed down the ladder to see just who the cute young lady was. They were married 8 Mar 1946 and Tom moved into the house on Ohio Street. Child of Thomas and Dorothy Groves:

    3. **Margaret Ann "Peggy" Groves**
        b. 14 Jun 1948, Warren, Trumbull Co., Oh.

Dorothy and Tom loved to travel and took many trips once their girls were grown. They also loved dancing, and joined a soon group of cloggers. The group traveled together (in a motor home train!) and gave performances in several states. Dorothy's goal was to visit every state in the US, and she was able to see forty two of them before she died 6 Dec 1976 after a long and courageous fight against cancer. She is buried in Oakwood Cemetery, between Howard Tilton and Morris Moser. Tom rented out the house, remarried and moved to Largo, Florida, where he died 4 Dec 1985. He was cremated and his urn was returned to Warren where it was interred on top of Dorothy's grave.

1. Anita Louise Tilton Mott

Anita Louise Tilton, oldest daughter of **Howard Mills Tilton** and **Dorothy Evelyn Moser**, was born 19 Oct 1937 in City Hospital (now Trumbull Memorial), Warren, Trumbull County, Ohio. Her mother shared the maternity ward with **Mildred Lucille (Rogers) Mott**, who had just given birth to her second son, **W. Lloyd Mott**. The two women soon became friends. When Dorothy left the hospital, she promised that Anita would one day marry the oldest son and that she would have another daughter to marry the newborn son. The two families visited each other often. During one of these visits, Anita fell in awe of the oldest son, **Alfred Roger Mott**. In those days, it was the fad to administer a daily dose of cod liver oil to all young children. Anita hated the taste and did all she could to avoid that punishment. However, as she watched "Roger" (as he was called by the family) take his dose, lick the spoon and ask for more, she decided that he was her hero for ever more.

After her father's death in 1941, the visits with the Mott family became less frequent, and the teenage Anita dated other boys, even becoming engaged to one for a time. Destiny finally prevailed however, and the two were married on 24 Aug 1956 at the First Baptist Church with Rev. Charles French officiating. The young couple moved to Pittsburgh, Pennsylvania where Roger was enrolled in Pharmacy school at the University of Pittsburgh. In 1960, they moved to Indiana, where Roger would eventually obtain a PhD in Pharmacology from Purdue University, and where their first two children were born. Children of Alfred Roger and Anita Mott:

    a. **Vernon Stuart Mott**
        b. 13 Oct 1961, Lafayette, Tippecanoe Co., In.
        m. 1 Sep 1985, New Vernon, Morris Co., In. **Carol Ahl**
        Children of Vernon and Carol Mott:
            1. **Kristin Nicole Mott**
                b. 1 Dec 1988, Morristown, Morris Co., NJ
            2. **Melissa Joyce Mott**
                b. 10 Oct 1992, Morristown, Morris Co., NJ
    b. **Catherine Marie Mott**
        b. 12 Nov 1962, Lafayette, Tippecanoe Co., In.
        m. 18 Jun 1983, Morristown, Morris Co., NJ
        Alan Richard Erickson (b. 30 Jun 1961, Redwing, Mi,
        son of **Elwood Erickson** and **Wilma Sue Evans**)

Children of Catherine and Alan Erickson:
1. **Matthew Alan Erickson**
   b. 16 Jul 1984, Lancaster, Oh.
2. **Emily Anne Erickson**
   b. 13 Nov 1985 Morristown, Morris Co., NJ
3. **Tahlia Sue Erickson**
   b. 12 Jan 1987 Morristown, Morris Co., NJ
4. **Evan Roger Erickson**
   b. 25 Nov 1990 Warren, Trumbull Co., Oh.
5. **Maxwell Thomas Erickson**
   b. 25 Mar 1993 Warren, Trumbull Co., Oh.
6. **Katherine (Cadie) Louise Erickson**
   b. 23 Oct 1994 Warren, Trumbull Co., Oh.

Anita and Roger (now known professionally as "Al") next moved to Sudbury, Massachusetts, stopping off in Ohio long enough for their third child to be born there.

   c. **David Alfred Mott**
   b. 9 Sep 1965, St. Joseph's Hospital, Warren, Trumbull Co., Oh.
   m. 31 Dec 1987, Virgin, Washington Co., Utah
   Tammy Wynett Gifford
   (b. 23 Jul 1968, dau. of **Lawrence Ray Gifford** and
   Tauna Spendlove)
   Child of David and Tammy Mott:
   Jordan Davis Mott
   b. 19 Apr 1993, St. George, Washington Co., Ut.

Al worked as a professor at the Massachusetts College of Pharmacy in Boston, Mass., and at the University of Illinois' Medical campus in Chicago, Illinois, before he decided to move on to the pharmaceutical industry. The family moved to New Jersey, where he was employed by Ciba-Geigy Corporation (now Novartis) in Summit, New Jersey. While there, Anita was surprised by the birth of three more children in her later years:

   d. **Brian Alfred Mott**
   b. 12 Jan 1976, Summit, Morris Co., NJ
   m. 23 Aug 1997, St. George, Washington Co., Ut
   Jennifer Sue Nelson, b. 2 Jan 1979, Las Vegas, Clark, Nev.
   dau. of **Clair Nelson** and **Susan Felton**
   Child of Brian and Jennifer Mott:
   Justin Allen Mott, b. 11 Oct 1998, Orem, Utah Co., Ut

   e. **Dorothy Renee Mott** (twin)
   b. 1 Nov 1977, Summit, Morris Co., NJ
   m. 10 Feb 1996, Hurricane, Washington Co., Ut
   Barry Alexander Oakes, III
   Child of Dorothy and Barry Oakes:
   Kirsten Louise Oakes b. 19 Mar 1997, St. George,
   Washington Co., Ut

   f. **Elizabeth Lucille Mott** (twin)
   b. 1 Nov 1977, Summit, Morris Co., NJ

The members of the family were so impressed with the weather in southern Utah at the time of David's marriage, that they decided to move there when Al retired from Ciba-Geigy. This event came a bit earlier than planned for, due to a company downsizing, and they made the move in June 1993.

2. Donna Jean Tilton Kittle Rable

Donna Jean Tilton, the only other child of **Howard Mills Tilton** and **Dorothy Evelyn Moser**, was born 27 Nov 1938 at St. Joseph's Hospital, Warren, Trumbull County, Ohio. Donna attended Dickey Avenue, West Junior High, Warren G. Harding Senior High and Kent State University, where she majored in English education.

Donna suffered a ruptured appendix at age seven, which required five weeks in the hospital and nearly a year of continued care afterwards. The resulting infection left her unable to have children. She married (1) 27 Jul 1957 **Donald Kittle**, son of **Summie Kittle**, at the First Baptist Church in Warren, with Rev. Charles French officiating. He was born on 14 Feb 1932 in Elkins, W. Va. Donna and Don adopted two children:
- **a. Barbara Jean Kittle**
    - b. 29 Jul 1961 in Mahoning Co., Oh.
    - m. 2 Feb 1980, **Michael Stephen Stredney**
    - Child of Barbara and Michael Stredney:
        - **Melissa Marie Stredney**, 10 Aug 1980, Ohio
- **b. Thomas Gary Kittle**
    - b. 25 Apr 1964, Cleveland, Cuyohoga Co., Oh.
    - m. (1) 6 Sep 1984 **Michella Baker**
    - (2) 24 Dec 1994 **Kammie Davis**
    - Children of Thomas and Shelly Kittle:
        - **Megan Rae Kittle**, b. 31 Mar 1985
        - **Heather Lynn Kittle**, b. 30 Jun 1988
        - **Amber Christina Kittle**, b. 27 Nov 1990
        - **Samantha Kittle**, b. 17 Jan, 1991
    - Children of Thomas and Kammie Kittle:
        - **Bethanie Karolyn Kittle**, b. 1 Dec 1994
        - **Tiffany Noel Kittle**, b. 8 Dec 1995

Donna and Don Kittle were divorced in 1974, after which she married 22 Aug 1974, **Alex Mondak**, who left for California shortly after the marriage. They were divorced in July 1976. Donna then married 12 Jul 1977 in Warren, Ohio, **Andrew Michael Rable**, a surgical nursing assistant at St. Joseph Hospital in Warren. "Mike" died 4 Apr 1991 following surgery. He was the father of a son, **Brian Rable** from a previous marriage. The lonely widow married 26 Mar 1994 **Charles L. Jewel**, whom she divorced in 1996.

Donna spent twenty-five years doing general office work and then had a successful ten year career in advertising with the Tribune, Warren's newspaper. She left that to open a dress shop, but had to close it during her husband's illness and subsequent death. Donna has had several poems published over the years and is currently employed as a home health nurse in Warren.

3. Margaret Ann "Peggy" Groves Weller

Margaret Ann "Peggy" Groves, the only daughter of **Thomas Hill Groves** and **Dorothy Evelyn Moser**, was born 14 Jun 1948 at Trumbull Memorial Hospital in Warren, Trumbull County, Ohio. She attended Dickey Avenue, West Junior High and Western Reserve High Schools is Warren before spending a year at Kent State University. She married (1) 14 Sep 1968 **Ernest Tamarro** (who was also born 14 Jun 1948 at Trumbull Memorial Hospital). They did a bit of traveling while he served in the armed service, but finally settled down in Warren, where their daughter was born:
- **Pamela Tamarro**
    - b. 8 Oct 1971, Trumbull Memorial Hospital
    - m. 2 Jul 1994, Warren, Trumbull Co., Oh
    - **Eric Paul Layfield**

Peggy married (2) 20 Jul 1975 **Lance Jensen** of Jensen's Flower & Gifts, Inc. Because of her creative and artistic talents, Peggy happily went to work in the florist business. Unfortunately, Lance died at an early age, leaving the greiving young widow to run the business alone. Peggy and Lance had no children. Peggy married (3) 8 Apr 1983, **Thomas Weller**, a friend she knew from church. They have continued to successfully operate the business. Tom is the father of two children, born of a previous marriage.

D4. Lewis Dewey Moser

Lewis Dewey Moser, the youngest child of **Owen Nelson Moser** and **Lucy Manda Long**, was born 15 Apr 1898 on the family farm in Leavittsburg, Trumbull County, Ohio. He married 7 Aug 1918 **Vena Rose Swab** in Trumbull County, Ohio. He died in Warren on 21 Dec 1949. Children of Lewis and Vena Moser:
- **a. Lucy Mae Moser** (twin)
  - b. 21 May 1920, Warren, Trumbull Co., Oh.
  - d. shortly after birth
- **b. Lucille Rose Moser** (twin)
  - b. 21 May 1920, Warren, Trumbull Co., Oh.
  - m. 25 Aug 1945 in Silica, Oh. **Ralph Henry Lynn**
  - d. bef. 1976
  - Child of Lucille & Ralph Lynn:
    - **James Nelson Lynn**
      - b. 26 Jul 1954 Warren, Oh

D5. Helen Clara Moser Eaton

Helen Clara Moser, only child of **Owen Nelson Moser** and **Effie Eloise Beegle**, was born 11 Jun 1904 in Leavittsburg, Trumbull County, Ohio. After the death of her father in 1915, she moved with her mother into the house directly across the street from her half-brother, **Morris Moser**. A family feud erupted over the settlement of Owen's estate, so that the two families rarely spoke to each other for nearly fifty years. A truce was reached only a few years prior to Morris' death in 1968.

Helen married 1 Sep 1923 **Lawrence Edwin Eaton** (b. 11 Jan 1901, d. 10 Jun 1992) in Warren. Helen died 7 Jul 1985 in Warren. Children of Helen and Larry:
- **a. Wanda Jean Eaton**
  - b. 17 Jan 1925, Warren, Trumbull Co., Oh.
  - m. (1) 11 Apr 1950, **Donald Frances Butchko** (b. 10 Apr 1926)
  - (2) **Rick Loveredge** (d. bef. 1996)
  - Children of Wanda and Donald Butchko:
    - **1. Debra Jean Butchko**, b. 1950, died young
    - **2. Jeffery John Butchko**, b. 19 Dec 1956
    - **3. Patricia Ann Butchko**, b. 27 Jul 1958
    - **4. Edward Donald Butchko**, b. 7 Aug 1960
      - m. 19 Jul 1982 **Elaine Marie Fulton**
- **b. Eileen Elizabeth Eaton**
  - b. 29 Oct 1926, Warren, Trumbull Co., Oh.
  - m. 23 Nov 1946, Warren, Trumbull Co., Oh.
  - **Emil Joseph Skocik** (b. 12 Aug 1942)
  - Children of Eileen and Emil Skocik:
    - **1. Carol Ann Skocik**, b. 1 Oct 1947
      - m. **Joseph Fasanelli**
      - Children of Carol & Joseph Fasanelli:
        - **Nicolette Fasanelli**
        - **Joseph Fasanelli**

2. **Ellen Jean Skocik**, b. 29 Oct 1948
   m. (1) **Don Clark**
     (2) **Dr. David Brown**
   Children of Ellen & Don Clark:
     Carrie Lynn Clark
     Danielle Clark
   Child of Ellen & David Brown:
     Robert Brown

3. **Michael Skocik**, b. 30 May 1950
   m. (1) **Jill** _____
     (2) **Terri** _____
   Children of Michael and Terri Skocik:
     Michael Skocik
     Joey Skocik

4. **David Skocik**, b. 15 Dec 1954
   Adopted child of David and his wife:
     Jonathan Skocik

5. **Mary Christine Skocik**
   b. 1 Nov 1958
   m. (1) 1975 **Philip Chelsea**
     (2) **John Longberry**
   Child of Mary & Philip Chelsea:
     Philip "Chip" Chelsea
   Children of Mary & John Longberry:
     Joshua Longberry
     Breanna Longberry

6. **Christopher Skocik, Md.**
   b. 4 Oct 1962
   m. **Monica** _____
   Children of Christopher & Monica:
     Jessica Skocik
     Jordanne Skocik
     Natalie Skocik

c. **Beverly Jane Eaton**
  b. 14 Jul 1929, Warren, Trumbull Co., Oh.
  m. 30 Jun 1951, Warren, Trumbull Co., Oh.
  William Leonard Fetterman, (b. 21 Mar 1926, d. 13 Jan 1994)
  d. 11 Dec 1980
  Children of Beverly & William Fetterman:
    1. **Suzette Marie Fetterman**, b. 6 Aug 1954
      m. 2 Jun 1973, **Norman James Darak**
        (b. 28 Jan 1954)
      Children of Suzette & Norman Darak:
        Jayson Matthew Darak, b. 28 Apr 1975
        Lori Marie Darak, b. 2 Oct 1976
        Rebecca Sue Darak, b. 16 Jul 1979
    2. **William Leonard Fetterman, Jr.**, b. 11 Feb 1958
      m. (1) **Tina Gray** (no children)
        (2) 5 Aug 1985 **Janet Elaine Campbell**
      Children of William & Janet:
        Beverly Ann Fetterman, b. 1 Jul 1988
        Troy William Fetterman
          b. 20 Dec 1990, d. 21 Aug 1991

d. Lawrence Edwin Eaton, Jr.
>
> b. 18 Jul 1940, Warren, Trumbull Co., Oh.
>
> m. 21 Oct 1963, Warren, Trumbull Co., Oh.
>
> **Faith Louise Luptak** (b. 12 Jun 1940)
>
> Children of Larry & Faith Eaton:
>
>> **Christine Marie Eaton**, b. 24 Jun 1964
>>
>> **Kathy Ann Eaton**, b. 18 Jun 1966

E. Owen Moser

Owen Moser, son of **Philip Moser** and **Elisabeth Schnobel**, was born 10 Mar 1827 in Lehigh County, Pennsylvania. In "*Trumbull Co. Atlas and Directory, 1899*" he declared that he was born in Allentown. In 1834 he moved from Pennsylvania to Ohio with his family, locating on the McKee farm just south of Warren.

By 1850, both Owen and his brother, David were living in the boarding house of **Lewis** and **Sarah Hoyt** at 684 South Street in Warren, Trumbull County, Ohio. He signed the marriage certificate of his brother in 1851. Owen started in the grocery business, but his place of business was destroyed during the 1860 fire in Warren which nearly wiped out the whole business district. Owen then entered the employ of Anderson & Rupp and traveled extensively for the firm. For a number of years, he ran restaurants on Main Street in Warren and in Leavittsburg. At one time he tried running a hotel in Girard, Ohio. Owen was a Republican, and in 1899 was listed as one of the oldest men living in Warren.

Owen was married 28 Jul 1850 **Laura Lane** in Canfield, Mahoning County, Ohio by the Mayor of Canfield, **John Wetmore**. Laura, born 16 Jan 1830, was the daughter of **John Lane** and **Mary Caldwell**, who went from Ireland to Connecticut, finally settling in Weathersfield, Trumbull County, Ohio. Laura died 28 Dec 1907. Owen died of a stroke 28 Apr 1909 in Warren. They are both buried in Oakwood Cemetery in Warren. Children of Owen and Laura Moser:

1. **Alice L. Moser**
>
> b. 1851, Warren, Trumbull Co., Oh.
>
> d. from measles at 22 mos.
>
> bur. 29 Jan 1853, Oakwood Cemetery, Warren, Oh.

2. **P. A. (Albert) Moser**
>
> b. abt. 1854

3. **Charles W. Moser**
>
> b. 26 Oct 1857, Warren, Trumbull Co., Oh.
>
> m. (1) 30 Aug 1884 **Anna McNulty** (b. 24 Jul 1858)
>
>> (dau. of **Michael** & **Margaret McNulty** of Mt. Savage, Md.)
>>
>> (2) 24 Nov 1909 **Millie L. Wilson**
>
> d. 19 Sep 1921
>
> bur. Oakwood Cemetery
>
> Charles was apprenticed to **Henry Strong** and learned the blacksmith trade. His successful shop was on Canal Street in Warren. He was a and served his community as a member of the Warren City Council in 1894 and as Trumbull County Sheriff in 1905. He was a member of I.O.O.F. Lodge #29, B.P.O.E. #295 and Eagles #311. Known children of Charles and Anna Moser:
>
>> 1. **Fred Jameson Moser**, b. 2 Mar 1886, Warren, Oh
>>
>> 2. **Laura J. Moser**, b. 30 Oct 1887, Warren, Oh
>>
>> 3. **William C. Moser**, b. 12 Jan 1891, Warren, Oh

4. **Lewis K. Moser**
   b. 27 Dec 1859, Warren, Trumbull Co., Oh.
   d. 19 Jan 1861 of croup
5. **Delos Kinney Moser**
   b. 22 Oct 1862, Warren, Trumbull Co., Oh.
   m. 10 Sep 1884 **Rose A. Garghill**
   d. 31 Mar 1941, Warren, Trumbull Co., Oh.
   bur. St. Mary's Cemetery, Warren, Oh.
6. **George Moser**
   b. 1864, Oh., d. between 1893-1907
7. **Daniel B. Moser**
   b. 1866, Oh.
   m. 21 Oct 1890, **Estelle Brobst**
   d. abt. 1907
   Daniel was a Trumbull County Sherrif
   Children of Daniel B. & Estelle Moser:
       John B. Moser, b. 5 Jul 1891
       Alice Moser, b. 1 Jan 1895
       Olive L. Moser, b. 25 Apr 1897
       Owen D. Moser, b. 24 May 1900
           Child of Owen and his wife:
           Owen E. Moser, b. 1933
       Paul Daniel Moser, b. 28 Feb 1903
       Fred J. Moser, b. 26 Jun 1906, d. May 1971, Florida
8. **Edward David Moser**
   b. 7 Aug 1875
   m. 1 Apr 1897 **Anna E. Evans**
   d. Dec. 1907
   Children of Edward D. & Anna Moser:
       Jessie Mae Moser, b. 25 Mar 1890
       Laura O. Moser, b. 29 Mar 1901
       (female) Moser, b. 10 Jan 1905
9. **(male) Moser** (possibly named John.)

E5. Delos Kinney Moser

Delos Kinney Moser, son of **Owen Moser** and **Laura Lane**, was born 22 Oct 1862 in Warren, Trumbull County, Ohio. He received his schooling in the home schools and went to work at the Warren Packard Co. when he ws nineteen years of age. He also became a master of the lumber and planing mill business, joining with **S.B. Loveless** to form the Loveless & Moser Co. The property was sold two years later to the Warren Packard Co. His next venture was in the grocery business, operating the store "Moser & Garghill". Delos joined the volunteer fire brigade when he was twenty years old and was later appointed the first chief of the paid fire department. Delos was a staunch Republican, a member of the Elks, the Eagles, the Modern Woodmen, and the Knights of Columbus, where he was made the first Grand Knight on 5 Jan 1902. He married 10 Sep 1883, **Rose Garghill**, daughter of **Philip** and **Isabella Garghill**. Rose was born in 1855 in Brownsville, Pennsylvania and died 14 May 1890 of complications following childbirth. Delos never remarried after her death. He died 31 May 1931 in Warren, Ohio of heart problems. Delos and Rose are buried in St. Mary's Cemetery in Warren. Children of Delos K. and Rose Moser:

a. **Philip Owen Francis Moser**
   b. 22 Dec 1885, Warren, Trumbull Co., Oh
   bp. 1 Jan 1886, St. Mary's Church, Warren, Trumbull, Oh
   m. 3 Mar 1907, Youngstown, Mahoning, Co., Oh, **Mary C. Cotter**
   d. 6 Jan 1968, Detroit, Wayne Co., Mi

b. **Isabella Moser**
      b. 1 Jan 1889, Warren, Trumbull Co., Oh.
      m. **Charles Richard Sexton**
      She was raised by an aunt in Warren.
      They moved to Birmingham, Alabama.
      Children of Isabella & Charles Sexton:
            John Sexton, b. abt. 1909
            Richard P. Sexton, b. abt. 1910

E5a. Philip Owen Francis Moser

Philip Owen Francis Moser, son of **Delos Kinney Moser** and **Rose Garghill** was born 22 Dec 1885 in Warren, Trumbull County, Ohio. He was baptized 11 Jan 1885 and confirmed 10 May 1898 at St. Mary's Catholic Church in Warren. His mother died in childbirth when he was five years old and he was raised by **Mamie Garghill** (believed to be an aunt). He married **Mary C. Cotter**, daughter of **Edward F. Cotter** and **Catherine Joyce** on 3 Mar 1907 in Youngstown, Mahoning County, Ohio.

Philip worked as a sales engineer for the Modine Manufacturing Co. before going to work at B. F. Goodyear Aerospace of Akron, Ohio. He retired in 1956. He was a member of St. Mary's Church, a fourth degree Bishop of the McFadden Assembly and a life member of the Knights of Columbus, Council #620. Mary died 15 Jan 1958 and Philip died 6 Jan 1968 of heart disease in Detroit, Wayne County, Michigan. Children of Philip and Mary Moser:

1. **Rose Mary Moser**
      b. 12 Oct 1908
      m. 25 Jan 1933, **Elmer Louth**
      d. 13 Oct 1969, Cleveland, Ashtabula Co., Oh
      bur. Calvary Cemetery, Cleveland, Oh
      Children of Rose Mary and Elmer Louth:
            Joyce Louth, b. 23 Feb 1933
                   m. _____ **Rohr**
                Children of Joyce Rohr:
                   Michael Leonard Rohr, b. 4 Aug 1952
                   Kathleen Margaret Rohr, b. 28 Dec 1955
                   Diane Rohr, b. 5 Mar 1957
                   Karen Joyce Rohr, b. 3 Oct 1959
            Nancy Louth, b. abt 1934
2. **Philip Francis Moser**, b. 11 Apr 1911
      m. 22 Jul 1939 **Alice E. Aborgast**
      d. 12 May 1963
      bur. Crown Hill Cemetery, Warren, Trumbull Co., Oh
      Children of Frank and Alice Moser:
            Richard Kenneth Moser, b. 4 Jun 1936
            Children of Richard Moser and his wife:
                Philicia Rae Moser, b. 18 May 1961
                Richard Kenneth Moser, b. 30 Mar 1963
3. **Catherine Jane Moser**, b. 21 Sep 1912
      m. 12 Apr 1936 **George C. Biggers**
      They moved to Atlanta, Georgia. Children of Catherine and George:
            Isabel Rose Biggers, b. 29 May 1937
                m. _____ **Ward** and had 2 sons and 1 daughter
            Mary Katherine Biggers, b. 1938
            George C. Biggers, III, b. 13 Oct 1940
                m. _____
                Child of George and his wife:
                 Clinton Bradley Biggers, b. 11 Oct 1963

4. **Edwin Delos Moser**, b. 29 Sep 1913
   m. 23 Oct 1948, **Carol Hochelt**
   d. 25 Mar 1991, San Diego, California
   Children of Edwin and Carol Moser:
     a. **Edwin Cotter Moser**, b. 25 Jun 1950
       Children of Edwin Moser:
         Brenna Ann Moser, b. 22 Sep 1977
         Alyssa Carol Moser, b. 12 Sep 1979
         Erin Michelle Moser, b. 14 Apr 1981
         Joshua Edward Moser, b. 30 Apr 1984
         Myles David Moser
     b. **Dennis Kevin Moser**, b. 23 Jan 1953
       Children of Dennis Moser:
         Adrienne Megan Moser, b. 22 Feb 1981
         Kevin Raymond Moser, b. 30 May 1984
         Scott James Moser, 29 Sep 1990
     c. **Philip Gerhard Moser**, b. 23 Aug 1958
       Child of Philip Moser:
         Adam Joseph Moser, b. 26 Mar 1984
5. **Isabel Moser**, b. 15 Feb 1916
   m. 10 Jan 1947, **Lester Wallace**
   Children of Isabel and Lester Wallace:
     a. **Mary Kathleen Wallace**, b. 24 May 1948
       m. _____ **Park**
       Children of Mary Kathleen Park:
         Jeffrey Charles Park, b. 19 Apr 1973
         Jennifer Ann Park, b. 27 Apr 1976
         Jacqueline Suzanne Park, b. 29 Aug 1977
     b. **David Burton Wallace**, b. 3 Feb 1950
       Children of David Wallace:
         Michelle Ann Wallace, b. 17 Apr 1976
         Michael David Wallace, b. 15 Jan 1977
     c. **Suzanne Patrice Wallace**, b. 8 Feb 1951
       m. _____ **Clayton**
       Children of Suzanne Clayton:
         Michael Clayton, b. 15 Jan 1977
         David Clayton, b. 21 Mar 1985
6. **Eugene Cotter Moser**, b. 27 Jul 1920
   m. **Dolores Baca** (b. 1944, Albueguerque, New Mexoco)
   d. 26 Jun 1993, Albuequerque, NM
   Children of Gene and Dolores Moser:
     a. **Eugene Joseph Moser**, b. 9 Jan 1947
       Children of Eugene Moser:
         Michella Ann Moser, b. 21 Feb 1975
         James Patrick Moser, b. 19 Mar 1980
         Patrick Michael Moser, 15 Jan 1982
         Benjamin Luis Moser, 21 Jul 1989
         Jessica Claire Moser, b. 22 Sep 1991
     b. **Margaret Jane Moser**, b. 29 Nov 1948
       m. **Robert Hay, II**
       Children of Margaret and Robert Hay:
         Robert Hay, III, b. abt. 1974
         Jennifer Hay, b. abt. 1976

      c. Philip Francis Moser, b. 12 Jan 1950

           Children of Philip Francis Moser:

              David Moser, b. 13 Oct 1973

              Lisa Moser, b. 10 Feb 1979

              Kimberly Moser, b. 8 Jul 1981

    d. Mary Louise Moser, b. 22 May 1951

           m. _____ **Geautreaux**

           Children of Mary Geautreaux:

              Michelle Geautreaux, b. 27 Jun 1978

              Meghan Geautreaux, b. 27 Jun 1981

              Elizabeth Geautreaux, b. 1 Feb 1984

              Matthew Geautreaux, b. 10 Jun 1986

              Monica Geautreaux, b. 15 Jun 1989

    e. Nancy Elizabeth Moser, b. 22 Sep 1953

    f. Patrick Joseph Moser, b. 16 Mar 1958

7. Jane Moser, b. 1923, d. Feb. 1923

8. Thomas Owen Moser, b. 12 Jan 1917

    m. 12 Nov 1941, Warren, Trumbull Co., Oh.

    Dorothy Louise Davis (b. 22 Jan 1920)

    d. 18 Mar 1986, Tucson, Arizona

           Children of Thomas and Dorothy Moser:

              a. Thomas Owen Moser, Jr., b. 5 Jan 1944

                Child of Thomas Owen, Jr.:

                Elyse Marie Moser, b. 15 Mar 1966

              b. Patricia Ann Moser, b. 3 Sep 1946, Akron, Oh.

                m. (1) 11 Aug 1972, Lansing, Mi.

                Gary Laycox Taylor

                (2) 2 Sep 1983, Den Burg, Netherland

                Johannes Albertus Dernison

              c. Daniel Kent Moser, b. 14 Jun 1951

                Children of Daniel Moser:

                Aragorn Shawanesse Moser

                  b. 29 Jun 1970

                Nathan Thomas Moser, b. 19 Dec. 1978

                Joshua James Moser, b. 5 Jun 1981

              e. Karen Sue Moser, b. 10 Mar 1962

G. Lydia Moser Rowe Brobst

Lydia Moser, daughter of **Philip Moser** and **Elisabeth Schnobel,** was born
3 Apr 1836 in Trumbull County Ohio. She married (1) **Jackson Rowe,** a lawyer and
lived in Warren Township between her brothers, Owen and David. Jackson died
between 1870-1880. Known Children of Lydia and Jackson Rowe:

      William Ellis Rowe, b. abt. 1859, Oh.

           d. 26 Sep 1860 in Leavittsburg, Trumbull Co.,

           Oh. of dysentery

      Anne Rowe, b. abt. 1863

      Henry Rowe, b. abt 1865

Lydia married (2) before the 1880 Trumbull County Census **Isaac Brobst,** (son of **John
Brobst** and **Polly** _____), a widower with four children still at home. Known
children of Isaac Brobst, raised by Lydia Moser:

      Mary L. Brobst, b. abt. 1859

      Alice Brobst, b. abt. 1864

      George F. Brobst,   b. abt. 1866

      Lizzie J. Brobst, b. abt. 1868

H. Fiern Anna Moser Hower

Fiern Anna Moser, daughter of **Philip Moser** and **Elisabeth Schnobel,** was born March 1839 in Trumbull County, Ohio. 12 She married 10 Dec 1863, Branch County, Michigan, **Emery Hower/Hauer** (born 28 Feb 1839, Ellsworth Township, Trumbull County, Ohio. He was a son of **Jacob Hower/Hauer** and **Anna Barbara Kimmel,** a younger brother of the **Susan Hower,** who married Fiern's brother, Gideon. Emery became a farmer in Ohio. Emery died 3 May 1903 and is buried in Oakwood Cemetery, Warren, Ohio. Children of Emery and Fiern Anna Moser:

Dora J. Hower, b. abt. 1864
    m. 9 May 1889, Warren, Trumbull Co., Oh **William Griffin**
    They had four children.
        Ada Griffin, b. abt. 1865
        M. Zeffa Griffin, b. 8 Aug 1866
        Nellie K. Griffin, b. abt. 1868
        Arthur E. Griffin, b. 13 Apr 1869
            d. 25 Nov 1898, Warren, Trumbull Co., Oh
        Annie R. Griffin, b. abt. 1872
            m. _____ **Rose**
            d. 6 Aug 1892
            Child: **Elizabeth Rose**
        Henry C. Griffin, b. 6 Jan 1875, d. 8 Aug 1927
            bur. Oakwood Cemetery, Warren, Trumbull Co., Oh
        Lucy S. Griffin, b. 14 Apr 1879

A. Johann Christian Mosser

Johann Christian Moser, according to his deposition filed in support of his Revolutionary War pension application, was born in Berks County, Pennsylvania on 10 Feb 1756. The records of Falkner Swamp Church, New Hanover Township, Montgomery County, Pennsylvania reveal that he was actually born on 10 Feb 1758 and christened on 16 April 1758, and that his parents were **Christian** and **Anna Maria Mosser**.

His father arrived on the "*St. Andrew*" from Rotterdam and took the oath of allegiance 18 Aug 1750 at Philadelphia and was naturalized in 1765, along with his brother, **Peter**. Records of the father's land purchases in Pottsgrove (now Pottstown) began 24 Dec 1755. He died and was buried at Falkner Swamp on 4 Nov 1765. The estate papers were not filed until 1769 because all official recordings were kept on hold until after the repeal of the Stamp Act. His mother married (2) 11 April 1769 **Heinrich Fuchs** at Falkner Swamp. The three brothers, **Peter, George** and **Christian Moser**, sold their father's five acres to their brother-in-law, **George Neiman**, on 13 Mar 1779. The family of Johann Christian and Anna Maria Mosser were:

1. **Barbara Moser**, b. abt. 1734 in Germany
   m. abt. 1759 **George Neiman** (wp. 24 Aug 1803)
   probably son of immigrant **Hans George Neiman**
   of the "*Henrietta*" in 1754.
   Known children of Barbara and John Neiman:
   a. **Johann Philip Neiman**
      b. 15 Mar 1760
      bp. 26 Apr 1760, Falkner Swamp
   b. **Maria Agnes Neiman**
      b. 17 Apr 1762
      bp. 6 Jun 1762, Falkner Swamp
      m. _____ **Bunn**
   c. **Johann Peter Neiman**
      b. 11 Feb 1764
      bp. 22 Apr 1764, Falkner Swamp
      Sponsor: **Peter Moser**, uncle
   d. **Johannes Neiman**
      mentioned in his father's will of 1803
2. **Peter Moser**, b. abt. 1741, Germany
   m. 9 Feb 1767, St.Michaels, Germantown (now Philadelphia),
   Philadelphia Co., Pa. **Margaretha Lamp** (b. abt. 1749, dau. of
   Johannes and **Anna Lamp**, d. bet. 1812-1825.)
   d. 30 May 1829, Amity Twp., Berks Co., Pa.
   Known child of Peter and Margaretha Moser:
   Anna Maria Moser
      b. 13 Apr 1768
      bp. 5 Jun 1768, Falkner Swamp
      Sponsor: **Anna Maria Moser**, grandmother
   Peter enrolled in the Revolutionary War, but was fined as not
   served. He was then double-taxed as a loyalist.
3. **Johann Christian Moser**, b. 20 Feb 1758
   bp. 16 Apr 1758, Falkner Swamp
   m. **Margaretha** _____
      (b. abt. 1645, d. 11 Apr 1830 Centre Square, Montgomery Co., Pa.)
   d. 22 Dec 1838, Swedesburgh, Upper Marion Twp, Montgomery Co., Pa.
   Only living children of Christian and Margaretha Moser:
   (Two other sons died in infancy)

a. Johannes Moser, b. 1 Apr 1789

    bp. 20 Jun 1789, Emmanuel Lutheran Church, Pottstown, Pa.

    m. **Hannah Weidner**

    Had a daughter, **Hannah Moser** who m. **Jacob Spiese.**

b. Elisabeth Moser, b. 2 Dec 1791

    bp. 22 April 1792, Emmanuel Lutheran, Pottstown, Pa.

    m. **Benjamin F. Harry**

    Children of Elisabeth and Benjamin Harry:

        John Harry

        Samuel Harry

        Rees Harry

c. Anna Maria Moser, b. 13 Sep 1793

    bp. 3 Nov 1793, Emmanual Lutheran, Pottstown, Pa.

    m. **Jacob M. Hurst**

    Children of Mary and Jacob Hurst:

        Margaret Hurst

        Jacob Hurst

        Christian Hurst

A DAR application claiming that Christian had another son, **Henry Moser** who married **Mary Clemens**, has been invalidated by the will of Christian Moser. Please see the following page for other invalid information on these children.

B. Hans Michael Mosser/Mauer

Hans Michael Mosser arrived 16 Oct 1751 on the *Duke of Wurtenberg*. It is important to note that while *Strassburger and Hinke* have him listed as **Michael Mosser,** *Rupp* calls him **Michael Mauer.** His signature is included here to let the reader decide. Most of the information available on this man is incorrect, having been fabricated by the coal company in an effort to claim the land of **Burkhard Mosser.** The false information reads as follows:

He was b. 2 Jan 1716, lived in Amityville, Pa., and died there on 27 Jun 1793. He had a wife named **Anna Maria.** His supposed children are:

1. **George Moser**
   b. 1740
   m. 9 May 1782 at Trappe, Montgomery Co., Pa.
   by Rev. Henry Muhlenberg **Margaret Lower**
   (d. Trappe, Pa. the age of 104)
   d. 1807, Montgomery Co., Pa.
   bur. St. John's Cemetery
   According to his will of 1807, this George had no children.
2. **Barbara Moser**
   b. 1735
   m. **George Newman**
   d. 1828, Pottstown, Pa.
   Note: She is the daughter of Christian Moser, not Michael, as was proven by Christian's will.
3. **Peter Moser**
   b. abt. 1742
   Note: This is probably also the child of Christian Moser.
4. **Johann Christian Moser**
   b. 10 Feb 1758
   bp. 16 Apr 1758, Falkner Swamp
   Note: This is the son of Christian Moser.
5. **Burkhard Moser**
   b. 1748
   unmarried
   d. near Tamauqua, Pa.

This is the fake Burkhard, made up by the coal company. He was supposedly an eccentric old bachelor who lived as a hermit in the hills. It was said that he died and was buried on his land by the neighbors who found him. However, this has never been substantiated, and the land in question belonged to Burkhard, son of **Hans Martin Mosser.**

signature of Hans Michael Mosser

C. Michael Moser

Michael Moser (<u>possibly</u> the son of **Simon** and **Christina Moser**, b. 18 Jun 1765 and baptized 30 Jun 1765 in the Heidelburg Church, was born in 1765 and married **Barbara Kistler**, widow of **Philip Brobst**. They lived in Unionville Township, North Whitehall, Bucks Co. (now Schuylkill), Pennsylvania and were the parents of the following children:

1. **Maria Barbara Moser**
   b. 7 Jan 1780
   bp. 4 Feb 1780, Schlossers Reformed, N. Whitehall, Pa.
   m. **Peter Frey**
2. **Margaretha Moser**
   b. 4 Apr 1783
   bp. 21 Apr 1783 Schlossers Reformed, N. Whitehall, Pa.
   m. **Jacob Peter**
   Children of Margaretha and Jacob Peter:
     a. **Elisabeth Peter**
        b. 13 Oct 1802
        bp. 5 Sep 1802, Heidelberg, Pa.
     b. **Daniel Peter**
        b. 4 Apr 1806
        bp. 14 May 1806, Heidelberg, Pa.
        sponsors: **Philip Moser & Catherine Hausman**
     c. **Magdalena Peter**
        b. 22 Apr 1807
        bp. 10 May 1807, Heidelberg, Pa.
     d. **Abraham Peter**
        b. 10 Oct 1807
        bp. 24 Oct 1807, Heidelberg, Pa.
        Sponsors: **Abraham Moser & Maria Hoatz**
     e. **Jonas Peter**
        b. 8 Apr 1809
        bp. 7 May 1809, Heidelberg, Pa.
     f. **Susanna Catharina Peter**
        b. 1 Jun 1811
        bp. 17 Jun 1811, Heidelberg, Pa.
        m. **Jacob Moser**, son of **Jacob Moser**
                   and _____ **Oswald**
3. **Daniel Moser**
   b. 6 Oct 1784
   bp. 6 Nov. 1784, Schlossers Reformed, N. Whitehall, Pa.
   Sponsors: **John & Maria Eva Kistler**
   m. **Maria** _____
4. **Philip Moser**
   b. 14 Apr 1786
   m. **Catharine Mohr** (b. 14 Mar 1787, d. 2 Feb 1862)
   d. 23 May 1855, Unionville, Lehigh Co., Pa.
   bur. Neff's Cemetery, Unionville, Lehigh Co., Pa.
   They had a son:
     John Moser
        b. 21 Nov 1812
        d. 6 Oct 1876 Schuylkill Co., Pa.
        m. **Abigail Sensinger** (dau of **John & Maria
           Barbara Sensinger** (b. 5 Sep 1812, d. 3 Oct 1858)
        Bur. Ebenezer Church, Lehigh Co., Pa.

Children of John & Abigail Moser:

Polly Moser, b. abt. 1831
   m. **Israel Meyerle**
Lydia Moser, b. abt. 1833
   m. **David Steigerwald**
David Moser, b. abt. 1835
Feyanna Moser, b. 29 Oct 1836
   bp. 4 Dec 1836, Schlossers
      Reformed Sponsors: **Nicholas**
      & Elisabeth Hensinger
Jacob Moser, b. 13 Mar 1838
   bp. 23 Apr 1838, Schlossers
      Reformed Sponsors: **Philip &**
      Catharine Moser,
   m. **Susan Gilbert**
Levina Moser
   b. 3 May 1849
   bp. 24 Dec 1860, Ebenezer Church
   d. 24 Dec 1860
Sarah Ann Moser
   b. 23 Feb 1844 New Tripoli, Lehigh, Pa.
   m. 8 Jun 1868 **Amandes Ebert**
   d. 5 May 1919, New Tripoli, Lehigh
Angelina Moser
   b. 1 Apr 1860, New Tripoli, Lehigh, Pa.
   d. 16 Feb 1896, Allentown, Lehigh, Pa.
Amanda Moser
   b. 1 Apr 1860, New Tripoli, Lehigh., Pa.
   m. 1 Jul 1888 **John Miller**

5. **Abraham Moser**
   b. 28 Jan 1788
   bp. 13 Mar 1788, Heidelberg Lutheran
   Sponsors: **Kistler & Wife**

D. Thirteen More Michael Mosers

1. **Michael Moser** and **Anna Maria**, and had a son, **Emanuel Moser** baptized at Falkner Swamp on 21 Aug 1764.

2. **Michale Moser** and **Mariga** (possibly **Horner**) had three children baptized at Ebeneezer Church:
> **Johannes Moser**, b. 4 Nov. 1785, bp. 27 Nov 1785
> Sponsors: **Jacob & Catharina Barbara Horner**
> **Elisabetha Moser**, b. 6 Sep 1790, bp. 26 Dec1790
> **Maria Magdalena Moser**, b. 18 Dec 1799, bp. 22 Feb 1801
> Sponsors: **Jacob & Catharina Barbara Horner**

3. **Michael Moser** (no wife listed), had the following child baptized:
> **Philip Moser**
>> b. 24 Jun 1773
>> bp. 4 Jul 1773, Lehigh Co., Pa.
>> Sponsors: **Philip Peter & Wife**

4. **Michael** and **Catharina Moser** had:
> **Philip Moser**
>> b. 22 Dec 1793
>> bp. 12 Jun 1840, Ebeneezer Church, Lehigh Co., Pa.
5. **Michael** and **Elisabeth Moser** had:
> **Lydia Moser**, bp. 23 Sep 1804, Schlossers, Unionville, Pa.
> **Jacob Moser**, b. 12 Sep 1810, bp. 18 Nov 1810
> Sponsors: **Abraham & Catharine Moser**

6. **Michael** and **Barbara Moser** sponsored a child at the Jerusulam Lutheran Church, Berks County, Pennsylvania in 1795. (Not Barbara Kistler).

7. **Michael Moser**, son of **Peter** and **Catharine Moser**, was baptized in 1792. His sponsors were **Paul** and **Magdalena Moser**.

8. **Johann Michael Moser** m. **Barbara Bollweber**, 1714, in Wuertt, Jagstkiers, Bopfingen, Germany.

9. **Michael** and **Eva Moser** had the following children baptized in Unionville:
> **Magdalene Moser**, 1795
> **Elisabeth Moser**, 20 Jul 1798, d. 24 May 1798
> **Margareth Moser**, 11 Jun 1800

10. **Michael** and **Sophia Moser** had **John Jacob Moser** baptized in Heidelberg in 1782

11. **Johan Michael Moser**, son of **Johann Michael Moser** and **Wife** was baptized in 1761 at the Jordan Lutheran Lutheran Church Weissberg Township, Pennsylvania.

12. **Michael Moser**, married **Sarah Wohlford**. He was born in Centre County, Pennsylvania in 1844.

13. **Michael Musser** married **Catherine Musser** (daughter of **John J. Moser**) and went to Stephenson County, Illinois.

E. The Mosers Of The *Adventure*

The "Adventure", arrived in Philadelphia on 23 Sep 1732 from Rotterdam. The ship master, **Robert Curson,** had kept one of the earliest detailed passenger lists available today. Several Mossers were listed among the passengers. The following list refers to lists as published by Strassburger and Hinke (1), Walter Allen Knittle (2) and new research done by Lila Robinson of Matla, Montana, who claims they were all from Eckerweiler, Rotenburgischen, Germany (3).

Males: **George Mosser (48) (no age) (not listed)**
       Michael Mosser (38) (40) (38)
       Tobias Mosser (30) (not listed) (30)
       Leonart Mosser (no age) (not listed) (no age)
       Paulus Mosser (no age) (24) (no age)
       John Mosser (not listed) (23) (not listed)

Males under sixteen:
       Bastian Mosser (6) (no age) (6)
       Simon Mosser (11) (no age) (not listed)
       Hans George (8) (12) (12)

Females: **Eve Mosser (40) (not listed) (40)**
       Eva(n) Barbara Mosser (16) (40) (16)
       Christian Mosser (24) (34, listed as Christina) (not listed)
       Magdalena Mosser (28) (28, listed as Matthew) (not listed)
       Susanna Mosser (40) (53, listed as Susan Barbara) (40)
       Meirna Mosser (not listed) (28) (not listed)
       Hanna Margaret Mosser (12) (12) (not listed)
       Anna Maria Mosser (10) (10) (not listed)
       Anna Margaret Mosser (8) (8) (not listed)

Perhaps a fresh look at the original documents would be helpful.

1. Johann Michael Moser

Johann Michael Moser arrived 23 Sep 1732 on the *Adventure* when he was thirty eight years old, according to Strassburger and Hinke , or forty years old, according to Walter Allen Knittle. According to Lila Robinson, a researcher recently hired to do research in Germany, he was born 4 Mar 1690 in Weissenkirchberg, Bavaria, Germany, and was a son of **Adam Moser** and **Maria Strobel** . He married **Susanna Barbara Baumann** (also on the *Adventure*) 24 Oct 1719 in Germany, who must have died shortly after their arrival. Rev. Johann Casper Stoever declared that the Michael Moser of the *Adventure* married on 6 Jun 1734 **Ursula Dumb** in New Goshenhoppen, Pennsylvania. (It is possible that the wife was **Ursula Stumb,** as there were other Stumb families (and no one else surnamed Dumb!) in the area at that time. Since the European letters "St" can often be confused with a present day capital letter "D", it would have been a simple mistake to make.) Ursula was probably his second wife.

One researcher has declared that they had two sons, named Michael. This is doubtful, as he was already seventy-three years old and Ursula must have been at least fifty when the two Michaels were born. The two Michaels are:
       Michael Johann Moser, bp. 1765, m. **Catharina Wassum**
       Johann Michael Moser, b. 1765, m. **Barbara Kistler**

[signature]

2. Simon Moser

Simon Moser was also a passenger on the *Adventure*. He was naturalized 30 Sep 1765 and lived in Falkner Swamp, then in Lynn, Northampton County, Pennsylvania. Simon bought 203 acres of land in Heidelberg (now Lehigh County) in 1748. In 1766, he purchased an additional 33 acres from **Frederick Moser** (son of **Hans Martin Moser**). Strassburger and Hinke list his arrival age as eleven, making his date of birth about 1721. Simon had a wife named **Christina**, with whom he sponsored children in 1762, 1764, 1766 and 1767 at the Heidelberg Lutheran Church. They were the parents of two known chidren:

> **Christina Margaret Moser**
>> b. 1 Oct 1758
>> bp. at the Lehigh Church near Alburtis
>
> **Johan Michael Moser**
>> b. 18 Jun 1765
>> bp. 30 Jun 1765, Heidelberg Lutheran Church, Lehigh, Pa.

Signature of Simon Mosser

3. Sebastian Moser

Sebastian Moser, another passenger on the *Adventure*, arrived at the age of six. He married 29 Mar 1748 at New Hanover Church in Lehigh County, Pennsylvania, **Susanna Hill**. He took land in New Tripoli in 1750, which he sold to a **Philip Moser** 10 Jun 1761. According to the records of Bob Kunkel, Sebastian died 10 Nov. 1784 at the age of fifty eight and is buried at the New Hanover Church Cemetery. Sebastian and Susanna had the following children baptized at the New Hanover Church:

> **Johannes Moser**, bp. 3 Jul 1748
> **John George Moser**, b. 25 Feb 1760, bp. 11 Apr 1760
> **Paulus Moser**, bp. 5 Jun 1763
> **Jacob Moser**, b. 1766

Note: If these children really belong to this Sebastian and Susanna, were there other children born between 1748 and 1766?

4. George Philip Moser

George Philip Moser, also a son of **Adam Moser** and **Maria Strobel**, born 24 Apr 1683, was forty-eight years old when he arrived in Philadelphia aboard the *Adventure*. He married **Eva Ebert** (age forty on the *Adventure*, dau of **Michael Ebert**), in Eckartsweiler, Germany 19 Mar 1712. Eva died 10 May 1762. They are buried at Augustus Lutheran Church, Trappe, Pennsylvania.

Signature of George Philip Mosser

5. Lorentz (Leonard) Moser

This **Lorentz Moser** also arrived on the *Adventure* in 1732. He is among the males over sixteen in the ship's manifest. He married 30 Jan 1744 **Maria Sara Kocher**. He was confirmed a member of the Graceland, Maryland Moravian Church on 8 Oct 1758, where a Maria Sara (possibly his second wife) is listed as a probationerand confirmed on 11 Jan 1761. These four are probably children of Maria Sara Kocher:

a. Anna Margaretha Moser
  b. Feb. 1745, Pa.
  m. (1) **Henry Demuth**
    (2) 6 Apr 1786 **Peter Freiser**
b. Leonard Moser m. **Maria Elisabeth Schenkel**
c. Peter Moser
  b. 23 Jun 1743, Pa.
  m. (1) **Catherine Volk/Folk** (d. 9 Sep 1805)
    (2) **Margaret** _____
  d. 4 Feb 1821
d. Jacob Moser
  b. abt 1754, Pa., d. 2 Jul 1813

He married (2) **Maria Sarah Binkley** (daughter of **Peter Binkley** and **Maria Anna Werle**, b. 24 Sep 1733 in Switzerland). Their children were:

e. John Michael Moser
  b. 1 Aug 1759 at 2:30 am
  bp. 5 Aug 1759, Graceland Moravian Church, Md.
  m. 3 Feb 1785 **Catherine Koller**
  d. 11 Jun 1816
  Had a daughter, **Elisabeth Moser**, b. abt. 1777.
  They went to Kreagerstown, Md. in 1789.
f. Samuel Moser
  b. 11 Apr 1761
  bp. 12 Apr 1761, Graceland Moravian Church, Md.
g. Francis Moser
  b. 15 Mar 1763 at 9:00 am
  bp. 17 Mar 1763, Graceland Moravian Church, Md.
  m. (1) **Elisabeth Miller**
    (2) 1 Oct 1820, **Mary Sipes**
h. Christian Moser
  b. 5 Jan 1765 at 11:00 pm
  bp. 6 Jan 1765, Graceland Moravian Church, Md.
  m. **Elisabeth Fuller**
i. Anna Elizabeth Moser
  b. 30 Jan 1767 at 8:00 am
  bp. 1 Feb 1767, Graceland Moravian Church, Md.
  m. **John Jacob Hess**
j. Henry Moser
  b. 12 Sep 1769 in the afternoon
  bp. 17 Sep 1769, Graceland Moravian Church, Md.
  m. **Magdalene Schenkel**
  d. 1820
  He went to Kreagerstown, Md. with his brother, Michael about 1778, before settling in Stokes County, North Carolina.
k. Joseph Moser
  b. 21 Jul 1772 at 8:00 am
  bp. 26 Jul 1772, Graceland Moravian Church, Md.
  d. 17 Apr 1773, bur. 18 Apr 1773, Moravian Cemetery, Graceland, Md.

l. **Christina Moser**
    b. 17 Mar 1774, Md.
m. **Sarah Moser**
    m. before 1778, **Johann Adam Volk**
n. **John Moser**
    b. 3 Jun 1776, Stokes Co., N.C.
    bp. Moravian Church, Bethania, N.C.
    m. (1) **Mary Smithe**
      (2) 12 Aug 1824, **Thaleta Wagner**

Leonard's will is dated 16 Jul 1782, in which is mentioned his wife, Sarah and his children. Also mentioned are daughters **Sarah** and **Christina** (no other records found for these two daughters). Leonard died 18 Jul 1782, just two days after making the will. After his death, Sarah married **Edward Bartley**.

signature of Lorentz Mosser

5b. Leonard Moser

Leonard Moser, son of **Leonard Moser** and his first wife, **Maria Sara Kocher** was born prior to his father joining the Moravian Church in Graceham, Maryland. He married **Maria Elisabeth Schenkel**. A child named **Christian Moser** was born 16 Apr 1767 and baptized 26 May 1767 at Falkner Swamp, Lehigh County, Pennsylvania, whose parents are listed as Leonard and Maria Elisabeth Moser. It is not known if this is the same Leonard. However, when the following children were baptized at the Moravian Church, they were listed as "Lutherans". At least two other children must have been born before the Christian, listed as "4" below.

  3. **Leonard Moser**, b. 17 Sep 1785
  4. **Christian Moser** (listed as their fourth son)
      b. 22 Dec 1787, bp. 27 Dec 1787
  5. **Margaret Moser**
      b. 24 Dec 1797, bp. 21 Jan 1798
      m. **Jonas Nathanael Eyler**
  6. **Sophia Theresa Moser**
      b. 25 Dec 1802, bp. 30 Dec 1802
      m. **Jonas Nathanael Eyler**
  7. **Elizabeth Christina Moser**
      b. 7 Sep 1805, bp. 20 Oct 1805
      m. **David Wilhide**
  8. **Elias Moser**
      b. 24 Feb 1809, bp. 23 Apr 1809
  9. **Magdalena Moser** (no dates given)
      m. **Jeremiah Maloney**
      Magdalena had a son by **Jacob Wilhide**. (no dates given)
      Known children of Jeremiah & Magdalena Maloney:
          Elisabeth Maloney, b. 24 Apr 1809, bp. 7 Jun 1809
          Sarah Maloney, b. 30 Jan 1811, bp. 31 Mar 1811
Other possible children of Leonard and Maria Elizabeth are:
          Henry Moser, b. 23 Aug 1794, d. 18 Jul 1853
          Catherine Moser, b. 30 Jun 1800

5j. Henrich Moser

Henrich (Henry) Moser, son of **Leonard Moser** and **Sarah Maria Binkley**, was born 16 Sep 1769 in Graceham, Maryland. He spent three years in North Carolina with his parents before going to Keagerstown, Maryland to live with his married brother, Michael. In 1789, Michael moved his family to Stokes County, North Carolina, and Henry again went along. He married before 1802 **Magdalena Schenkel**. In 1805 he purchased land in Benzcin, just three miles from the farm of another brother, Peter. Four of his children were baptized at the Bethania Moravian Church:

1. **Peter Moser**, bp. 21 Nov 1802
2. **Johann Leonard Moser**, bp. 11 Mar 1804
   Sponsors: **Adam** and **Christina (Moser) Geiger**
   m. **Elizabeth Scott**
   Children of Leonard and Elizabeth Moser:
   > **William Moser**, b. 1830
   > **John L. Moser**, b. 1836
   > **James R. Moser**, b. 1838
   > **Sarah Catherine Moser**, b. 1844

John Moser

John Moser (possibly a son of **Leonard Moser** and **Maria Elizabeth Schenkel**, m. **Hannah Ruth Williams**, who was baptized 26 Jun 1815 as an adult. They had the following children baptized at the Graceland Moravian church:

1. **David Moser**, b. 4 Feb 1808, bp. 24 Apr 1808
2. **John Moser**, b. 29 Sep 1809, bp. 12 Nov 1809
3. **Amy Moser**, b. 25 Mar 1812, bp. 31 May 1812
4. **William Moser**, b. 7 May 1814, bp. 16 Mar 1817
   > m. **Martha "Mattie" Gough** (b. 29 Apr 1816, d. 8 Dec 1905)
   > d. 13 Sep 1881
   > Child of William and Mattie Moser:
   > > **John Percival Moser**
   > > b. 5 Jul 1844, Emmitsburg, Md.
   > > m. **Elizabeth Delilah Barton**, dau of **Hammond Barton** and **Harriet Fogle** (b. 5 Dec 1851, d. 18 Nov 1931, Emmitsburg, Md.)
   > > d. 1 Feb 1905, Emmitsburg, Md.
5. **Thomas Moser**, b. 18 Nov 1816, bp. 16 Mar 1817
6. **Cyrus Moser**, b. 22 Dec 1821, bp. 7 Apr 1822
   > m. **Susan Heffner**
   > They lived in Mechanicstown, Maryland.
   > Children of Cyrus and Susan Moser:
   > > a. **Phoebe Ann Moser**, b. 10 May 1846, bp. 2 Jun 1846
   > > b. **Ruth Ann Amelia Moser**, b. 14 Jan 1854, bp. 16 Feb 1854
   > > d. 17 Feb 1854, bur. Apple's Church, Maryland
   > > c. **Agnes Savanah Moser**, b. 2 Aug 1860, bp. 10 Aug 1860
   > > d. **Charles Cyrus Moser**, b. 20 Apr 1863, bp. 31 Jul 1863
7. **Mary Ann Moser**, b. 24 Jan 1824, bp. 27 Jan 1824

A **Susanna Herzog Moser**, daughter of **Anna Catharina Herzog**, had an illegitimate son, **Alfred Moser**, b. 13 Jun 1852, bp. 30 Jan. 1853 at Graceland, who d. 28 Jan 1854. The father was **Joseph Alfred Wilhide**, son of **David Jacob Wilhide** and **Elisabeth Christina Moser**.

6. Tobias Moser

Tobias Moser, according to two different sources, was age thirty when he arrived in Philadelphia on the *Adventure*. He was born in Germany in 1702 and died in Pennsylvania in 1757. Tobias married 29 Jan 1734 in Goshenhoppen, Pennsylvania, **Ursula Margaretha Meyer**. He died 14 Apr 1757 in Lowhill, Northampton County, Pennsylvania. They are buried in the Lowhill Cemetery. Grave stones give his birth as 6 Aug 1702 and hers as 10 Sep 1704. Tobias was a land owner in what is now Lehigh County, Pennsylvania. Known children of Tobias and Margaretha Moser:

  a. Johannes Moser
     b. 24 Jun 1741, Guthsville, Pa.
     bp. 14 Jul 1741, Jordan Lutheran Church
     sponsors: **Johann & Barbara Lichtenwallner**
     m. 19 Jul 1762, Guthsville, Lehigh, Pa., **Elisabeth Moyer**
     d. 11 Oct 1810, Lowhill, Lehigh Co., Pa.
     Children of Johannes & Elisabeth Moser:

      1. Christina Moser
        b. 27 Oct 1765, Guthsville, Pa.
        bp. 27 Oct 1765, Jordan Lutheran
        Sponsors: **Tobias & Christina Moser**
      2. Johannes Moser
        b. 3 Oct 1766, Guthsville, Pa.
        bp. 2 Nov 1766, Jordan Lutheran
        Sponsors: **Tobias & Christina Moser**
        m. 5 Feb 1793, Guthsville, Pa., **Maria B. Moyer**
        d. 26 Apr 1811, Moserville, Lehigh, Pa
      3. John Martin Moser
        b. 4 May 1778, Guthsville, Pa.
        bp. Jordan Lutheran (no date given)
        Sponsors: **Tobias & Christina Moser**
        d. 21 Dec 1778, Guthsville, Pa.
      4. Maria Barbara Moser
        b. 7 Nov 1780, Guthsville, Pa.
        bp. 20 Nov 1781, Jordan Lutheran
        Sponsors: **Tobias & Christina Moser**
      5. Elisabeth Moser
        b. 1 Oct 1786, Guthsville, Pa.
        bp. Jordan Lutheran (no date)
        Sponsors: **Tobias & Christina Moser**

  b. Tobias Moser
     b. 26 May 1743, Guthsville, Lehigh Co., Pa.
     bp. 26 Jun 1743, Jordan Lutheran, Whitehall, Lehigh, Pa.
     m. 31 May 1764, **Christina Lichtenwallner**, daughter of
     Johannes and **Barbara Lichtenwallner**
     Children of Tobias and Christina Moser:

      1. Maria Catharina Moser
        b. 12 Apr 1766, Guthsville, Lehigh, Pa.
      2. Elisabetha Moser
        b. 26 Dec 1768, Guthsville, Lehigh, Pa.
        bp. 15 Jan 1769, Jordan Lutheran
        Sponsors: **Johannes & Elisabeth Acker**
      3. (female)
        b. 13 Aug 1771, Guthsville, Lehigh, Pa.
        bp. 18 Aug 1771, Jordan Lutheran
        Sponsors: **Johannes & Elisabeth Acker**

4. **Tobias Moser**
> b. 25 Apr 1781, Guthsville, Lehigh, Pa.
> bp. 4 May 1781, Jordan Lutheran
> Sponsors: **Johannes & Elisabeth Acker**
> m. **Maria Magdalena _____**
> Children of Tobias & Magdalena:
>> **Jonas Moser**, b. 2 Aug 1804
>> **Judith Moser**, b. 27 Sep 1806
>> **Salome Moser**, b. 3 Nov 1808
>> **Hannah Moser**, b. 14 Sep 1815

5. **Daniel Moser**
> b. 8 Feb 1785, Pa.
> bp. 27 Feb 1785, Jordan Lutheran
> Sponsors: **Johannes & Elisabeth Acker**
> m. **Magdalena Seiss**
> Known children of Daniel and Magdalena:
>> **David Moser**, b. 23 Jan 1814, Lowhill, Pa.
>> **Susanna Moser**, b. 14 Nov 1829, Lowhill, Pa.

c. **John Jacob Moser**
> b. 25 Jul 1747, Guthsville Pa
> bp. 16 Aug 1747, Jordan Lutheran (No sponsors listed)

b. **Johann Michael Moser**
> b. 19 Aug 1749, Guthsville
> bp. 27 Aug 1749, Jordan Lutheran
> Sponsors: **Michael & Anna Margaretha Moser**
> m. (1) **Catharina _____**
> (2) **Eva Burz/Boorz**
> Michael was a miller and lived at Cedar Creek.
> Children of Michael & Catharina:
>> 1. **Michael Moser**
>>> b. 25 Nov 1765, Pa.
>>> bp. Jordan Lutheran
>>> Sponsors: **Tobias & Christina Moser**
>>> (It has been claimed that this is the Michael who married **Barbara Kistler**, but this is not proven.)
>> 2. **Elisabetha Moser**
>>> b. 10 Aug 1778, Pa.
>>> bp. 18 Oct 1778, Christ Lutheran Reformed Shoenersville, Lehigh, Pa
>> 3. **Johann Moser**
>>> b. 10 Sep 1780, Pa.
>>> bp. 29 Oct 1790, Christ Lutheran Reformed Shoenersville, Lehigh, Pa
> Children of Michael & Eva:
>> 4. **John Heinrich Moser**
>>> b. 12 Feb 1786, Pa.
>>> bp. 12 Mar 1786, Jordan Lutheran Reformed Shoenersville, Lehigh, Pa
>> 5. **Magdalene Moser**
>>> b. 23 Dec 1795, Pa.
>>> bp. 28 Mar 1796, Schlossers Reformed, Unionville, North Whitehall, Pa.
>> 6. **Elisabeth Moser**
>>> b. 7 Feb 1798, Pa.
>>> bp. 17 May 1798, Schlossers Reformed, Unionville, North Whitehall, Pa.
>> 7. **Esther Moser**

The will of this Tobias Moser (#144) was administered in 1757, Folks Township., Northampton County, Pennsylvania.

Signature of Tobias Mosser

Note: A Tobias Moser was listed on the 1772 Lowhill, Northampton (now Lehigh) County, Pennsylvania tax list as a farmer. In 1785, a Tobias owned a distillery and 135 acres in Lowhill. In 1790, there were two men named Tobias living in Lowhill, Pennsylvania. One had a wife and one son, while the other had a wife, three daughters and two sons. One of them left a will (#1991) in 1800 in Lowhill, Northampton County (now Lehigh) County. A look at this will might help to clarify which Tobias is which. Another will for a Tobias Moser is #5378, made in 1845.

F. Peter Moser

There are two Mennonites named **Peter Moser**, father and son, on the Palatine
Mennonite Census lists, dated 1664-1793. They came to Philadelphia, Pennsylvania in
1747 on the *Restauration* from Schrockenhof, Switzerland. The father was fifty-seven
and had a broken bone at the time; the son was thirty. The son became the father of at
least three sons, **Peter, Jacob** and **Henry**. A <u>possible</u> son of Peter (the son above) is:
(see pp. 132 & 133 for other possibilities)

1. **Peter Moser**
   b. about 1742, Germany or Pa.
   m. _____ **Dietz**
   d. 1829 Pottstown, Montgomery, Pa.
   Children of Peter Moser:
   a. **John Moser**
      m. 1793 **Hanna Weidner**
      Children of John and Hanna Moser:
      1. **Peter Moser**, b. abt. 1742
         m. **Magdaline Horlacher II**
      2. **Mary Moser** . _____ **Bunn**
      3. **Margaret Moser** _____ **Weidner**
      4. **Elizabeth Moser** _____ **Bunn**
      5. **Eleanor Harrison Moser** _____ **Green**
   b. **Peter Moser**, b. 29 Nov 1796
      m. **Elisabeth Rohrer**
      d. 2 Jul 1848
   c. **Jacob Moser**, b. abt. 1785, Pa.
      m. **Elisabeth Gresh**
      d. 1843, Amityville, Pa.
      He was a farmer at Monocacy Hill.
      Children of Jacob and Elisabeth:
      1. **Henry Moser**
      2. **Margaret Moser** m. **Israel Boyer**
      3. **George G. Moser**, b. abt. 1820, Pa.
         m. **Willi deTruck**
         Children of George and Willi:
         a. **Thompson Moser** (died young)
         b. **Emma Moser**
            m. **Martin Groff**
         c. **Margaret Moser** (no issue)
         d. **Esther Moser**
         e. **Ira Moser, M.D.** b. abt 1855
            d. 1907, Reading
         f. **Willi Moser** m . **Samuel**
            Francis Sassman
         g. **Henry G. Moser**
            b. abt 1860, Perry Co.
            m. **Margaret Sasaman**
      4. **Eliza Moser** (2nd wife of **Israel Boyer**)
      5. **Peter Moser** (lived in Pottstown, Pa.)
      6. **Sarah Moser** m. **Joshua Gehr**
      7. **Jeremiah Moser** m. **Rebecca Epler**
      8. **Mary Moser** m . **John Coover**
      9. **Angeline Moser** m. **Henry Walter**
      10. **Harriet Moser** (never married)
      (and four others who died young)

d. **Anna Maria Moser** m. _____ **Greiger**
e. **Catherine Moser** m. _____ **Pyfer**
f. **Hanna Moser** m. _____ **Weidner**
g. **Margaret Moser** m. _____ **Neidig**
h. **Eliza Moser** m. _____ **Yokum**
    they went to Ohio
i. **Anna Moser** m. _____ **Egolf**
j. **Lydia Moser** m. _____ **Brunner**

G. Hans Moser of Bavaria, Germany

Hans Moser was born about 1623 and died 26 Sep 1696 in Bavaria, Germany. He married **Maria** _____ (died 30 Jul 1686 in Bavaria) in 1652, Weissenkirchberg. They were the parents of the following known children:

1. **Adam Moser**
   - b. 14 Jul 1653, Hetzweiler, Bavaria, Germany
   - m. 26 Mar 1675 **Maria Strobel**, of Kloster Sulz, in the Weissenkirchberg Church
2. **Johann Phillip Moser**
   - b. 30 Jun 1656, Hetzweiler, Bavaria
   - m. 4 Aug 1689 **Rosina Mittelmeyer** (d. 17 Nov 1742)
   - d. 21 Aug 1727, Hetzweiler, Bavaria
3. **Johann Michael Moser**
   - b. 19 Pct 1658, Hetzweiler, Bavaria
   - m. 15 Jul 1683 **Eva Mittelmeyer**, of Neuweiler in the Weissenkirchberg Church
   - d. 5 Apr 1717, Altengreuth, Bavaria

G1. Adam Moser

Adam Moser, son of **Hans** and **Maria Moser**, was born 14 Nov 1653 in Altengreuth, Germany. He married 26 Mar 1675 **Maria Strobel** of Kloster Sulz in Weissenkirchberg, Bavaria, Germany. Known children:

Adam Moser, b. 13 Apr 1675, Hetzweiller
Anna Maria Moser, b. 20 Jun 1678, Altengreuth
Eva Moser, b. 2 Dec 1680, Altengreuth
George Philip Moser, b. 24 Jun 1683, Altengreuth
   m. 19 Mar 1712 **Eva Ebert**, dau of **Michael** (passengers on the *Adventure*)
Maria Barbara Moser, b. 25 Dec 1686, Altengreuth
Johann Michael Moser, b. 4 May 1690, Altengreuth
   m. 24 Dec 1719 **Susanna Barbara Baumann** dau of **Hans Fredrich Baumann** (passengers on the *Adventure*)

G2. Johann Philip Moser

Hans Philip Moser, son of **Hans** and **Maria Moser**, was born 30 Jun 1656 in Hetzweiler, Germany. He married **Rosina Mittlemeyer** of Eckartsweiler on 4 Aug 1689. He died 21 Jul 1727 and Rosina died 17 Nov 1742. Known children of Philip and Rosina Moser:

Jacob Moser, b. 18 Nov 1691, Altsengreuth
Hans Philip Moser, b. 4 Feb 1692, Altsengreuth
   m. 1 Oct 1719 **Anna Eva Kinds**
Hans Michael Moser, b. 3 Jun 1695, Hetzweiler
   m. 21 Jan 1724 **M. Margt. Grindaker**, dau of **Anton**
    (d. Apr 7 1750)
   d. 6 Aug 1763 in Eckartsweiler
   Known children of Hans Michael and M. Margt:
    J. Michael Moser, b. 17 Mar 1726
    M. Barbara Moser, b. 1 Jul 1728
    J. _____, b. 28 Sep, 1730
    Eva M., b. 20 Oct 1734
    M. Margt., b. 31 Mar 1739, d. 14 Sep 1741
Johann Moser, b. 2 Apr 1698, Eckartsweiler
J. Moser, b. 1 Aug 1700, d. 1 Mar 1700/1, Eckartsweiler
Margaret Moser, b. 11 Aug 1704, Eckartsweiler

G3. Johan Michael Moser

Johann Michael Moser, son of **Hans** and **Maria Moser**, was born 19 Oct 1658 in Germany. He married 4 Aug 1683 **Eva Mittelmeyer**, daughter of **Hans Mittlemeyer**, Weissenkirchberg, Bavaria, Germany. Known children of Michael and Eva Moser:

Johann Philip Moser, b. 24 Jun 1683, d. 24 Aug 1683
Eva Moser, b. 29 Jun 1686, d. 9 Sep 1686
M. Barbara Moser, b. 16 Jul 1687
Eva Moser, b. 4 Apr 1690, d. 1 May 1710
Margaretha Moser, b. 17 Apr 1692
A. Mg. Moser, b. 9 Feb 1693, d. 6 May 1699
Johann Michael Moser, b. 22 Feb 1699, m. **A. Regina Lutz**
M. Anna Moser, b. 11 Feb 1702
Jakobina Moser, b. 26 Sep 1704, d. 9 Nov 1706
Elisabeth Moser, b. 21 Jul 1706, d. 22 Jul 1706
Anna Moser, b. 23 May 1709, d. 23 May 1708

H. Abraham Moser

Abraham Moser of Maryland had a brother named **Samuel Moser** and a wife named
Mary. He went to Washington County, Pennsylvania and then to Tuscarawas County,
Ohio, where his will was dated 14 Jan 1822. Abraham and Mary had three daughters:
Mary Moser m. **John Taylor**
Elizabeth Moser m. **C. Hormish**
Eve Moser m. **Jacob Good**

I. Samuel Moser

Samuel Moser, son of **Samuel Moser** of Maryland and nephew of **Abraham Moser**
(above), was born about 1770 in Maryland. He married **Catrena** _____ and went to
Tuscarawas County, Ohio. His will is dated 14 Jan 1811. Children of Samuel and
Catrena Moser:
Elizabeth Moser m. **John Kline**
Joseph Moser (went to Quincy, Ill in 1884)
Jacob Moser
Samuel Moser
Catherine Moser m. _____ **Himes**
John Moser
Michael Moser
Abraham Moser b. abt. 1800

J. Henry Moser

Henry Moser was born between 1790 and 1800 in York County, Pennsylvania. He
moved to Washington County, Pennsylvania when he was very young. He married about
1818 **Margaret Smith** of Dauphin County, Pennsylvania and was in Richland County,
Ohio by 1819. Only known child of Henry and Margaret Moser:
Nancy Moser
    b. 1819, Richland Co., Ohio
    m. 1839 **Andrew Donaldson**
    d. 1843, Ohio

K. Julia Ann Moser Danley

Julia Ann Moser was born 20 Oct 1794 in Washington County, Pennsylvania. She
married **John Danley** and died 10 Oct 1886 in Jasper County, Iowa. Children of Julia
Ann and John Danley:
    Hannah Danley m. **Watson Mosgrove**
    Anna Danley m, **Peter Kempel**
    Margaret Danley m. **Charles McQuary**
    William Danley m. **Harriet Totten**
    Mary Judith Danley m. **Thomas J. Waters**
    Peter Danley m. **Jane Collins**

L. John (Hans) Musser

The will of John Musser was probated on 5 Apr 1752. He was born in Germany in 1704 and is buried in Musser Cemetery, Manor Township, Lancaster County, Pennsylvania. According to this will, he had a wife named **Veronica "Frony"** and the following children:

1. **Jacob Mosser** m. **Mary Hersey**
   d. 1766, Hanover Township, Pa.
   Children of Jacob and Mary Mosser:
   - **Catherine Moser** m. **Capt. Thomas Copenhaver**
   - **Rachel Moser** m. **Adam Gutman**
   - **Elisabeth Moser**
   - **Jacob Moser**
   - **Eva Moser**
   - **Christine Moser**
2. **Peter Musser** m. **Anna** _____
3. **Henry Musser** m. **Mary** _____
4. **John Musser** m. **Margaret** _____

M. Valentine Moser

Valentine Moser lived in Frederick County, Maryland in 1790. He was the father of the following children:

Susannah Moser
   b. abt 1775, m. **George Hunsaker**
   d. 1811, Fayette Co., Ky.
   They went first to Muhlenberg Co., Ky, then to Fayette Co., Ky.
Abraham Moser
Jacob Moser m. **Christina** _____
Valentine Moser
John Moser
Christina Moser
Mary Moser
Nancy Moser
Julian Moser b. abt. 1775
Catherina Moser

N. John Mosier

John Mosier came from Germany to Northampton County, Pennsylvania. He served either in Capt. Abraham Miller's Company or Colonel William Thompson's Battalion of Riflemen during the Revolutionary War. On 12 Jul 1785 he surveyed 400 acres in Allegheny County, where the city of Pittsburgh lies today.

O. John Mosier

John Mosier was born 7 May 1755, Middle Smithfield Twp., Monroe Co., Pa. He married **Sarah Overfield**, dau. **Paul Overfield** and **Rebecca Marshall**. John died 10 Nov 1785 near Easton, Pa. Their son, **Samuel Overfield Mosier**, inherited the homestead. Samuel had only one known son:

> **Daniel Dimmick Mosier**
>> b. 22 Aug 1816, Middle Smithfield Twp., Monroe Co., Pa.
>> m. 2 Jan 1842 **Elizabeth Ann Ward** (dau. of **Thomas Ward** and **Ann Wakely**. Thomas Ward served in Capt. Samuel Wright Co., Col. Sam Wylly Reg., Revolutionary War.), b. 27 Nov 1821, Trumbull, Conn.
>> d. 6 Mar 1909, Pa. , bur. Hollenbeck Cemetery, Wilkes-Barre, Pa.
>> Children of Daniel Dimmick and Elizabeth Mosier:
>>> **Georgia Mosier**
>>>> b. 18 Oct 1842, Pa.
>>>> m. 31 Oct 1865, **Conrad Sax Stark**
>>>> d. 14 Jul 1896, Florida
>>> **Frank C. Mosier**
>>>> b. 8 Oct 1846, Pa.
>>>> m. **Lydia Ellen Stark**
>>>> They had only one child:
>>>>> **Ruth Mosier**, b. 2 Apr 1893
>>> **John B. Mosier**
>>>> b. 9 Aug 1844, Pittston Twp., Pa.
>>>> d. 27 Sep 1889, never married
>>> **James H. Mosier**, m. **Fannie Field**

P. David J. Mosser

David J. Mosser was born 12 Jul 1826 in Lehigh County, Pennsylvania. He married 25 Dec 1849 **Elisabeth Anna Housman**, daughter of **Jacob Housman** and **Julia A. Schmidt**. She was born 17 Mar 1829 in Lehighton, Pennsylvania. and died 19 May 1914 in Lock Haven, Huntington County, Pennsylvania. David was a tanner. In 1871 he moved his family from Lehigh County to Lock Haven, where he died 1 Feb 1907. Both are buried in Highland Cemetery in Lock Haven. Children of David and Elizabeth:

> 1. **Albert Moser**
>> b. 2 Jan 1852, Mosserville, Lehigh Co., Pa
>> m. 6 Jun 1871, Lock Haven, Pa **Anna E. Reiling**, dau of
>> **Levi** and **Mary Reiling**
>> d. 11 Dec 1932, Lock Haven, Huntington Co., Pa
>> Children of Albert and Anna Moser:
>>> **Oswill Franklin Moser**
>>>> b. 4 Sep 1874, Lock Haven, Pa
>>>> d. 10 Jun 1879, Lock Haven, Pa
>>> **William Albert Moser**
>>>> b. 14 Sep 1876, Lock Haven, Pa
>>>> m. 10 May 1905 **Mabel C. Morris**
>>>> d. 28 Nov 1958, Buffalo, NY
>>>> child of William and Mabel Moser:
>>>>> **Ethel M. Moser**

Milton Wallace Moser
    b. 28 Jan 1879, Mt. Jewett, Pa
    m. 12 Apr 1905 **Estella Othelia Sheats**
    d. 10 Mar 1971, Ashland, Ky
    Childrenof Milton and Estella Moser:
        Joseph Sheats Moser
        Kenneth Wilson Moser
Edwin Garfiled Moser
    b. 1 Sep 1880, Lock Haven, Pa
    d. 20 Jul 1905, Lock Haven, Pa
    unmarried
Wilson David Moser
    b. 4 Jun 1882, Lehighton, Pa
    m. 28 Sep 1912 **Maude Mae Hager**
    d. 3 Feb 1963, Lock Haven, Pa
    No children
Gertrude Martha Moser
    b. 9 Apr 1884, St. Mary's, Pa
    d. 22 Jul 1931, Lock Haven, Pa
    unmarried
Joseph Anderson Moser
    b. 21 Apr 1887, Lock Haven, Pa
    d. 3 Apr 1892, Lock Haven, Pa
Mary Elizabeth Moser
    b. 3 Mar 1888, Lock Haven, Pa
    d. 10 Apr 1892, Lock Haven, Pa

2. **Oswill B. Moser**
    b. 28 Jan 1854, Mosserville, Pa
    m. 25 May 1881 **Emma Alpha Rippy**, dau. of **Frank Rippy** and **Frances Stringfeller**
    d. 13 Jul 1896, Mt. Jewett, Pa
    Children of Oswill and Alpha Moser:
    a. **Frank David Moser**
        b. 1 Jul 1882, Nossville, Pa
        m. 27 Mar 1948, Hagerstown, Md
            (1) Lola Patton
            (2) Esther E. Drew
        d. 19 Oct 1942, Washington DC
        No known children.
    b. **Duard Albert Moser**
        b. 9 Mar 1884, Nossville, Pa.
        m. 11 May 1913, Cordova, Ak **Catherine Scott** dau. of **George E. Scott & Sophia Stanley**
        d. 11 Sep 1948, Seattle, Wa
        Children of Duard and Catherine:
            Alberta C. Moser m. **Eugene P. Boyer**
            Oswilla Moser m. **Duncan W. Herr**
            Jane Moser m. **Jack D. Havens**
            Joseph F. Moser
                 m. **(1) Nancy B. Leonard**
                     (2) Hazel Hoak
    c. **Joseph Belmont Moser**
        b. 30 Jun 1885, Nossville, Pa
        m. 22 Feb 1917, St. Mary's, Pa **Effie Mae Wilson**
        d. 13 Feb 1950, St. Mary's, Pa
        No known children.

      d. **Mable Leona Moser**
          b. 21 Jul 1894, Mt. Jewett, Pa
          m. 15 Jul 1918, St. Mary's, Pa **Eldred Roy Crow**
          d. 5 Mar 1922, Westfield, NJ
          Son of Mable and Eldred Crow:
               Eldred Ray Crow
      e. **Oswilla Moser**
          b. 13 Sep 1896, Mt. Jewett, Pa
          m. 27 Jan 1917, Ridgeway, Pa **Marshall O. Price**
          d. 10 Jan 1981, New London, Oh
          No known children.
3. Elias Peter Moser
      b. 1 Jan 1856, Leighton, Lehigh Co., Pa
      m. 10 Jun 1885, Lock Haven, Pa **Chestie E. Strayer**
      d. 6 Feb 1929, Ashland, Ky
      Children of Elias and Chestie Moser
        (born Lock Haven, Pa.):
          Oliver D. Moser, b. 7 Oct 1877
          Sedgwick Moser, b. 12 Apr 1897
          Elwyn Lester Moser, b. 26 Oct 1892
4. Joseph F. Moser
      b. 31 Jul 1858, Mosserville, Lehigh Co., Pa
      m. 1 Jun 1879, Lock Haven, **Elizabeth Clayton**
      d. 13 Oct 1943, Montoursville, Pa
      Children of Joseh F. and Elizabeth Moser:
          Edward G. Moser
          Oswill F. Moser
          Oliver D. Moser
5. Martha Elizabeth Moser
      b. 1 Jan 1871, Lock Haven, Huntington Co., Pa
      m. 15 Sep 1892, Lock Haven, **Isaac A. Shaffer**
      d. 13 Dec 1855, Williamsport, Pa
      They had no children.

Q. Nathan Moser

S. Nathan Moser was born about 1805 in New York. He married **Clarissa** _____
(b. about 1809 in NY) before 1830. Children listed in the 1850 Federal Census of
Spring Township, Crawford County, Pa:
    Rufus Moser, b. abt. 1830, NY
    Jeromi Moser, b. abt. 1832, NY
    Alamo Moser, b. abt. 1835, NY
    Rudolphus Moser, b. abt. 1837, Pa
    Cornelius Moser, b. abt. 1839, Pa
    Amanda Moser, b. abt. 1841, Pa
    Dennison Moser, b. abt. 1844, Pa
    George Moser, b. abt. 1846, Pa

R. Edwin Henry Musser

Edwin Henry Musser was born Oct 1871/2 in Lancaster County, Pennsylvania and died in West Chester, Chester County, Pennsylvania on 21 Dec 1841. He married **Anna E. Glissen**, daughter of **Wilmer W. Glisson** and **Hanna Heck**. She was born 22 Aug 1874 in West Chester, Pennsylvania and died there in May 1955. Edwin was the warden of the Chester County Prison, while his wife was the matron. They are buried in West Chester. Children of Edwin and Anna Musser:

1. **Edwin Glisson Musser**, b. 9 Aug 1899
   m. (1) **Edna Unk**
   (2) **Alvina Unk** (d. 1979)
   Child of Edwin and Edna Musser:
   Unk Musser (died young)
   Children of Edwin and Alvina Musser:
   Edwin Glisson Musser, Jr.
   Gordon Musser
   Anna Musser
   Doris Musser
2. **Kathryn Hanna Musser**
   b. 12 Mar 1901, West Chester, Pa.
   m. 9 Nov 1925 **William Harper Reinhold**, son of **Daniel Gensemer Reinhold** & **Lena M. Mack**
   (b. 1901, d. 1978)
   Children of Kathryn and William Reinhold:
   William Harper Reinhold, Jr.
   Carolyn Ann Reinhold
   Daniel Gensemer Reinhold, III
   Dorothy Musser Reinhold
   Edwin Musser Reinhold
3. **Helen Martha Musser**
   b. 30 Aug 1902, West Chester, Pa.
   m. **Carl Blum**
   d. d. abt. 1979
4. **Dorothy Pearce Musser**
   b. 16 Aug 1905
   m. **Henry Stewart** (b. Island of Guernsey)
   d. abt. 1974
5. **Erma Anna Musser**
   b. 16 Aug 1906
   d. 16 Feb 1910
6. **Wilmer Glisson Musser**
   b. 14 Sep 1909, West Chester, Pa.
   m. **Ethyl Thomas**
   d. 1973
   Children of Wilmer and Thomas:
   Tom Musser
   Dick Musser
   Harry Musser
7. **Elizabeth "Bizzie" Howell Musser**
   b. 26 Oct 1910
   m. **Adone Febo** (b. Italy)
   d. 8 Jan 1978

8. **Harry "Hoppy" Warren Musser**
    b. 17 May 1912, West Chester, Pa
    m. 16 Sep 1936 **Josephine Elizabeth Bannan**, dau of
        William Stephen Bannan Jr, and **Nellie Ida Pennell**
        (b. 26 Oct 1916, d. 19 Apr 1982)
    Children of Harry and Josephine Musser:
        Barbara Bannan Musser
        Jean Wagner Musser
        Warren Stephen Musser

S. Elizabeth Moser Jewell

Elizabeth Moser, daughter of **Jonathon Moser** and **Catherine Swinehart**, was born 19 Apr 1838 in Ohio. She married 17 Oct 1861 in Van Wert County, Ohio **Seth Jewell**. Seth, a son of **Gershom Jewell** and **Jane E. Vogan**, was born in Allegheny County, Pennsylvania on 22 Mar 1832 and died 26 May 1919 in Merrill, Michigan. Elizabeth died 15 Aug 1901. They are buried in Riverside Cemetery in Rockford, Ohio.
Children of Seth and Elizabeth Jewell:

Samuel Vogan Jewell
    b. 18 Jul 1862, Oh.
    d. 1952, Midland Co., Mi.
    bur. Poseyville Cemetery, Poseyville, Mi.
Hannah Elizabeth Jewell
    b. 17 Dec 1863, Oh.
    m. 2 Jan 1887, Mercer Co., Oh.
        Matthias Allspaugh
    d. 7 Jul 1955, Midland, Midland Co., Mi.
    bur. Poseyville Cemetery, Poseyville, Mi.
Sarah Ellen Jewell
    b. 26 Feb 1865, Oh.
    d. 11 Nov 1918, Oh.
    bur. Poseyville Cemetery, Poseyville, Mi.
Franklin M. Jewell, b. 20 Oct 1867, Oh.
Cornelius Bryon "Neil" Jewell
    b. 20 Sep 1869, Oh.
    m. 30 Jul 1893, Mercer Co., Oh.
        Amanda E. Stetler
    d. Jun 1946
Charles Seth Jewell
    b. 18 Jan 1873, Willshire, Mercer Co., Oh.
    m. 11 Jan 1905, Eau Clair, Wisc.
        Ella Fouser
    d. 24 Aug 1975, Saginaw Co., Mi.
    bur. 27 Aug 1975, Roselawn Memorial Cemetery, Saginaw, Mi.
James Henry Jewell
    b. 15 May 1875, Rockford, Oh.
    m. **Minnie Z. "Peggy"** _____
    d. 6 Jan 1957
Madora Jewell
    b. 21 Oct 1877, Oh.
    m. **Earl K. "Jeff" Trimble**
    d. 26 Jan 1963
Ada Ann Jewell
    b. 23 Aug 1879, Oh.
    m. 15 Mar 1900, Mercer Co., Oh.
        William Henry Hoblet
    d. 27 Dec 1981, Oh.

T. Johann Paul Moser

Johann Paul Moser, only child of **Nicholas Moser** and **Maria Elizabeth Ritter** (b. abt.1675), was born 29 May 1697 at Kohthal bey, Wingen, Germany. He married **Maria Barbara Cassel** 1 May 1723 at Kohthal bey. She was born 1 May 1702, daughter of **Wilhelm Cassel** and **Maria Catharina** _____. They came to America on the *"Molley"* in 1727. He served as a deacon at St. Joseph's Church (the Red Church), located near Bechtelsville, Pennsylvania. Children of John Paul and Maria:

1. **Maria Elizabeth Moser**, b. Nov. 1724
2. **Franciscus "Frantz" Moser**, b. 10 Jun 1733
   m. **Maria Elizabeth Busch**
3. **Maria Christina Moser**, b. 19 Apr 1740
   bp. 7 Jan 1740, Hill Church, Berks Co., Pa
4. **Johann Michael Moser**, b. Jul 1743, d. 27 Jul 1744

T2. Franciscus "Frantz" Moser

Franciscus "Frantz" Moser, son of **Johann Paul Moser** and **Maria Barbara Cassel**, was born 10 Jun 1733 in Pennsylvania and confirmed 1749, Falkner Swamp, Montgomery Co., Pa. He married 20 Apr 1756, at the Hill Church, New Hanover, Berks Co., Pa., **Maria Elizabeth Busch** (dau. of **Jacob Busch**). At the time of the 1790 census, they were living at Earl Township, Berks County, Pa. Children of Francisus & Elizabeth Moser:

a. **Catharine Moser**, b. 7 Jan 1756
   bp. 7 Jan 1757, Hill Church, Berks, Pa
b. **Johannes Moser**, b. 16 Oct 1758
   bp. 16 Oct 1758, Hill Church, Berks, Pa
   m. **Anna Maria Huter**
c. **Johann Michael Moser**, b. 19 Dec 1760
   bp. 19 Dec 1760, Hill Church, Berks, Pa
   m. **Margaretha** _____
   d. 1817
d. **Johann George Moser**, b. 1 Jan 1763
   bp. Hill Church, Berks, Pa
   m. **Salome** _____
   d. 21 Jan 1829
e. **Franciscus "Frantz" Moser**, b. 19 Mar 1765
   bp. 19 Mar 1765, Hill Church, Berks, Pa
   m. **Susanna** _____
   d. 1847
f. (?) **Christian Moser**, b. 15 Apr 1767, New Hanover, Berks Co., Pa
   m. **Eva Elizabeth** _____ (b. 2 May 1760, d. 23 Sep 1841)
   (Note: He is omitted from this family in some sources)
g. **Magdalena Moser**, b. 6 Mar 1772
   bp. 6 Mar 1772, Hill Church, Berks Co., Pa
h. **Daniel Moser**, b. 21 Aug 1772
   bp. 6 Mar 1772, Hill Church, Berks Co., Pa
   m. **Rosina Wagner**
i. **Barbara Moser**, b. 5 Apr 1779
   bp. 5 Apr 1779, Hill Church, Berks Co., Pa
j. **Christina Moser**, b. 4 Dec 1782
   bp. 4 Dec 1782, Hill Church, Berks Co., Pa

T2b. Johannes Moser

Johannes Moser, son of **Franciscus Moser** and **Maria Elizabeth Busch**, was born in Berks County, Pennsylvania and baptized at Hill Church on 19 Dec 1760. He married **Anna Maria Huter** before 1783. Children of Johannes and Maria Elizabeth Moser:
1. **Catharina Moser**, b. 8 Feb 1783
2. **Magdalena Moser**, b. 16 Oct 1784
3. **Johannes Moser**, b. 22 Dec 1789, d. bef. Dec. 1794
4. **Jacob Moser**, b. 22 Jan 1792, m. **Rebecca** _____
   Only child of Jacob and Rebecca Moser:
      Maria Moser, b. 1 Oct 1820
5. **Johannes Moser**, b. 29 Dec 1794, m. **Magdalena** _____
   Children of Johannes and Magdalena Moser:
      Wilhelm Moser, b. 15 Mar 1820, d. 1 Feb 1887
      Daniel Moser, b. 30 Oct 1821
      Isaac Moser, b. 24 Dec 1824
        m. **Caroline** _____
        Children of Isaac and Caroline Moser:
          Melinda Moser, b. 1 Feb 1852
          Joel Moser, b. 7 Oct 1856
          William Moser, b. 3 Nov 1858
          Jonathan Moser, b. 9 Jul 1860
          Hannah Moser, b. 20 Aug 1862
          Mary Moser, b. 6 Nov 1865
          Anna Moser, b. 22 Dec 1868
          Jacob Moser, b. 12 Jan 1872
6. **Susanna Moser**, b. 7 Apr 1797
7. **Maria Moser**, b. 9 Nov 1799

T2c Johann Michael Moser

Johann Michael Moser, son of **Franciscus Moser** and **Maria Elizabeth Busch**, was born in Berks County, Pennsylvania and baptized at the Hill Church on 19 Dec 1760. He married **Margaretha** _____. His will was probated in 1817. Children of Johann Michael and Margaretha Moser:
   Johann Carl "Charles" Moser, b. 27 Jul 1784
   Elizabeth Moser, 9 Sep 1786
   Maria Moser, 26 Jul 1788
   Susanna Moser, b. 10 Jun 1790
   Adam Moser, b. 14 Jul 1792
   Magdalena Moser, b. 10 Mar 1797
   George Moser, b. 10 Oct 1799
   Margaretha Moser, b. 14 Nov 1802*
   Sarah Moser, b. 15 Feb 1805*

(* Not mentioned in their father's will of 12 Mar 1817.)

T2d. George Moser

George Moser, son of **Franciscus Moser** and **Maria Elizabeth Busch**, was born 1 Jan 1763 and baptized at Hill Church, Berks County, Pennsylvania. He married **Salome** _____. In 1828, George was living in Center Township, Union County, Pennsylvania (now Franklin Townshiip, Snyder County) when he deeded his land to his son John. George died 21 Jan 1829. Children of George and Salome Moser:

1. **Elizabeth Moser**, b. 19 Apr 1783
2. **Susanna Moser**, b. 27 Dec 1784
3. **John Musser**
   b. 12 Nov 1786
   m. **Deborah Stetler**
   d. 15 May 1855
   Children of John and Deborah Musser:
   a. **Henry Musser**, b. abt. 1813
   b. **George Musser**, 20 Jan 1815
      m. **Sarah Swartz**
      d. 4 Jan 1885
      Children of George and Sarah Musser:
      Lucy Ann Musser, b. 1842
         m. **Uriah Moyer**
      Joseph Musser, b. 1844
         m. **Catherine Kratzer**
      Mary "Polly" Musser, b. 1846
         m. **John McMullen**
      Matilda Musser, b. Apr 1850
         d. 3 Jul 1904
         m. **Paul Sampsell Bogar**
      Edward Musser, m. **Amanda Moyer**
      John Henry Musser
         m. **Margaret P. Kratzer**
      Isaac Musser
      Pharus Musser
      Eliza Musser
   c. **Adam Musser**
      b. 3 Apr 1816
      d. 30 Jul 1908
      m. **Mary Gloss**
      Children of Adam and Mary Musser:
      Hugh Musser
         b. 22 Apr 1836
         m. **Mary Louise Dale**
         d. 22 Dec 1921
      Reuben Musser, b. 28 Jun 1838
      Sophia Musser m. **Jacob Long**
      Lydia Musser m. **Henry Rearick**
      Levina Musser m. **Charles Teighman**
      Delilah Musser m. **George Zimmerman**
      Isaiah Musser
      Amelia Musser m. **Samuel Long**
      Nathan Musser
   d. **Jeremiah Musser**
      b. 6 Mar 1817
      m. **Mary Dinius**
      Children of Jeremiah and Mary:
      John Musser
      Robert Musser
      Matilda Musser
      Elizabeth Musser
      Daniel Musser
      Charles Musser

> e. **Reuben Musser**, b. 1823
>> m. **Elizabeth Ranck**
>> Child of Reuben and Elizabeth:
>>> **William Henry Moser**, b. 14 Feb 1846
>>>> m. **Barbara Elizabeth Ickes**
>>>> d. 1 Apr 1909
>> f. **Sarah Musser**
>> g. **Lydia Musser**
>> h. **Amelia Musser**
>> i. **Matilda Musser**
>> j. **Sophia Musser**
> 4. **George Moser**, b. 18 Jul 1789
> 5. **Anna Maria Moser**, b. 9 Oct 1792
> 6. **Anna Catharina Moser**, 7 Jun 1795

T2e. Franciscus "Frantz" Moser

Franciscus "Frantz" Moser, son of **Franciscus Moser** and **Maria Elizabeth Busch**, was baptized at the Hill Church, Berks County, Pennsylvania on 19 Mar 1765. He married **Susannah _____** about 1787, and died in 1847. Children of Frantz and Susannah Moser:

> **Matthais Moser**, b. 25 Jan 1788
> **Catharina Moser**, b. 27 Jul 1790
>> m. **Georg Klauser**
> **Magdalena Moser**, b. 25 Nov 1792
>> m. **Rubin Dotterer**
>> Children of Magdalena and Rubin Dotterer:
>>> **Susanna Dotterer** m. **Johannes Reitenauer**
>>> **Sarah Dotterer** m. **Daniel Meyer**
> **Johannes Moser**, b. 9 Jan 1795, d. 29 Apr 1874
> **Elizabeth Moser**, b. 1 Apr 1797*
> **David Moser**, b. 1 Sep 1801*
> **Frederick Moser**, b. 4 Nov 1804
> **Sara Moser**, b. 29 Jan 1808*

(* Not mentioned in their father's will of 1847.)

T2f. Christian Moser

Christian Moser, thought to be a son of **Franciscus Moser** and **Maria Elizabeth Busch**, was born 15 Apr 1767 at New Hanover, Berks County, Pennsylvania. He married **Eva Elizabeth _____**, who was born 2 May 1760 and died 23 Sep 1841. Children of Christian and Eva Moser:

> **George Moser**, b. 13 Feb 1787
> **Elisabeth Moser**, b. 21 Oct 1788
> **Susanna Moser**, b. 12 Jan 1794
> **Catharina Moser**, b. 15 Jun 1796
> **Jacob Moser**, b. 6 Jan 1800, d. 11 Apr 1885
> **Daniel Moser**, b. 4 May 1802

T2g. Daniel Moser

Daniel Moser, son of **Franciscus Moser** and **Maria Elizabeth Busch**, was baptized 21 Aug 1774 at Hill Church in Berks County, Pennsylvania. He married **Rosina Wagner**. They were the parents of:

Daniel Moser, He became a Lutheran minister
Mary Moser m. _____ Shook
Katherine Moser m. _____ Shook
Susannah Moser m. _____ Reed
Annie Moser m. _____ Bailey
Eva Moser m. **Benjamin Wion**

1. The Family of Rev. Johann Philip Boehm

Johann Philip Boehm was a son of **Philip Ludwig Bochm** and **Maria Englehard** of Wachenbuchen, Germany and was baptized in 25 Nov. 1683 in Hochstadt, Hesse, Germany. He was received as a citizen of Lambsheim on 14 Apr 1706 where he operated the Stag Inn. He served as the Reformed schoolmaster at Worms from 1708-1715 and then as schoolmaster at Lambsheim from 1715-1720. The family emigrated to Pennsylvania in 1720, where he had a farm in Whitpain Township, Montgomery County, Pennsylvania. He was ordained by the Dutch Reformed authorities in New York and served several German Lutheran congregations in Pennsylvania.

He was married about 1706 **Anna Maria Stehler**, daughter of **Hartmann** and **Anna Maria Stahler** of Lambsheim, Germany. After her father's death, her mother married (2) **Philip Scherer**, and she is the **Anna Maria Scherer** whom early researchers have thought to be the second wife of Rev. Boehm. The family emigrated to Pennsylvania in 1720, where Rev. Boehm died 29 Apr 1749 at the home of his son, **Johann Philip Boehm** in Hellertown, Pennsylvania.

The Rev. Boehm made several voyages across the ocean, escorting members of his faithful flock from religious persecutions in Germany to the freedom in Pennsylvania. On one of these trips, he took with him several sons of the *Goodwill* (1728) immigrants, including **John Adam Moser** and his own son, **Johann Philip Boehm**, returning 2 Sep 1743 on the *Loyal Judith*.

Signature of John Boehm

The Rev. Boehm is <u>thought</u> to have been the father of (not listed in order of birth):
1. **Johann Philip Boehm**
   b. 1728, Whitpain, Montgomery Co., Pa
   m. **Anna Barbara _____**
   He was naturalized on 11 Apr 1741.
   known children of John Philip and Anna Barbara:
   Johann Philip Boehm, b. 1774
   Susanna Boehm, b. 14 Jun 1776, Lower Saucon
   David Boehm, b. 1778, Lehigh Co., Pa
   Catherine Boehm, b. 1780, Lehigh Co., Pa
   Mary Boehm, b. 1782, Lehigh Co., Pa
   Elisabeth Boehm, b. 28 May 1784
   bp. 28 Sep 1784, Lower Saucon

2. **Rev. Charles Lewis Boehm**
   m. 5 Feb 1772 **Catherine Moser**, First Reformed Church, Race St., Philadelphia, Pa
3. **Anna Maria Boehm** m. (1) **Johann Adam Moser**
4. **Sabina Boehm**, m. **Ludwig Bitting**
5. **Elisabeth Boehm**
6. **Maria Philippina Boehm**
7. **Anton Wilhelm Boehm** b. 27 Apr 1714, Worms, Germany
   d. Upper Saucon Twp., Lehigh Co., Pa.

Johann Philip Boehm, Jr.

Johann Philip Boehm, Jr. (probably a grandson of the Rev. Boehm) m. 16 Feb 1800 at the Lower Saucon Church, located in what is now Allentown, Lehigh County, Pennsylvania, **Elisabeth Resser/Kosser**. Known children of John Philip, Jr. and Elisabeth Boehm:

Peter Boehm
   b. 12 Oct 1800, Pa
   bp. 14 Dec 1800, Lower Saucon Church, Lehigh Co., Pa
Magdalena Boehm
   bp. 1 Jan 1808, Lower Saucon Church, Lehigh Co., Pa
Juliana Boehm
   b. 30 Apr 1809, Pa
   bp. 11 Jun 1809, Lower Saucon Church, Lehigh Co., Pa
Henrietta Boehm, b. 14 Dec 1810, Pa
   bp. 13 Oct 1810, Lower Saucon Church, Lehigh Co., Pa
Thomas Boehm, b. 8 Jan 1813, Pa
   bp. 2 Feb 1813, Lower Saucon Church, Lehigh Co., Pa
Sarah Boehm, b. 21 Apr 1823, Pa
   bp. 9 Sep 1823, Lower Saucon Church, Lehigh Co., Pa

Other baptims at the Lower Saucon church:
   John Boehm and **Margaret** were the parents of the following:
      Henrietta Boehm, bp. 24 Jun 1810
      Israel Boehm, bp. 6 Apr 1814
      Henry Boehm, bp. 6 Jun 1823

John Boehm and **Rebecca** had **Levi Boehm** baptized 5 Nov 1812.

There are many Boehms buried in the cemetery of the Lower Saucon Church.

2. The Family of Thomas Everett

Thomas Everett, believed by some researchers to be the son of **John Everett** and **Bathsheba Sands**, was born about 1720, probably on Long Island, New York. He married **Catherine Albrecht** about 1744 and lived in Linn, Northampton (now Lehigh) County, Pennsylvania. He owned the property where Everett Fort was located. There is only a sign left to designate the site. Eighteen men were stationed there in 1764 to help protect the residents from the indian raids. Children of Thomas and Catherine Everett:

    a. Samuel Everett
        b. abt. 1745, Linn, Northampton Co., Pa
        m. **Maria Barbara Moser**
        d. 1808, Liberty Twp., Trumbull Co., Oh
        He served in the Revolutionary War.
    b. Peter Everett m. **Catherine Miller**
    c. Magdalena Everett m. **Lt. Col. Michael Brobst** (d. 1814)
    d. Catherine Everett m. **Rev. John Roth**
    e. Susanna Everett m. **Jurg Daniel Wannemacher**
    f. John Everett
        b. 1761, Linn, Northampton Co., Pa
        m. **Maria Magdalena Miller** (b. 1766, d. 1836)
        d. 1810, Lynn, Lehigh Co., Pa
        Known Child of John & Maria Everett:
            Daniel Everett, b. 1794
                m. **Elisabeth Wannemaker**
                    b. 1801, d. 19 Nov 1840 (dau. of
                    Jurg Daniel Wannemacher, above)
                d. 31 Oct 1837, Oh
                Children of Daniel & Elisabeth:
                    Sarah Everett, m. **Samuel Brown**
                    Mary Everett
                    Eliza A. Everett
                    John Everett
                    Daniel S. Everett
                    Adeline Everett

3. The Family of Jacob E. Everett

Jacob E. Everett was born 4 Mar 1811 in Fannettsburg, Franklin County, Pennsylvania. He married 6 Jun 1845 in Trumbull County, Ohio **Susannah Oswald**, daughter of **Jonathan Oswald** and **Maria Everett**. Susannah was born 11 Mar 1822 in Liberty, Tioga County, Pennsylvania and died 13 Jun 1903 in Trumbull County, Ohio. Jacob died 18 Aug 1897 in Newton Falls, Trumbull County, Ohio. They are buried in Newton Falls. Children of Jacob and Susannah Everett:

a. **John Javan Everett**
    b. 25 Sep 1846, Howland, Trumbull Co., Oh
    m. **Ellen Biekle**
    d. 13 Jun 1903, Trumbull Co., Oh
    bur. Newton Falls, Trumbull Co., Oh
    John was an undertaker in Newton Falls. They had no children.

b. **Samuel Charles Everett**
    b. 5 Mar 1848, Howland, Trumbull Co., Oh
    m. **Mary Holley**

c. **William Harrison Everett**, b. 5 Sep 1850, Howland, Trumbull Co., Oh

d. **Michael Moser Everett**
    b. 13 Nov 1852, Howland, Trumbull Co., Oh
    m. (1) 23 Dec 1880 **Celestina Ida Long**
       (2) **Mrs. Barbara Housman Brown**
    d. 21 Jan 1931, Warren, Trumbull Co., Oh

e. **Rebecca Caroline Everett**
    b. 22 Aug 1854, Howland, Trumbull Co., Oh
    m. **William H. Whitney**

f. **Jacob Clayton Everett**
    b. Feb 1856, Howland, Trumbull Co., Oh
    m. **Flora Daly**, dau. of **John Daly**
    d. 1924, Newton Falls, Trumbull Co., Oh
    They had no children.

g. **George Washington Everett**
    b. 1 Jun 1858, Howland, Trumbull Co., Oh
    m. **Ida Ames**, dau. of **Mark Ames**
    d. 7 Oct 1896, Meadville, Pa
    They had no children.

h. **Frank Everett**
    b. 10 Jul 1861, Howland, Trumbull Co., Oh
    m. **Elda** _____
    d. 25 Mar 1901

i. **Cora Ella Everett**
    b. 10 Feb 1865, Howland, Trumbull Co., Oh
    m. **Martin Allworth Holcomb**
    d. 16 Feb 1930, Milwaukee, Wi

j. **Eugene Everett**
    b. 4 Apr 1866, Howland, Trumbull Co., Oh
    d. 30 Aug 1889, Howland, Trumbull Co., Oh

d. Michael Moser Everett

Michael Moser Everett, son of **Jacob E. Everett** and **Susannah Oswald**, was born 13 Nov 1852 in Howland, Trumbull County, Ohio. He married 23 Dec 1880 in Trumbull County, Ohio, **Celestina Ida Long**, daughter of **Lewis W. Long** and **Rebecca Shoup** and sister of **Lucy Manda Long**. Celestina died in Newton Falls, Trumbull County, Ohio on 1 Oct 1918. Michael then married (2) **Mrs. Barbara Housman Brown**. He died in Warren, Trumbull County, Ohio on 21 Jan 1931 and is buried in Newton Falls. Barbara moved to Pocatello, Idaho after Michael's death.

Children of Michael and Celestina Everett:
Blanch May Everett
>
> b. 15 Sep 1881, Newton Falls, Trumbull Co., Oh
> m. 28 Dec 1900, **Orris O. Hewitt**
> d. 10 Jul 1944, Niles, Trumbull Co., Oh
> Children of Blanch and Orris Hewitt:
>> **Delphine Hewitt**, b. 28 Sep 1905, Niles, Trumbull, Oh
>> **Lee Hewitt**, b. 17 Sep 1907, Niles, Trumbull, Oh
>> **Ruth Hewitt**, b. 9 Aug 1910, Niles, Trumbull, Oh
>>> m. **Martin Hudtloff**
>>
>> **Walter Hewitt**, b. 10 Jan 1923, Niles, Trumbull, Oh

Dora Everett
>
> b. 20 Jan 1883, Newton Falls, Trumbull Co., Oh
> m. (1) 27 Oct 1907 **Patrick W. Jones**
> (2) **Walter Herzog**

Clayton Ralph Everett
>
> b. 18 Jun 1885, Newton Falls, Trumbull Co., Oh
> m. 3 May 1905 (1) **Mary Margaret Livingston**
> d. 30 Dec 1958, Pocatello, Idaho

Ida Rebecca Everett
>
> b. 10 Jan 1888, Newton Falls, Trumbull Co., Oh
> d. 2 Mar 1888, Newton Falls, Trumbull Co., Oh

Carrie Ellen Everett
>
> b. 11 May 1889, Newton Falls, Trumbull Co., Oh
> m. (1) 6 Aug 1906 **Henry W. Waggner**
> (2) 15 Jul 1924 **Peter Morales**
> (3) 26 Mar 1943 **David Evans**

Mary Lola Everett
>
> b. 30 Dec 1893, Warren, Trumbull Co., Oh
> d. 27 Jun 1935

Charlotte Leah Everett
>
> b. 17 Sep 1895, Newton Falls, Trumbull, Oh
> m. (1) 26 Nov 1913, **Fred J. King**
> (2) 17 Apr 1937, **Joseph Dean**
> (3) 1946, **Fred P. Mitchell**
> (4) **S. M. Pittman**

Elmer Blake Everett
>
> b. 19 Apr 1898, Newton Falls, Trumbull Co., Oh
> d. 7 Jul 1898, Newton Falls, Trumbull Co., Oh

Gladys Iona Everett
>
> b. 15 Jul 1902, Newton Falls, Trumbull Co., Oh
> m. 2 May 1918 **Thomas Siering**
> Only child of Gladys and Thomas Siering:
>> **Adelade Siering**
>>
>> b. 17 Feb 1919, Newton Falls, Trumbull Co., Oh
>> m. 2 Feb 1946 **John Hoostal**

4. The Family of Jacob Hower

Jacob Hower/Hauer was born 15 Jul 1801 in Pennsylvania. He married 5 Oct 1826 at the First Evangelical Lutheran Church, Carlisle, Cumberland Co., Pa. **Hannah Kimmell**. She was a daughter of **Anthony Kimmell** of Rye Township, Perry County, Pennsylvania. Jacob was a farmer and miller. In 1830, they were living in Juniata Township, Perry County, Pennsylvania. They moved to Trumbull County, Ohio in 1835 and then to Ovid Twp., Branch Co., Mi. where Jacob died on 1 Jul 1873. Children of Jacob and Hannah Hower:

1. **Susan Hower**
   b. 8 Jun 1825, Juniata Twp., Perry Co., Pa
   m. 8 Jan 1846, Trumbull Co., Oh **Gideon Moser**
   d. 23 Jun 1886, Ovid Twp. Branch Co., Mi

2. **Adam Hower**
   b. 10 Jun 1827, Juniata Twp., Perry Co., Pa
   m. 7 Oct 1852, Jackson, Trumbull Co., Oh **Mary Ann Brobst**
   d. 5 Apr 1903, Ovid Twp., Branch Co., Mi
   bur. Lockwood Cemetery, Branch Co., Mi
   Adam was a farmer and served in the Civil War, Co. G., 16th Reg., Michigan Infantry.
   Children of Adam and Mary Ann Hower:
   > **Edwin Hower**, b. 1863, d. 1864
   > **Alvin Hower**, b. @ 1866, d. 13 Feb 1871

3. **Anthony K. Hower**
   b. 18 Mar 1833, Juniata Twp., Perry Co., Pa
   m. 9 Jul 1857, Braceville, Trumbull Co., Oh **Harriet Stewart/Steward**
   d. 10 Jul 1915, Hillsdale Co., Mi
   He was a farmer, a miller, and served in the Civil War, Co. B., 11th Reg., Michigan Infantry.
   Children of Anthony and Harriet Hower:
   > **Charles Willis Hower**, b. 1859
   > **Emma Almira Hower**, b. 6 Jul 1861
   > **Jennie Margaret Hower**, b. 22 Feb 1863
   > **Harriet Alberta Hower**, b. 1865
   > **John Franklin Hower**, b. 1 Mar 1867
   > **Henry Eugene Hower**, b. 10 Apr 1869
   > **Jay Edward Hower**, b. 30 Jul 1871
   > **Homer Herman Hower**, b. 3 Aug 1877
   > **Jessie May Hower**, b. 1881

4. **Anna Barbara Hower**
   b. 21 Jul 1834, Juniata Twp., Perry Co., Pa
   m. 26 Sep1852, Newton Falls, Trumbull Co., Oh, **Henry Carlisle**
   d. 20 Mar 1908, Bluffto, Wells Co., In
   They had seven children.

5. **Margaret Hower**, b. abt. 1836
   m. 4 Mar 1842, Trumbull Co., Oh, **Pleman Cook**
   d. 1880
   Children of Margaret and Pleman Cook:
   > **Ellen Cook**, b. 1853
   > **Allison Cook**, b. 1855
   > **Jacob Cook**, b. 1857
   > **Joseph Cook**, b. Oct 1859
   > **Lester Cook**, b. 1862
   > **Alta Cook**, b. 1864/6
   > **Ira Cook**, b. 1869
   > **Frederick Cook**, b. 1871
   > **Frank Cook** (twin), b. 1874
   > **Martin Cook** (twin), b. 1874

6. Emery Hower
>   b. 28 Feb 1839, Ellsworth Twp., Trumbull Co., Oh
>   m. 10 Dec 1863 Branch Co., Mi **Fiern Anna Moser**
>   d. 3 May 1903, Trumbull Co., Oh
>   bur. Oakwood Cemetery, Warren, Trumbull Co., Oh

7. John Y. Hower
>   b. 22 Apr 1841, Jackson, Trumbull Co., Oh
>   m. 21 Sep 1865, Wells Co., In **Ethelinda Chalfant**
>   d. 10 Apr 1915, Bluffton, Wells Co., In
>   He was a city councilman in Bluffton, Indiana.

8. Leffenus/Levanus Hower
>   b. 1848, Newton Twp., Trumbull Co., Oh
>   d. 1909, Ovid Twp., Branch Co., Mi
>   He never married

5. The Family of Woolf Koppenheffer/Coppenhover

Woolf Koppenheffer and his family arrived in America 11 Sep 1732 on the *Pennsylvania Merchant*. He and his wife, **Maria** _____ settled in what is now Lebanon County, Pennsylvania. Known children of Woolf and Maria Koppenheffer:

    a. Thomas Koppenheffer
        m. (1) **Mary Ann** _____
           (2) **Elizabeth Holtsman**
    b. Michael Koppenheffer m. **Eva Margaret Staayer**
    c. Anna Barbara Koppenheffer m. 6 Oct 1735 **Johann Peter Kucher**
    d. Anna Catharina Koppenheffer m. 2 Aug 1738 **Matthias Smyser**
    e. Anna Rosina Koppenheffer m. 18 Dec 1734 **Christopher Myer**

5a. Thomas Coppenhover/Koppenheffer

Thomas Coppenhover, son of **Woolf** and **Maria Koppenheffer**, arrived on the *James Goodwill*, 11 Sep 1728 with **Hans Adam Mosser** and **Hans Martin Mosser**. He signed the ship manifesto with an "X", which indicates that he was possibly too ill to sign his name, a practice which was common due to the sad conditions of the accomodations. He married (1) **Mary Ann** _____ and (2) **Elizabeth Holtsman**. Another source identifies the first wife as **Anna Maria** and states that he was from Koeblingen, Wurttemberg, Germany. Children of Thomas and Mary Ann Coppenhover:

    Henry Coppenhover, b. 1731, m. **Christina Reith/Reed**
    Michael Coppenhover b. 1735, m. **Maria Elizabeth** _____
        They lived in Lancaster County, Pennsylvania. Their son,
        Simon Coppenhover (1758-1832)
           m. **Anna Elizabeth Wolff** (1763-1832)
    Thomas Coppenhover, b. 1739, m. **Catherine Moser**
    Regina Coppenhover, b. 1740, m. **John Tice**
    Eva Coppenhover, b. 1743, m. **Christian Lehman**
    Catharine Coppenhover, b. 1745, m. _____ **Bollinger**
    Jack Coppenhover

6. The Family of Johannes Lichtenwallner

Johannes Lichtenwallner, a blacksmith, arrived in Philladelphia on the *Samuel* in 1733, with his wife, **Barbara Burchard** and a one year old son. According to his passport, he was from Kreuth, Germany (now near Nuremberg, Bavaria). They were the parents of four sons and five daughters, but only the following are known:

    Margaret Lichtenwallner
        b. 3 Feb 1734, Goshenhoppen, Montgomery Co., Pa
        bp. 6 Feb 1734, New Hanover, Montgomery Co., Pa
        Sponsors: **Tobias** and **Margaretha Moser**
    Maria Agatha Lichtenwallner
        b. 1736, Pa
        m. (1) 5 Feb 1765 **Henrich Steininger**
           (2) abt 1760 **Johann Burchard Moser**
    Anna Christina Lichtenwallner
        b. 24 May 1743, Pa
        m. 31 May 1764 **Tobias Moser**
        d. 22 Jul 1810 Lowhill, Lehigh Co., Pa

The family moved to Whitehall Township, and then to Fogelsville, (now in Lehigh County), Pennsylvania in 1742.

7. The Family of Zachariah Long/Lang

Zachariah Long, according to burial records, was born 16 Mar 1759. He was a member of the Third Battalion, Montgomery County Pennsylvania Militia, under Llwellen Young in 1780, and the Third Battalion, Chester County Militia under Col. Richard Willing from 1784 to 1787. He married 31 Aug 1784 **Sarah Albrecht**, daughter of **Rudolph** and **Apollonia Epright** at St. Michaels Church in Germantown, Philadelphia County, Pennsylvania. He operated a tavern in Montgomery County in 1792, and from 1803 until 1810 he also operated a ferry for Henry Zook. He purchased land from **Samuel Everett** and moved his family to Lynn in Northampton (now Lehigh) County, Pennsylvania. He sold his land to his five sons in 1821 and died on 8 Oct 1827. Sarah refused the executorship of the estate in November. Children of Zachariah and Sarah Long:

1. **Abraham Long**
   b. 4 Aug 1785, Pa
   m. abt 1805 **Anna Maria Fetherwolf**
   d. 28 Feb 1861, Lewis Twp., Lycoming Co., Pa
2. **Charles Long**
   b. 1787, Pa
   m. (1) **Catherine Anna Gehringer**
   (2) **Martha _____**
   d. 21 May 1864, Wayne Co., NY
3. **Henry (Henrich) Long**
   b. 3 Mar 1791, Norristown, Montgomery Co., Pa
   bp. 26 Jun 1791, St. Paul's Lutheran Church, Ardmore, Pa
   m. 21 Jun 1818 **Maria Magdalena Hermany**
   d. 8 Nov 1867, Lynn, Lehigh Co., Pa
4. **Maria Long**
   b. 23 May 1793, Pa
   bp. 4 Aug 1793, St. Paul's Lutheran Church, Ardmore, Pa
   m. **George Reagan**
   d. 8 Nov 1867, Lynn, Lehigh Co., Pa
5. **Magdalena Long**
   b. abt 1795, Pa
   m. **Daniel Hermany**
   They went to Lockport, NY
   (She could be the one called Anna listed below)
6. **Sarah Long**
   b. abt. 1797, Pa
   m. **Johannes Fetherwolf**
   They went to Berks County, Pa
   (She also could be the one called Anna listed below)
7. **Anna Long**
   b. 20 Nov 1796, Pa
   bp. 30 Jul 1797
8. **Zachariah Long**
   b. 18 Mar 1801, Pa
   m. 30 Dec 1827 **Mary Magdalena "Polly" Straub**
   dau. of **Mathias Andreas Straub** and **Mary
   Magdalena Carl/Correl** (b. 29 Jan 1810 in Lynn, Pa
   d. 3 Sep 1883, Warren, Trumbull Co., Oh)
   d. 18 Mar 1878, Lynn, Lehigh Co., Pa

Children of Zachariah and Magdalena Long:
a. Lewis W. Long
    b. 26 Oct 1828, Lynn, Lehigh Co., Pa
    m. 9 Oct 1889, Southington, Trumbull Co., Oh
      Rebecca Shoop, dau. of **Jacob Shoop** and his second wife,
          Maria Witherstone (b. 4 Nov 1834,
          Weathersfield, Trumbull, Oh, d. 28 Apr 1896,
          Phalanx Station, Trumbull,Oh)
    Lewis was a carpenter and served during the Civil War in
    Company "B", Regiment 105 of the Ohio Volunteers. He was
    taken prisoner in Oct. 1862 and transfered to the Second
    Battalion, 126th Regiment of the Ohio Veteran's
    Reserve Corp. Children of Lewis and Rebecca Long:
    Jacob Ami Long
        b. 11 Dec 1858, Southington, Oh
        m. 1828 **Florence Lentz**
        d. 10 Jan 1931, Phalanx Station, Oh
    Celestine Ida Long
        b. 11 Jun 1860, Southington, Oh
        m. 23 Dec 1880 **Michael Moser Everett**
        d. 1 Oct 1918, Newton Falls, Oh
    Lucy Manda Long
        b. 10 Aug 1862, Southington, Oh
        m. 7 Sep 1887, Southington, Oh
          Owen Nelson Moser
        d. 23 Nov 1899, Leavittsburg, Oh
    Rhoda Ann Long
        b. 8 Nov 1865, Phalanx Station, Oh
        m. **Warren Klingerman**
        d. 20 Feb 1926
    Charles Allen Long
        b. 26 Nov 1867, Phalanx Station, Oh
        m. **Nellie Brown**
        d. 11 Feb 1923
    Myrtle Long
        b. 10 Jun 1871, Braceville, Oh
        m. **Walter Saltzman**
        d. 10 Oct 1924 Braceville, Oh
    Lewis Long
        b. 27 Sep 1872, Braceville, Oh
        died young.
    Nellie Adelle Long
        b. 23 Apr 1874, Braceville, Oh
        m. 30 Jun 1896 **James E. Moody**
        d. 28 Jan 1939
b. James M. Long
    b. 6 Sep 1830, Lynn, Lehigh Co., Pa
    m. 31 Jul 1856, Trumbull Co., Oh. **Esther Hurd**
    d. 19 Oct 1889, Southington, Trumbull Co., Oh
c. Maria Anna Long
    b. 23 Jun 1834, Lynn, Lehigh Co., Pa
    m. 29 Jan 1865, Warren, Trumbull Co., Pa
      Warren Richards/Richart

d. Helena Mahateth Long
    b. 30 Dec 1836, Lynn, Lehigh Co., Pa
    m. 9 Oct 1859, Trumbull Co., Oh
    Emanuel Cariher
    d. 24 Mar 1908, York Twp., Medina Co., Oh

e. Allen H. Long
    b. 7 Feb 1839, Lynn, Lehigh Co., Pa
    m. 28 Jun 1866, Trumbull Co., Oh
    Eliza Shoup (sister of Rebecca, above)
    d. 5 Nov 1902, Weathersfield, Trumbull, Oh

f. Sarah Long
    b. 24 Feb 1841, Lynn, Lehigh Co., Pa
    m. 3 Jan 1867, Trumbull Co., Oh
    Sylvester Wesley Peffers
    d. 21 Nov 1901, Trumbull Co., Oh

g. Elias Long
    b. 5 Jun 1843, Southington, Trumbull Co., Oh
    d. 11 Feb 1874, Ft. Dodge, Ia

h. Zachariah Long
    b. 14 May 1845, Southington, Trumbull Co., Oh
    m. 23 Dec 1869, Trumbull Co., Oh
    Emma Westwood
    d. 4 Oct 1902, Trumbull Co., Oh

i. Henrietta Long
    b. 1845, Oh

j. Rebecca Long
    b. 19 Dec 1847, Braceville, Trumbull Co., Oh
    m. 14 Oct 1875 Trumbull Co., Oh
    William W. Dray
    d. 1934, Trumbull Co., Oh

k. Charles Long
    b. 28 Apr 1850, Braceville, Trumbull Co., Oh
    d. 14 Oct 1862, Trumbull Co., Oh

l. John Long
    b. 2 Aug 1853, Braceville, Trumbull Co., Oh
    m. 31 Jul 1895, Trumbull Co., Oh
    Cora Taylor Dunn
    d. 28 Nov 1913, Trumbull Co., Oh

9. Rudolph Long
    b. 4 Jul 1805, Pa
    bp. 13 Oct 1805, St. Michael's Lutheran Church,
        Germantown, Philadelphia Co., Pa
    d. 1867

8. The Family of Daniel Oswald

Daniel Oswald, son of **Henrich Oswald** and **Elisabeth Peter** who arrived in Philadelphia 29 May 1735 on the *Mercury*, was born abt. 1742 in Pa. He married **Catharine Everett**, daughter of **Peter Everett** and **Catharina Miller**. Children of Daniel and Catharine Oswald:

    Johannes Oswald, b. 1765, Weissenburg, Northampton Co., Pa
        m. 8 May 1788 **Anna Maria Moser** (b. 18 Apr 1770, d. 21 Apr 1861)
        d. 10 Nov 1834, Lehigh Co., Pa
        Children of John and Anna Maria Oswald:
            Johann Oswald, b. 2 Oct 1789, d. 24 Mar 1827
                m. **Elisabeth Steigerwalt**
            Anna Maria Oswald, b. 10 Mar 1791, d. 1 Nov 1868
                m. (1) **Christian Klingerman**
                   (2) **Andrew Reitz**
            Daniel Oswald, b. 12 Oct 1792, d. 18 Apr 1861
            Samuel Oswald, b. 4 Nov 1794, d. 6 Dec 1880
                m. **Catharina Fetherolf**
            Benjamin Oswald, b. 11 Oct 1796, d. 28 Apr 1872
            Jacob Oswald, b. 15 Nov 1798, d. 4 Apr 1876
                m. **Polly Everett**
            Joseph Oswald, b. abt 1800, d. 1818
            Elias Oswald, b. abt 1800, d. young
            Catherina Oswald, b. abt 1804, m. **Reuben Lutz**
            Gideon Oswald, b. 1 Mar 1807, d. 9 Nov 1892
                m. **Salome Wehr**
    Magdalena Oswald, b. 15 Dec 1767, Weissenburg, Northampton Co., Pa
        m. 17 Oct 1787 **Daniel Moser, son of Philip** and
                Maria Barbara Moser
        d. 16 Nov 1842, Centre Co., Pa
        bur. Wolf's Chapel, Penn Valley, Centre Co., Pa
    Catharine Oswald, b. 7 Apr 1770, Lynn, Northampton Co., Pa
        m. 1 May 1795 **David Moser, son of Philip** and **Maria Barbara Moser**
        d. 14 May 1851, Pa
        bur. Ebeneezer Cemetery, Lehigh Co., Pa
    Elisabeth Oswald, b. 9 Mar 1771, Lynn, Northampton Co., Pa
        m. 11 Nov 1785 **Philip Moser, son of Burchard Moser** and **Maria**
                Agatha Lichtenwallner
        d. 26 Feb 1843, Gregg Twp., Centre Co., Pa
        bur. Heckman's Cemetery, Penn Valley, Pa
    Barbara Oswald
    Susanna Oswald m. **Peter Lichtenwallner**
    David Oswald m. **Susan Miller**
    Jacob Oswald b. 27 Apr 1781, Lynn, Northampton Co., Pa.
        m. 22 Feb 1802 **Maria Elisabeth Everett**, daughter of **Samuel Everett**
            and **Maria Barbara Moser**
        d. 13 Jul 1852, Liberty Twp., Trumbull Co., Oh

9. The Family of Jacob Friedrich Oswald

Jacob Freidrich Oswald, son of **Johann Martin Oswald** (a tax collector) and **Christina Kindler**, was born 21 Aug 1713 in Germany. He married in Offenhausen, Germany, **Anna Maria Rebstock** (b. 7 Oct 1709 in Germany), whose father is listed as **Cloister Cooper**. The family went to Nova Scotia on 11 Apr 1752 with one child. Known children of Jacob and Anna Oswald:

> **Frederich Oswald**
>> b. abt. 1736 in Germany
>> arrived in Philadelphia in 1753 on the *Patience*
>
> **Frederica Barbara Oswald**
>> b. 2 Nov 1740, Steinhulben, Germany
>
> **Johan Jacob Oswald**
>> b. 29 Dec 1747, Germany
>> d. 14 Nov 1825, New Tripoli, Pa.
>> bur. Ebeneezer cemetery, Lehigh Co., Pa.

10. The Family of Jonathan Oswald

Jonathan Oswald, son of **Jacob Oswald** and **Rebecca Huston** married **Maria Everett**, daughter of **Samuel Everett** and **Maria Barbara Moser**. They were the parents of at least one daughter:

> **Susanna Oswald**
>> b. 1 Mar 1822, Liberty, Tioga Co., Pa
>> m. 6 Jun 1845, Trumbull Co., Oh, **Jacob E. Everett**
>> d. 13 Jun 1903, Trumbull Co., Oh
>> bur. Newton Falls, Trumbull Co., Oh

11. The Family of Christian Seiberling

Christian Seiberling, son of **Michael Seiberling** (1704-1791) who arrived at Philadelphia on the *Molly* in 1741*)*, was born in 1733 and died in Pennsylvania in 1820. He married **Ernestine Louisa Holben** (1728-1824). He purchased 200 acres of land in Weissenberg Township, Northumberland Co., Pa., where the following son was born:

    Frederick Seiberling (1760-1837)
      m. **Catherine Weiss**
      They had a son, **John Seiberling** m. **Catherine Bear**
      He was a shoemaker and the postmaster of Lynn in Lehigh County. They were the parents of:
        Joshua Seiberling m. **Catherine Moser**
        Mary Elisabeth Seiberling
          b. 28 Jan 1804, Northampton Co., Pa
          m. **Daniel Moser** (b. 8 Feb 1790, Pa
            (d. 30 Dec 1834, Wadsworth, Medina, Oh)
            d. 9 Aug 1873, Wadsworth, Medina
          bur. High Church Cemetery, Doylestown, Oh
          Children of Daniel and Mary Elisabeth:
            John F. Moser b. 1824, Pa
            Mary A. Moser b. 1828, Pa
            Sarah Ann Moser b. 22 Aug 1833, Oh
              m. **Jacob Henry Miller**
            James Moser b. 30 Aug 1838, Oh
              m. 19 Sep 1858 **Adelina**
                Emilie Kemmerer
           David Moser b. 1842, Oh
           Joshua Moser b. 1844, Oh
           Emily Moser b. 1856, Oh

12. The Family of Jurg Daniel Wannemacher

Jurg Daniel Wannemacher, son of **Marx Wannemacher** and **Catharina** _____,
was born 1 Aug 1755 in Lynn Township, Northampton County, Pennsylvania and
baptized 12 Oct 1756 by Rev. Daniel Schumacher. Sponsors at his baptism were **Jurg
Falck** and **Dorothea Wannemacher** (both single). He served in the Northampton Co.
Militia, 6th Co., First Battalion as a fifer during the Revolution War.

Daniel married abt. 1786 **Susanna Everett**, (sister of **Samuel Everett**) daughter of
Thomas Everett and **Catherine Albright** of Lynn Township, (now Lehigh County), Pa.
They lived in Lynn Township, but moved to Liberty Township, Trumbull County Ohio,
where he owned land, possibly as a reward of his Revolutionar War service. He served
as the appraiser for the estate of his brother-in-law, Samuel Everett, in 1807.

Daniel died before18 Jun 1816 in Liberty, Trumbull County, Ohio, when **Conrad
Miller** was appointed by the Orphan's Court, as guardian of two minor children, **Daniel
Jr.** and **Elizabeth Wannamacher**. **Christian Wannamacher**, a son of Daniel, was
appointed as guardian of his sister, **Susannah**, and **Philip Wannamacher**, another son,
became guardian of his siblings **Samuel** and **Sarah**. His estate was administered
25 Apr 1817. Children of Daniel & Susanna Wannamacher:

1. **Philip Wannamacher**
   b. abt. 1787, Lynn Twp., Northampton Co., Pa
   m. 30 Nov 1813, Trumbull Co., Oh. **Magdalena Everett**
   dau. of **Samuel Everett** and **Maria Barbara Moser**
2. **Christian Wannamacher**
   b. 23 Apr 1789, Lynn Twp., Lynn Twp., Northampton Co., Pa
   m. (1) **Catherine "Katy" Fusselman**
   (2) 11 May 1837, Trumbull Co., Oh **Pamelia St. John Barnes**
3. **Jacob Wannamacher**
   b. 17 Sep 1793, Berks Co., Pa
   bp. 3 Nov 1793, Jerusalem Lutheran Church, Albany Twp., Berks Co.
   Sponsors: **Daniel Segler** and **Catherine Probst/Brobst**
   m. **Elizabeth "Betsy" Sechler**, dau of **Henry** and **Juliana Sechler**
   d. bef. 1860, Southington, Trumbull Co., Oh
   Children of Jacob and Betsy Wannamacher:
   a. **Daniel Wannamacher**
      b. 23 Jun 1818, Lynn Twp., Lehigh Co., Pa
      m. 4 May 1845 **Jane C. Trusdell**
      They had seven children.
   b. **Samuel Wannamacher**
      b. 6 Apr 1821, Pa
      m. 22 Oct 1849 **Elizabeth Waggoner**
   c. **Henry Lewis Wannamacher**
      b. 18 Sep 1822, Oh
      m. 31 Dec 1843 Trumbull Co., Oh
      Hannah Chatfield
   d. **Lucy Ann Wannamacher**
      b. abt 1826, Oh.
      m. (1) 21 Apr 1852, Trumbull Co., Oh
      Samuel Downs, of England,
      They had four children
      (2) 14 Jul 1880 **William Dent** of Warren, Oh.
      d. 2 Feb 1874
   e. **Charles Wannamacher**
      b. 9 Dec 1828, Oh
      m. 23 Sep 1857 **Martha D. Norton**

      f. **Julia Ann Wannamacher**
         b. abt. 1833, Oh.
         m. **Harmon Brecht**
         They moved to Emmett Co., Mi.
      g. **Susanna Wannamacher**
         b. 1837, Oh.
         m. 16 Jul 1864 **Eri O. Smith**
      h. **Mary Elizabeth Wannamacher**
         b. 1849, Oh
         m. _____ **Fusselman**
4. **John Wannamacher**
    b. abt. 1794/5, Pa
    m. **Mary "Polly" Sauer**
5. **Daniel Wannamacher**
    b. abt. 1798, Pa
    m. 21 Nov 1820 Trumbull Co., Oh **Sarah "Sally" Dustman**
    d. 25 Nov 1861
    bur. Old North (Zion) Cemetery, Canfield, Mahoning Co., Oh
    Children of Daniel and Sarah Wannamacher:
        a. **Lydianna Wannamacher** b. 1821, Oh
             m. 1841 **Nathan Moyer/Myers**
        b. **Reuben Wannamacher** b. 1823, Oh
             m. 15 Sep1844 **Sarah Fox**
             d. 12 May 1849
        c. **Elias Wannamacher** b. 1824 Oh
             d. 30 Aug 1860
             (unmarried)
        d. **Sarah Wannamacher** b. 1827/8, Oh
             m. 30 Apr 1843 **Ethen Bowen**
        e. **Martin Wannamacher** b. 1831 Oh
             d. 13 Oct 1852
             (unmarried)
        f. **Nathan Wannamacher** b. 1834/5, Oh
        g. **Juliatt Wannamacher** b. 1845
    6. **Jonas Wannamacher**
        b. 28 Mar 1796, Berks Co., Pa
        bp. 29 Jun 1796, Jerusalem Lutheran Church,
           Albany Twp., Berks Co., Pa
           Sponsors: **Johannes & Magdalena Hartinger**
        m. **Ester Everett**
    7. **Mary "Polly" Wannamacher**
        b. abt. 1799, Pa.
        m. 18 Nov 1817 **Peter Riehl/Reel**
        d. 23 Jun 1822, Weathersfield, Trumbull Co., Oh
    8. **Elizabeth "Betsy" Wannamacher**
        m. 2 Sep 1825 **Daniel Everett**
        of Hubbard, Trumbull Co., Oh
    9. **Susannah Wannamacher**
    10. **Sarah Wannamacher**
    11. **Samuel E. Wannamacher**
        b. 19 Feb 1804
        m. (1) **Mary Barbara Hake**
           (2) 15 Jan 1842 **Minerva Williams**

The Great Coal Caper

Burkhard Moser, son of **Johann Burchard Moser** and **Maria Agatha Lichtenwallner**, married **Catharine** and lived in Lynn, Northampton (now Lehigh) County, Pennsylvania, where his children were born. After the Revolutionary War in which he served, he pushed over the Blue Mountains into what was then wild country. He purchased two tracts of land, one in what is now Penn Township, Centre Co., and the other in Tamaqua where he built a saw mill in 1799 at the junction of the Tamaqua River and Panther Creek. Because of Indian trouble and the primitive condition of the area, his wife and children remained behind in Lynn, Lehigh County. By 1804, he had cleared enough land and built a cabin in what is now Tamaqua, Schuylkill County, Pennsylvania, and brought his family there to live.

In 1817, Burkhard and his son, Jacob, discovered coal on their property, which they began to mine and sell to local blacksmiths. Soon they had enlarged their operation and began selling the coal on the other side of the mountain. Unfortunately, this came to the attention of the Lehigh Coal & Navigation Company, who managed to run them off the land, probably through the forceful methods used by coal companies in those days.

The owners of the coal company then made up a Burkhard who was supposed to be an eccentric old bachelor, supposedly a brother to **Christian** and **Peter Moser**, sons of the **Hans Michael Moser** who arrived on the "*Duke of Wurtemberg*" in 1752. (Straussberg and Hinke, who are considered to be the foremost authority on German Immigration, have this Hans Michael listed as "*Mosser*". Rupp, which is supposedly full of errors, is the one who has declared him to be a "*Mauer*".) In a very scholarly article for the American Genealogist Magazine, April, 1987, pp. 82-88, Walter R. Mattfeld has proven that this Michael, whom he believes is really a Moser, never had a son named Burkhard.

To prove their claim, the coal company also created a fake deed for the 420 acre tract was drawn up and dated 17 January 1815. (This deed was written on a typewriter, which had not even been invented in 1815!) This story is repeated in many printed books, including Roberts "*History of Lehigh County, Pennsylvania*" on page 923. The coal company then claimed that Burkhard paid taxes on this land until he died in 1828 at which time his neighbors, believing that he was without kith or kin, just buried his body on his land.

It is interesting to note that all of the church records between 1820 and about 1824 which are now on microfilm, contain notes regarding pages torn from the record books during that time period. The microfilm of the 1850 Schuylkill County Federal Census is very clear and easy reading -- except for Tamaqua, which is so covered with ink blotches that it cannot be read at all!

In the 1820 Centre County Federal Census, Burkhard was listed as owning no land, but was levied taxes on it anyway. The coal company claimed that they built the log cabin in 1804, that they paid the taxes on the land for two years, then took possession under "squatters rights". If this is true, the taxes on the property were paid twice, once by Burkhard, and again by the coal company.

Burkhard's wife, Catharine is believed to have died between 1811 and 1814, as she signed a deed with Burkhard in 1811, giving land to a son, but did not sign the 1814 deed. (These deeds may also be forged, as they are also typewritten.) These two pieces of land were supposedly leased to the Greenaugh Coal Company and the Little Schuylkill Company for ninety-nine years, expiring in 1883. Simple arithmatic proves that Burkhard's sons could not have leased land to anyone in 1784, as not only did they not yet own it, but they weren't even born yet! The leases would have to have expiration dates of 1920 and 1923 if this "story" were to be believed.

However, in 1840 Burkhard, was still very much alive living in West Penn Township (now Coaldale, Schuylkill County) with his son, John. He attended the St. John's Lutheran Church in Tamaqua. Burkhard died before the 1850 census was taken.

In 1973, we learned of a Margaret Spielman who possessed some old letters regarding a lawsuit being pursued by Moser heirs against a coal company. That began a twenty year search for copies of those letters. Thanks to the generosity of Carl Morr of Michigan, we have now acquired some copies of the Trumbull County, Ohio newsletter. These copies are reproduced on the following pages.

Mannechoir Hall,
Schuylkill Ave., Tamaqua, Pa.
April 9, 1927

A meeting of the heirs of the Burkhart Moser Jr., Estate was held at the above place on the date designated. Close to two hundred heirs were present, each of whom was permitted to voice his or her opinion concerning the Estate.

The meeting was called to order at 2.30 P. M by Mr. Burkhart Lee Moser, resident and heir, of Scranton, Pa. Mr. Moser read several letters received from relatives in the West concerning their opinions on the case. They conveyed to us as best they could just how much satisfaction and interest may be derived from meetings held by the heirs who have come together as one family to plan and exchange thoughts on the Estate. Furthermore, Mr. Moser stated, in a very appreciative manner, how well qualified Mr. Harry King would be as our legal advisor.

Mrs. Dora Becker was next introduced and thereon gave an itemized account of the money which had heretofore been collected, stating that travelling, stationery, etc., were the main items which naturally required money.

Next Mr. Harry King, Cleveland attorney, was introduced. Mr. King has volunteered his services in our own problem and does not hope for anything except that we can prove our claim. That object being achieved, he is at ease, knowing that he has accomplished his point. Mr. King is very well known in his particular profession—that of law—as having successfully settled cases of a similar nature.

Mr. King's introduction has evidently made a favorable impression on those in attendance, as an immediate motion was made to the effect that Mr. King be named our permanent legal advisor, which motion was unanimously accepted by the house.

In the course of Mr. King's most inspiring talk,

[1]

he frankly admitted that, although having heard stories from both sides involved, it was utterly impossible to make any definite statement concerning settlement until an abstract title could be secured. Mr. King made numerous visits to various people where an interview was quite necessary. Each interview consumed a fairly good portion of the money already contributed. Upon a visit to New York he met Mrs. Dora Moser Becker and spent quite some time with her, during which time he found that law suits had already been filed, but had been dismissed. Mrs. Olive Beardsley, of Ohio, was informed of the situation and advised that in her estimation an abstract title would be necessary, as well as various other papers which Mrs. Beardsley mentioned. Mr. King immediately set to work to secure the necessary information, but it was in vain. The papers had evidently been destroyed. From searches recently made it is reported that there were very bold irregularities discovered. Thus far, Mr. King stated that at this time he was not prepared to produce sufficient evidence as would justify action on our part, but he would tell us, to the best of his ability, just what he could do and what he had discovered.

Burkhart Moser, Jr., owned several hundred acres of property, part of which lays in this borough and in the adjoining towns and county. As times became hard, part of it was sold for taxes. It was taken by the Lehigh Coal and Navigation Company, although not legally purchased until years after. Not until 1892 did they have claim to the land. At this particular time, Mr. Tiffany, Scranton lawyer, was appointed to take care of the matter. Some settlement was made previous to this time. as has been proved. At the request of the Western folks Mr. King has set to work to obtain the abstract which is already being prepared at an approximate cost of from $100.00 to $150.00, $20.00 of which is paid. Before this title is obtained, Mr. King advises that it is absolutely useless to spend any more money. Mr.

[2]

King also stated that, outside of travelling expenses and necessary funds to cover charges required for titles, etc., he asked nothing whatever for himself.

Here it was moved that a fixed amount of money be collected from each family. The amount, which was arrived at, $5.00, will be used to defray expenses of those who have so nobly volunteered their efforts for our cause. The suggestion seemed favorable to the house and was passed by a majority.

————o————

RECEIPTS

Collected in Pennsylvania.................$645.00
Collected in Warren, O., $161.00; sent us.... 135.00
Collected in Cleveland, O., $105.00; send us.. 30.00
                                            ————
                                            $810.00

EXPENSES

Mr. Maneeley $250.00
Mr. Maneeley and Becker.......... 40.00
Our Expenses to Date............. 395.00
                                  ———— 685.00
                                        ————
Balance on Hand....................$125.00

————o————

The question then arose as to the organization of an association here in the East as has developed among the Western heirs, to promote the interests of we Eastern folks, who seemingly are at a loss to know anything about it, which fact was ably proven by several heirs at our meeting.

Mr. King, being a very good friend of Mrs. Beardsley, has accepted the case, stating that he would fight it to the end to prove our claim or title to the land in question.

With further reference to our proposed organization, after a little explanation and the usual arguments that naturally arise in a "family discussion," it

[3]

was decided that the following officers for our association be named: Mr. Burkhart Lee Moser, President; Mr. John Moser Barrett, of Coaldale, Pa., was nominated Secretary but declined in favor of Mrs. Dora Moser Becker. The declination being accepted, it was moved that she be appointed both Secretary and Treasurer. It was thought that both positions would afford considerable responsibility for one person, but our officer in charge was well aware of the fact that Mrs. Becker was ably qualified to perform the tasks of Secretary and Treasurer.

Several heirs were rather anxious to know how much land was covered by the Estate, which was a rather hard matter to say. Mr. Tiffany, during his "reign," made the statement that "it extended on the next neighbor's land." Rather absurd and indefinite statement to make when one seems as interested as some of the heirs seemed to be. Mr. John Moser Barrett stated that he would say it was comprised of approximately 932 acres. The question could not be settled without a legal survey, and that only part of it had been sold for taxes. It was then suggested that a lieutenant be appointed in each family to take care of their own immediate interests. This lieutenant is to attend to all affairs for his family and assume all responsibilities therein. Of course, it was generally understood that the Eastern Branch act entirely independent of the Western Branch.

The organization not being formed when the move was made concerning the $5.00 contribution, it was necessary to place the same question before the house again. It was regularly moved and seconded, and the sum fixed at $5.00, to be paid by each family.

The amount named was then contributed by many heirs, although there were some who did not contribute. The amount collected was $165.00, to be used for disbursements, etc., an account of which would be given out every six months to each lieutenant.

The meeting adjourned at 3.45. This report is

[4]

for the heirs only, and may we ask that each and every one try and help us by not giving this any publicity? Please look up all the data that you can, as all our forefathers kept records in the family Bible.

After Mr. King gets all the required information and the abstract, he will form his plans, and our President will call another meeting. We want you to know all there is to know, and if you know anything, please tell us. Every one who has not sent in their family data for the tree are requested to send it at once. We must get this tree together real soon.

We want to ask all who have not paid their second assessment of $5.00 to please do so at once. We also want to call your attention to the fact that the heirs from Ohio and Western States have all joined our Organization and that we are all working together.

Trusting you will comply with the above,

We remain,

BURKHART L. MOSER,
President.

DORA MOSER BECKER,
Secretary and Treasurer.
100 South 51st Street, Phila., Pa.

———o———

Cleveland, O., April 1, 1927.

Greetings From Your Ohio, Michigan and Indiana Moser Cousins:

Wishing you all a happy reunion—a greater success than ever before—we have sent to you our representative, Mr. Harry E. King, of Cleveland, O., a New York Central Railroad attorney of note, whom we highly recommend as a man of legal ability; one who is familiar with Pennsylvania land titles; one who has a sixth sense and makes valuable discoveries. Nearly all of us have known him since childhood. We invite you to co-operate with us to stand back of Dora M. Becker and Mr. King and help them

[5]

with our financial and moral support. We must have
a working capital. Will do our bit and want you to
act with us as one body, one mind and have con-
fidence in our captains. Mrs. Becker deserves a
crown. She's been loyal to Burkhart Moser's children and their children. She needs co-operation.
Together we will win our case against the Coal Company and come into the legacy left us by our dear
old grandparents — Burkhart Moser's children.
There is "full and plenty for all." It would be our
pleasure to meet you all face to face.

Sincerely yours,

OLIVE C. BEARDSLEY.

Pres. of Magdalene and Marie Moser heir,

Lakewood, O.

C. W. MOSER,.

Pres. of Philip. son of Michael Moser heirs,

Warren, O.

———o———

Warren, O., April 4, 1927.

Dear Mrs. Becker:

I received this letter, introducing Mr. King, from
Mrs. Beardsley this morning, and as Mr. King is
known by most of our family we feel that we have
secured one of the best lawyers we could find any-
where.

We all unite in sending our best regards to all
of our Eastern relatives, and all good wishes for great
success to you in this great undertaking, for it has
been your perseverance which will help us to reach
the goal.

We are awaiting the result of your reunion and
then we will all meet together here and endeavor to
help you to still carry on for the good of all.

Wishing we could all be together, I am

Very truly yours,

MISS LUCY M. HOWER,

Secretary for Phillip Moser Family.

[6]

THE BURKHART MOSER ESTATE ASSOCIATION

MRS. DORA M. BECKER, SECRETARY AND TREASURER

5024 CHESTNUT STREET

PHILADELPHIA, PA.

June 12-192,

Dear Friends and Relatives:

After many years of hard work, searching old records, etc., we have found everything necessary, and are now ready to bring suit to recover the Coal Lands owned by Burkhart Moser, Jr., which were taken and worked for many years by the Lehigh Coal & Navigation Company.

Now that all the preliminary work is finished, we expect a court date will be sent soon to our attorney, Mr. Harry E. King, of Cleveland, Ohio.

Mr. King is working on a contingent fee, and if we lose, he also loses. However, we have promised to pay all necessary expenses of the case.

We need more money at once; as our funds are practically exhausted. We must have the ready cash for Mr. King to come East, as well as to meet other expenses.

No doubt you realize it is the duty of everyone to help defray the expenses to bring about a satisfactory settlement.

Let us keep up our good work, and to this end we feel that if everyone were to contribute five dollars or more and make this the last appeal for funds we will be well paid for our honest efforts.

Trusting that you will give this your hearty co-operation and respond promptly. I am, thankfully yours,

Signed: Dora M. Becker

DESCENDANCY CHART FOR HANS MARTIN MOSER

Name	(Birth/Chr.-Death/Burial)	Birth/Chr. Place

```
1-- Hans Martin MOSER-152 (1699-1744) Germany
 sp-Maria Margaret KUNKEL-108 (1700-1762) Germany
  2-- Frederick MOSER-166 (1727-1800) Germany
   sp-Barbara Maria LOOSER-167 (    -    )
    3-- Jacob MOSER-286 (1751-1819) Pa
     sp-Nellie (MOSER)-287 (    -    )
     sp-Polly STEPHENS-288 (    -    )
    3-- Abraham MOSER-289 (1752-    ) Pa
     sp-Nellie (MOSER)-290 (    -    )
    3-- Michael MOSER-291 (1756-1828) Northampton Co.,Pa.
     sp-Sophie REINHARDT-292 (    -    )
    3-- Johann Philip MOSER-293 (1758-1828) Northampton Co.,Pa.
     sp-Catherine SCHNEIDER-294 (    -    )
     sp-Martha (MOSER)-295 (    -    )
    3-- Maria Barbara MOSER-296 (1760-    ) Linn,Northampton,Pa.
     sp-Samuel HUFFMAN-298 (    -    )
     sp-KECK-299 (    -    )
    3-- Jurg Frederick MOSER-297 (1760-    ) Linn,Northampton,Pa.
    3-- Mary Ann MOSER-300 (1761-1838) Orange Co.,NC
     sp-Conrad Frederick KECK-301 (    -    )
    3-- Nicholas MOSER-302 (1762-    ) Pa
     sp-Elisabeth LOW-303 (    -    )
    3-- Elizabeth "Lizzy" MOSER-304 (1767-1821) Orange Co.,NC
     sp-Henry SHARP [Jr.]-305 (    -    )
    3-- Eve MOSER-306 (1768-1822) Orange Co.,NC
     sp-Peter SHARP-307 (    -    )
    3-- Caty MOSER-308 (1769-    )
     sp-Henry KIMBRO-309 (    -    )
    3-- John MOSER-310 (1771-    ) Orange Co.,NC
     sp-Margaret KLEIN-311 (    -    )
    3-- Frederick MOSER-312 (1772-1839) Orange Co.,NC
     sp-Mary INGOLD-313 (    -    )
     sp-Barbara ANTHONY-371 (    -    )
  2-- Maria Margaretta MOSER-107 (1728-    ) Goshenhoppen,Philadelphia,I
   sp-Johann Jacob STEINBROOK-182 (    -1756)
    3-- George Frederick STANBROOK-393 (1742-1812) Pa.
     sp-Catharina (MOSER)-394 (    -    )
    3-- Maria Barbara STANBROOK-395 (1741-1821) Philadelphia Co.,Pa.
     sp-Johann Adam DIETRICH-396 (    -    )
```

```
  3-- Abraham STANBROOK-397 (1763-    ) Weisenberg Church,
  3-- Anna Barbara STANBROOK-398 (1763-    ) Weisenberg Church,
2-- Maria Barbara MOSER-171 (1729-    ) Goshenhoppen,Philadelphia,Pa.
 sp-SITTLER-172 (    -    )
2-- Johann Phillip MOSER-151 (1730-1817) Goshenhoppen,Philadelphia,Pa.
 sp-Maria Barbara (MOSER)-164 (    -    )
  3-- Christina MOSER-177 (1751-1833) Pa.
   sp-John Matthais PIKE-178 (    -    )
  3-- Maria Barbara MOSER-115 (1753-1811) Linn,Northampton,Pa.
   sp-Samuel EVERETT-114 (1745-1807) Northampton County,PA
  3-- Catharina MOSER-179 (1756-1826) Linn,Northampton,Pa.
   sp-Michael OHL-180 (1750-1825) Pa
  3-- Johann Philip MOSER-1369 (1757-1804)
   sp-Catherine Margaretha SCHOCH-1370 (1759-1839)
  3-- Johann Sebastian MOSER-169 (1760-1829) Linn,Northampton,Pa.
   sp-Anna Maria MILLER-436 (1762-1842) Linn,Northampton,Pa.
  3-- Johann Daniel MOSER-170 (1762-1804) Linn,Northampton,Pa.
   sp-Magdalena OSWALD-514 (1767-1842) ,Northampton,Pa.
  3-- David MOSER-176 (1766-1832) Linn,Northampton,PA
   sp-Catharine OSWALD-181 (1776-1857)
  3-- Johann Jacob MOSER-173 (1775-1833) Linn,Northampton,Pa.
   sp-Margaretha HAGENBACH-607 (1779-1851)
2-- Johann Michael MOSER-165 (1734-1820) Goshenhoppen,Philadelphia,Pa.
 sp-Catharina (MOSER)-168 (    -    )
  3-- Ertmann (Adam) MOSER-933 (1750-    )
  3-- Michael MOSER-934 (1752-1818) Pa.
   sp-Catharina WEIHMAN-935 (1751-1827)
  3-- Christina Catharina MOSER-936 (1754-    ) Pa.
   sp-Michael HOCHNLE-937 (    -    )
  3-- Anna Barbara MOSER-938 (1756-    ) Pa.
  3-- Eva MOSER-939 (1757-    ) Pa.
  3-- John MOSER-944 (1763-    ) Pa.
2-- Johann Burkhard MOSER-183 (1736-1807) Goshenhoppen,Philadelphia,Pa.
 sp-Maria Agatha LICHTENWALNER-184 (1734-1807) Pa.
  3-- Johann Burkhard MOSER-187 (1763-1849) Lynn Twp,Northampton,PA
   sp-Catharine HORNBERGER-188 (    -    )
  3-- Johann Phillip MOSER-189 (1765-1849) Lynn Twp,Northampton,PA
   sp-Elisabeth OSWALD-542 (1771-1843)
  3-- Anna Maria MOSER-185 (1769-1842) Lynn Twp,Northampton,PA
   sp-Christian MILLER-186 (    -1799)
   sp-John OSWALD-133 (    -    )
  3-- Jacob MOSER-191 (1772-1855) Lynn Twp,Northampton,PA
   sp-OSWALD-135 (    -1800)
   sp-Susanna HUNSICKER-280 (1775-1850) Pa.
  3-- Catharine Barbara MOSER-283 (1773-    ) Lynn Twp,Northampton,PA
   sp-George SITTLER-266 (    -    )
  3-- Michael MOSER-463 (1767-1853) Lynn Twp,Northampton,PA
   sp-Anna Margaretha WEBER-464 (    -    )
   sp-Catharina Elisabetha WASSER-240 (    -1801)
```

DESCENDANCY CHART FOR HANS ADAM MOSER

Name	(Birth/Chr.-Death/Burial)	Birth/Chr. Place

```
1-- Hans Adam MOSER-1 (1684-1770) ,,Germany
sp-Eva (MOSER)-2 (    -1759)
  2-- Hans Adam MOSER [Jr]-3 (1726-1758) Pa.
  sp-Anna Maria (MOSER)-5 (   -   )
    3-- Hans Adam MOSER-6 (1745-1804) Pa.
  2-- Anna Maria MUSSER-13 (1735-1804) Pa.
  sp-Michael RUTH-14 (1725-1803)
    3-- Michael RUTH-93 (   -   )
  2-- Nicholas MOSER-4 (1738-1824) Pa
  sp-Catherine LEY-8 (   -1788)
    3-- Anna Maria MOSER-34 (1763-1835) Pa.
    sp-J. Nicholas ALBERT-35 (1765-1831)
    3-- Michael MOSER-36 (1764-1843) Pa.
    sp-Margaret Ann COPENHAVER-37 (1766-   ) Pa.
    3-- Christena MOSER-38 (1773-   ) Pa.
    sp-William SIEBERT-39 (   -   )
    3-- Eva MOSER-40 (   -   )
    sp-Philip TICE-41 (   -   )
  sp-Margaret HAHN-9 (1747-1818) Pa.
    3-- Margaret MOSER-45 (1788-   ) Tulpehocken Church
  2-- Henry MUSSER-11 (   -   )
  sp-Elisabeth (MOSER)-12 (   -   )
  2-- Catharine MUSSER-15 (   -   )
  sp-Tobias BICKEL-16 (   -   )
  2-- Peter MUSSER-17 (   -1844)
  sp-Catherine SNIDER-18 (   -   )
  2-- Jacob MUSSER-19 (   -1780)
  sp-Maria HOSTETTLER-20 (   -   )
    3-- Christina MOSER-161 (1749-   ) Swatara,Pa.
    sp-John WALLNER-162 (   -   )
    3-- Catherine MOSER-165 (   -   )
    sp-Thomas COPENHAVER [Capt.]-44 (   -   )
    3-- Rachel Regina MOSER-166 (   -   )
    sp-Adam GUTMAN-167 (   -   )
    3-- Elisabeth MOSER-168 (   -   )
    3-- Jacob MOSER [Jr.]-169 (1757-   ) Pa.
    3-- Eva MOSER-170 (   -   )
    sp-WEIRICK-171 (   -   )
  2-- Hans MUSSER-21 (   -   )
  2-- Elizabeth MUSSER-22 (   -   )
```

```
2-- Daniel MUSSER-23 (    -    )
  sp-Anna Maria (MUSSER)-24 (    -    )
      3-- John Henry MOSER-172 (1771-    ) Swatara Reformed Chur(
      3-- Magdalena MOSER-173 (1775-    )  Swatara Reformed Chur(
2-- Weirley MUSSER-25 (    -1811)
  sp-Margaret EPLER-174 (    -    )
      3-- Anna Maria MOSER-175 (    -    )
        sp-William ALBRECHT-176 (    -    )
      3-- Barbara MOSER-177 (    -    )
      3-- Catherine MOSER-178 (    -    )
      3-- John MOSER-179 (    -    )
        sp-Elisabeth LAMM-180 (    -    )
      3-- Valentine MOSER-181 (1759-1833)  Lancaster Co.,Pa.
        sp-Rosina FISCHER-182 (    -    )

  sp-Anna Maria (MOSER)-26 (    -1759)
```

DESCENDANCY CHART FOR HANS PAULUS MÖSSER

Name	(Birth/Chr.-Death/Burial)	Birth/Chr. Place

```
1-- Hans Paulus MÖSSER-1 (1708-1780)    Germany
sp-Elisabeth (MOSER)-2 (    -1749)
    2-- Michael MUSSER-3 (1739-1814)    New Hanover,Montgomery,Pa.
    sp-Elisabeth (MOSER)-4 (    -    )
    sp-Mary (MOSER)-5 (    -    )
        3-- William MUSSER-32 (1764-1803)
        3-- Elisabeth MUSSER-33 (1765-1771)  Pa.
        3-- Frederich MUSSER-34 (1769-1785)  Pa.
        3-- Elisabeth MUSSER-35 (1771-    )  Pa.
        3-- John MUSSER-36 (1774-1813)  Pa.
        sp-Mary Catherine MUHLENBERG-37 (1776-1843)  Lancaster Co.,Pa.
        3-- Anna Maria MUSSER-38 (1778-    )  Lancaster Co.,Pa.
        3-- Catharine MUSSER-39 (1781-    )  Lancaster Co.,Pa.
        3-- Rebecca MUSSER-40 (1784-1797)  Lancaster Co.,Pa.
    2-- George MUSSER-6 (1741-1806)  Pa.
    sp-Christina YOUNG-7 (1748-1828)
        3-- Rebecca MUSSER-113 (1766-1846)  Pa.
        sp-Henry DERING-114 (1760-    )
        3-- John MUSSER-115 (1768-1773)  Pa.
        3-- Anna Maria MUSSER-116 (1771-1827)  Lancaster Co.,Pa.
        sp-John SINGER-117 (1763-    )  Lancaster Co.,Pa.
        3-- Elisabeth MUSSER-118 (1773-    )  Pa.
        3-- Salome MUSSER-119 (1774-1854)  Pa.
        3-- John MUSSER-120 (1775-    )  Pa.
        3-- George MUSSER-121 (1777-1868)  Pa.
        sp-Mary GRAFF-122 (1783-1817)
        sp-Sarah GRAFF-123 (1775-1854)
        3-- Jacob MUSSER-124 (1779-    )  Pa.
        3-- Catharine MUSSER-125 (1781-    )  Pa.
        sp-William HAVERSTICK [Jr.]-126 (    -    )
        3-- Jacob MUSSER-127 (1783-    )  Pa.
        3-- Mathias MUSSER-128 (1785-1833)  Pa.
        sp-Ann HAVERSTICK-129 (1786-    )
        3-- John Adam MUSSER-130 (1787-    )  Pa.
        sp-Margaret SCHAUM-131 (    -    )
        3-- William MUSSER-132 (1789-1881)  Pa.
        sp-Susan Elisabeth GREINER-133 (    -    )
        3-- Henry MUSSER-134 (1791-1822)  Pa.
        3-- Abraham MUSSER-135 (1793-1828)  Pa.
        sp-Maria DUCHMAN-136 (    -    )
```

```
  3-- Henrietta MUSSER-137 (1794-1886)  Pa.
    sp-William GLENN-138 (    -    )
    sp-John William KANE-139 (    -    )
2-- Eva MOSSER-26 (1743-    )  Pa.
  sp-Balthaser TRAUT-27 (    -    )
    3-- George TRAUT-28 (1764-    )  Pa.
2-- John Adam MUSSER-8 (1746-1823)
  sp-Christina PRUNNER-9 (1752-1823)
    3-- George MOSER-289 (1774-1853)  Lancaster,Pa.
      sp-Elisabeth MONTELIUS-290 (1779-1833)
    3-- Christina MOSER-291 (1776-1860)  Pa.
      sp-Samuel REAM-292 (    -    )
    3-- Elisabeth MOSER-298 (1777-1823)  Pa.
      sp-Christian HARTER-299 (    -    )

    3-- Adam MOSER-300 (1779-    )  Lancaster Co.,Pa.
      sp-Catharine (MOSER)-301 (    -    )
    3-- Susanna MOSER-302 (1781-    )
    3-- Sarah MOSER-304 (1783-    )  Pa.
      sp-John HOCKER-303 (    -    )
    3-- Rebecca MOSER-305 (1785-    )  Pa.
      sp-John RUTH-306 (    -    )
    3-- Henry MOSER-307 (1787-    )  Pa.
    3-- William MOSER-310 (1790-1847)  Pa.
      sp-Elizabeth SCHWEITZER-311 (    -1838)
    3-- Mary MOSER-312 (1792-1796)  Pa.
    3-- John MOSER-308 (1794-    )  Pa.
      sp-Catharine (MOSER)-309 (    -    )
    3-- Mary MOSER-313 (1796-    )  Pa.
2-- Andrew MOSSER-10 (1748-    )  Pa.
  sp-Maria Magdalena BIGN-11 (1754-1820)  Pa.
    3-- Anna Maria MOSER-465 (1776-    )  Easton,Northampton,Pa.
    3-- John Jacob MOSER-466 (1778-1852)  Pa.
      sp-Elisabeth NICKOM-467 (1781-1850)
    3-- Andreas MOSER-468 (1780-    )  Easton,Northampton,Pa.
      sp-Catharine NICKOM-469 (    -    )
    3-- Frederick MOSER-471 (1783-1830)  Pa.
      sp-Rosina LATTIG-472 (    -    )
    3-- Maria MOSER-473 (1785-    )  Williams Twp.,Northampton,Pa.
    3-- George MOSER-474 (1789-    )  Pa.
      sp-Maria SEIFFERT-475 (    -    )
    3-- Margaret MOSER-476 (1791-    )  Pa.
    3-- Paul MOSER-477 (    -    )
      sp-Maria DEILY-478 (    -    )
2-- Jacob MOSSER-12 (1750-1830)  Pa.
  sp-Catharine/Margaret (MOSSER)-13 (    -    )
```

```
3-- George MOSER-493 (1790-1869)  Green Co.,Pa.
 sp-Mary HANLIN-494 (1800-1869)
 3-- Mary MOSER [Polly]-495 (   -   )
 sp-Felix HANLIN-496 (   -   )
 3-- Catharine MOSER-497 (1792-1850)  Green Co.,Pa.
 sp-Christopher WAGNER-498 (1791-1862)
 3-- John MOSER-499 (   -   )
 sp-Lucinda MIKE-500 (   -   )
 3-- David MOSER-501 (   -   )
 sp-Elizabeth (MOSER)-502 (   -   )
 3-- Margaret MOSER-503 (   -   )
sp-Eva BEEHOLT-14 (   -   )
 2-- Magdalena MOSSER-16 (1753-   )  Pa.
 sp-John HEITER-17 (   -   )
 2-- Johannes Paulus MOSSER-18 (1756-1842)  Pa.
 sp-Maria Magdalena HEITER-19 (   -   )
 3-- MOSER-568 (   -   )
 sp-Joseph SWARTZ-569 (   -   )
 3-- Elizabeth MOSER-572 (1792-   )  Pa.
 sp-John MILLER-573 (   -   )
 3-- Joseph MOSER-574 (1794-   )  Pa.
 3-- William MOSER-575 (   -   )
 3-- Isaac MOSER-576 (   -   )
 2-- Tobias MOSSER-20 (1763-1811)  Pa.
 sp-Christina (MOSER)-21 (1771-1816)
 3-- John MOSER-578 (1789-   )  Pa.
 3-- Elizabeth MOSER-579 (1791-   )  Pa.
 sp-John DERR-580 (   -1880)
 3-- Jacob MOSER-581 (   -   )
 3-- John George MOSER-582 (1797-   )  Pa.
 3-- Tobias MOSER-577 (1802-1804)  Pa.
 3-- Rebecca MOSER-583 (1804-   )  Pa.
 3-- Daniel MOSER-584 (1807-   )  Pa.
 2-- John Peter MOSSER-23 (1766-1841)  Pa.
 sp-Catharine MILLER-24 (1767-1806)
 3-- Michael MOSER-588 (1792-1864)  Pa.
 sp-Elisabeth SCHICK-589 (1804-1871)
 3-- Susanna MOSER-590 (1794-   )  Pa.
 3-- Maria Eva MOSER-591 (1802-   )  Pa.
 3-- Peter MOSER-592 (   -   )
 sp-Magdalena HORLACHER-593 (   -   )
 3-- Henry MOSER-594 (1806-   )  Pa.
 3-- William MOSER-595 (   -   )
 2-- Christina MOSSER-22 (1766-   )  Pa.
 2-- Catharine MOSSER-29 (   -   )
 sp-Conrad REISER-596 (   -   )
```

```
          3-- Conrad REISER-597 (    -    )
           sp-Christina HARTENDORF-598 (    -    )
      2-- Johannes MOSSER-30 (1771-1839)  Pa.
       sp-Anna Maria NICKOM-31 (1773-1843)  Pa.
          3-- Susanna MOSER-626 (1797-1881)  Pa.
           sp-Joseph TROXELL-627 (1797-    ) Easton,Northampton,Pa.
          3-- Paul MOSER-628 (1799-    ) Easton,Northampton,Pa.
           sp-Sarah GRESS-629 (    -    )
          3-- Joseph MOSER-635 (1801-1838)
          3-- Andreas MOSER-630 (1805-    ) Easton,Northampton,Pa.
           sp-Elisabeth (MOSER)-631 (    -    )
          3-- Maria Susana MOSER-636 (1810-    ) Pa.
          3-- Hannah MOSER-634 (1813-    ) Pa.
          3-- Peter MOSER-633 (1818-    ) Williams Twp.,Pa.
```

REFERENCES

LDS Microfiche
AIS (Moser, Snoble surnames)
LDS IGI (Moser, Snoble surnames)
    Pa, Tenn, Indiana, N.C., Va, W. Va
#6048670 'Immigrants to Philadelphia Ports'
#6048784 'Early Trumbull County Newspapers'

LDS MICROFILM:
0022042 - 1800-1820 Northampton, Pa. County Marriage Records
0940443 - Allentown, Pa. Church Records
0387855 - Northampton County, Pa. Baptisms, 1825-1859
0021681 - Northampton County, Pa. Probate Records
1414861 - Schumacher Records
1035761 - Pa. Church Records
1294882 - Pa. Church Records
0060306 - Pa. Church Records
0129849 - Pa. Church Records
0010969 - Pa. Church Records
1320941 - Lehigh County, Pa. Church Records
0329925 - Heidelberg Church Records
0329926 - Heidelberg Church Records
1321380 - Heidelberg Church Records
1321128 - Pa. Church Records
1305959 - Lehigh Co., Pa. Church Records
1305846 - Lowhill & Heidelberg Church Records
0856829 - Lehigh County, Pa. Church Records
0824058 - Pa. Church Records as copied by Howard Graff
0856830 - Lehigh County, Pa. Church Records
0856840 - Schulykill County, Pa. Church Records
1029741 - Lehigh County, Pa. Church Records
0020518 - Heidelberg Church Records, 1752-1860
0317348 - Columbiana County, Ohio Marriages & Cemetery Records
0856840 - Berks County, Pa. Records
1320941 - Lowhill, Pa. Church Records
0961021 - Early Northumberland County, Pa. Records
1035928 - 'The Wengler Book'
0021343 - Heidelberg Church Records
1597981 - Heidelberg Church Records
1036443 - Pa. Church Records
1011917 - 'Mussers & Allied Families' by Dorothy Moser
1321128 - 'People of the Marsh' by Charles Recker
0904252 - Trumbull Co, Ohio Death Records
0904251 - Trumbull Co., Ohio Marriage Records
1306272 - Schuylkill Co, Pa. Church Records
1312861 - Schuylkill Co., Pa. Marriages & Baptisms
1305961 - Schuylkill Co., Pa. Church Records
0020527 - Schuylkill & Berks Co., Pa. Cemetery Records
0924629 - Schuylkill & Berks Co., Pa., Tombstones
0387907 - Schuylkill Co., Pa. Probate Records
0385062 - Rev. Daniel Schumacher's Record Book
0098994 - "Moser Family of Berks Co."
1017041 - "Tobias Moser"
0385032 - Obit Notices from early Pa. Newspapers
0020527 - Berks Co., Pa. Church Records
0032734 - Nelson Co., Va. Marriage Licenses

Books, Court Records, Churchs & Cemeteries:

"Abstract of Wills of Berks County, Pennsylvania", Vol II 1798-1825, Alfred Smith

"American Compendium of Genealogy", all Volumes

American Genealogist Magazine, April 1987, "Some Descendants of Johann Christiam
    Moser of Berks County, Pennsylvania", by Walter R. Mattfeld

"Atlas & Directory of Trumbull County, Ohio", by American Atlas Company, 1899

"Baptism Records of Jordan Lutheran Church", by John Kistler

"Baptisms of Lutheran Congregations in Lehigh, Berks and Northampton Countys, 1754-
    1774", by Daniel Schumacher (Salt Lake Library #385.062

"Beaver Valley Pioneers, Pike Co., Ohio", by Brill

"Berks County History" by Morton L. Montgomery, Vol. I (Salt Lake Library
    #974.816 D2m)

Berks County, Pennsylvania land records

"Berks County Soldiers in the Revolutionary War", by Hollenbeck

"Biographical Sketches of Stephenson County, Illinois"

"Blue Book of Schuylkill County", by Ella Zerby Elliott (Salt Lake Library #974.817 H2e)

"Book of Biographies", 1898

Breitbard/Brunner Notes'"The Mosser (Etc) Family in America", unpublished notes of the
    authors, indexed by Charles Recker, seen at Las Vegas Family History Center

"Central Pennsylvania Marriages, 1700-1896", by Charles Fisher"

"Centre & Clinton Counties", by John Blair Linn (Salt Lake Library #974.85 H2l)

"Colonial & Revolutionary Families of Pennsylvania", Vol. 1, by John W. Jordan, 1978

DAR Lineage Records

"Data Relating to German Settlers in Newspapers - 1743-1800", Edward W. Hocker

Daughters of American Colonists Records

"Descendants of Henry Oswald", 1907, Appendix, by Rev. Charles E. C. Oswald

"Descendants of Nicholas Moser", (unpublished manuscript) by John Hendricks, seen at
    Las Vegas LDS Family History Center

"Early Lutheran Baptisms & Marriages in Southeastern Pennsylvania", by John
    Casper Stoever

"Early Pennsylvania Births, 1675-1875", by Charles Fisher

"Early Trumbull County Marriages", by Mrs. Roscoe Winnagle

Easton, Pennsylvania cemetery records

"Eighteenth Century Emigrants from the Northern Alsace to America"
    by Annette K. Burgert

"Emigrants from Germany", by Knittle

"Engles Notes and Queries Annual", 1900

Family Bible of H. M. Musser, Gaithersburg, Md.

"Family Histories, Descendents of Daniel Moser, 1796", by Harold Honeyfield and
    Homer Hill

"From Stones of Help, 250th Anniversary of Ebeneezer Church", by Pennsylvania
    German Society

Genealogical Magazine of New Jersey, Vol. 41-42

"German and Swiss Settlement" by Oscar Kuhns, 1901 (Appendix)

German Lutheran Church Records of Easton, Pa

"Handy Book for Genealogists", Eighth Edition

"Hauer, Hower Family Genealogy", by C. C. Houch & Agnes Wells

"History of Berks County" as sent over Genie in 1992 to Anita from GeeGee Hughes

"History of Huntington County" 1882, J. Simpson Africa

"History of Lehigh County, Pennsylvania", Vol. 1, by Charles Rhodes Roberts

"History of Sussex County, New Jersey", 1881, by Snell

"Immigrants in Pennsylvania, 1727-1776", by Daniel Rupp

"Index of Berks County, Pennsylvania Wills & Administration Records 1752-1850",
    by Richard T. & Mildred C. Williams (Salt Lake Library #975.216 p2w)

Lehigh County Historical Society Library (located in Allentown, Pa.) -- indexes to large
     collection of typed early church records
"Lebanon County History", by Engle
Lower Saucon Reformed Church Records, Northampton County, Pa.
"Moravian Families of Graceham, MD", 1942, by Henry James Young
"Moser Family", an unindexed collection of family group sheets by Richard Stoneking found at the
     Lehigh County Historical Society in Allentown, Pa.
"Moser Family History, Descendants of the Pioneer - Paul Moser" unpublished manuscript by Helen
     Weaver Gould in 1978
"Moser Family History, Monroe Co., Tenn", by Francis I. Moser
"Mosers of Schuylkill", unpublished manuscript by Paul Moser
"Mosser, Moser, Musser Family", a letter to the DAR reproduced in "Steinbruch/Mosser
     Family History" by Dr. Gary Dickey
National Archive Civil War Records
New Hanover Church Records, New Hanover Twp., Northampton Co., Pa.
"New World Immigrants", by Michael Tepper, Vol. II
"Northampton Co. Newspaper Extracts, 1871-1884", Vol. 6, by Argus
Oakwood Cemetery, Warren, Ohio
"Old Stillwater Cemetery", transcript on file at Sussex County Main Library,
     filed 19 Jul 1985
Orphan Court Records, Meedville, Crawford Co., Pa.
"Passenger Arrivals at the Port of Philadelphia" by Elisabeth Bentley
Pennsylvania Archives, Third Series, all Volumes
Pennsylvania Archives, Fifth Series, Vol. 5.
"Pennsylvania Dutch History" in Academic American Encyclopedia, Grolier, 1982
"Pennsylvania Genealogical Findings, Berks & Lehigh County" by Warren Ziegler
"Pennsylvania German Church Records", Vol. II, by the Pa. German Society
"Pennsylvania German Immigrants, 1709-1876", 1980, by Don Yoder
"Pennsylvania German Marriages" by Donna Irish
"Pennsylvania German Pioneers" Vol. I & II, by Strassburger & Hinke
Pennsylvania Historical Magazine, Vol. 66
Pennsylvania German Society Genealogical Magazine, Vol XV & XXVIII
"Pennsylvania Marriages", Vol. II, (Salt Lake Library #HR929.3)
"People of the Marsh" by Charles Recker, a newsletter published during the 1970's
Philadelphia County, Pa. Estate Administrations, A60-1744,
Philadelphia County, Pa. Estate Administrations, Book E
"Records of Penn Creek Lutheran Church, Gregg Township, Centre Co., Pennsylvania"
     (to page 77 only) (Salt Lake Library #974.853/G1 K2w)
"Register of Marriages & Burials, 1790-1810" by Rev. Helffrich, in Pa. Vital Records,
     Vol. III
"Rhineland Emigrants, Lists of German Settlers in Colonial America" by Don Yoder
"Roster of Ohio Soldiers, War of 1812" published by the Adjutant General (book located at the
Lafayette, Indiana, DAR Library)
"Schuylkill County, Pennsylvania Archive'" by Philip A. Rice
     (Salt Lake Library #974.817 H2rd)
"Schuylkill County, Pennsylvania Vital Records" by Philip A. Rice
     (Salt Lake Library #974.817 H2r)
Shawnee Cemetery, Methodist Church, Sugar Valley, W. Va.
"Steinbruch/Moser Family History", 1993, unpublished manuscript by
     Dr. Gary Alan Dickey, 1993
Stroup Reunion Book
"The Demise of Johann Krangelich" by Charles Recker
"Tobias Bickel", Pensylvania Genealogical Magazine, Vol XXVIII
Trinity Lutheran Church Records, Lancaster County, Pa.

Trinity Lutheran Reformed Church Records, Lancaster County, Pa.
Trumbull County Probate Records, Warren, Ohio
"Trumbull County Cemetery Records" by Ruth Allen
Tulphoecken Cemetery Records
"Two Everett Families of Northampton County", by Alice Allen Everett in Pa. Genealogical
    Magazine
"Wannemacher/Wanamaker Families", unpublished manuscript by Jean Gurney Rigler,
    located at Lehigh County Historical Library in Allentown, Pa.
"Will of John Musser", in Pa. German Magazine, Vol. 10

Federal Census Records:

Ohio: 1820, 1830, 1840 Index
            1850, Ashtabula, Geauga, Mahoning, Ottowa, Pike & Trumbull Counties
            1860, Trumbull County
            1870, Stark, Summitt & Trumbull Counties
            1880, 1900, 1910, Trumbull County

Pennsylvania: 1790, all Counties
            1810, 1820, 1830 Index
            1840, Lehigh County
            1850, Berks, Centre, Crawford, Lehigh & Schuylkill Counties
            1860, Lehigh County

West Virginia: 1850, Tyler County

Family Records

Mrs. Margery S. Anger of Canada
George Benedict of California
Janet R. Binkley of Neward, Delaware
Larry Clapp of Genesee, Illinois
Tim Conway of Pennsylvania
Mrs. Suzette Fetterman Darak of Ohio
Mrs. Patricia Moser Dernison of Tuscon, Arizona
Mrs. Helen Moser Eaton of Warren, Ohio, now deceased
Mrs. John T. Hamner, Jr.
Mrs. Barbara Hausmann Everett of Pocatello, Idaho, now deceased
Mrs. Lois Hopkins
Bob Kunkel of Tamaqua, Pa.
Mrs. Terri McClellan of Ohio
Carl Moor of Michigan
Clarence Moser of Warren, Ohio
Mrs. Geri Moser
Mrs. Kathleen Musser
Mrs. Anita Tilton Mott of Hurricane, Utah
Mrs. Donna Tilton Rable of Warren, Ohio
Daniel G. Reihnold
Mrs. Mary Walters of Las Vegas, Nevada
Mrs. Margaret Groves Weller of Warren, Ohio
Mrs. Sheila Williamson of Tacoma, Washington

INDEX

209

John M., 40
John Wesley, 68
Kate, 40
Lewis, 36
Louisa, 68
Magdalena, 36
Margaret, 24
Mary Ann, 36
Mary Emma, 68
Masena, 36
Noah, 40, 68
Owen, 68
Polly, 69
Salome, 33, 37, 38, 69
Samuel, 40
Sara Ann, 38
Sarah Alice, 68
Stephanus, 34
Sylvesta, 36, 39
Thomas, 36
Wilson Alfred, 68
KITTLE, Amber Christina, 123
Barbara Jean, 123
Bethanie Karolyn, 123
Donald, 123
Heather Lynn, 123
Megan Rae, 123
Samantha, 123
Summie, 123
Thomas Gary, 123
Tiffany Noel, 123
KLAUSE, Elisabeth, 68
KLAUSER, Georg, 160
KLEIN, Margaret, 2
KLINE, John, 150
KLINGERMAN, Christian, 173
Jeremiah, 68
Warren, 177
KNAPP, Doris, 118
KOCH, Charles, 51
Hugh, 45
Lizzie, 51
Mr., 45
Rettia, 51
Thomas, 45
KOCHER, Maria Sara, 140, 141
KONIG, Kenneth Edward, 93
Kenneth Edward, Jr., 93
Kenneth Edward, III, 93
Michelle, 93
Sherrill Lee, 93
Patricia Lynn, 93
KOPPENHEFFER, see also
COPENHOVER
Anna Barbara, 169
Anna Catharina, 169
Anna Rosina, 169
Michael, 169
Simon, viii
Thomas, vi, viii, 76, 169
Woolf, 169
KORNS, Martha, 117

KOSSER see RESSER
KRAEMER, Elisabeth, 15, 16
KRAMER, Maria, 45
KRANGELICH, Maria Barbara, 9
KRATZER, Catherine, 159
Margaret, 159
KRAUSE, Mary, 10, 34, 40
KREIDER, Barbara, 29
Maria Catherine, 28
KRUM, Wilson P., 39
KRUMREISS, Eva Barbara, 98
Magdalena, 98
KRUMRINE, John W., 65
KUBLER see KIBLER
KUCHER, Johann Peter, 169
KUHNS, Daniel, 36
Susanna, 33, 36
KUNGEL, Margarthea, vi, viii,1, 6, 9, 47
KUNST, Mr., 58

LAMM, Elisabeth, 78
LAMP, Johannes, 136
Margaretha, 136
LANDBACK, Alice, 51
Clara, 51
David, 51
Ellen, 51
Mary, 51
LANDIS, Bill, 110
LANE, John, 126
Laura, 108, 126
LANG, Jonathan, 114
see also LONG
LAPHAM, Henry, 108
LATTIG, Rosina, 95
LAUCKS, Catherine, 74
LAUER, Anna Sophia, 73
LAYFIELD, Eric, 123
LEASE, Sarilda, 110
LEASER/LOESER, Jacob, 48
LEBO, Mr., 45
LECHERT, Harriet, 104
LEFFLER, Eve Catherina, 8
LEH, G. Edward, 41
LEHMAN, Christian, 169
LENHART, Louis, 39
LENTZ, Florence, 171
LEONARD, Nanacy B., 153
LEWIS, Belle, 109
Beverly, 118
James, 118
Mr., 109
Rosalyn, 118
Russell, 118
LEY, Catherine, 70, 71
Christian, 70
LICHTENWALLNER,
Anna Christina, 169
Christina, 143
Johannes, vii, 47, 143, 169
Margaret, 169
Maria Agatha 47, 59, 62, 169, 173, 178

CPSIA information can be obtained
at www.ICGtesting.com
Printed in the USA
FFOW01n1413181217
44153101-43517FF